Savage Words:
Invectives as a literary genre

All rights reserved.

Published under the aegis of the UCLA Center for Medieval and Renaissance Studies.

ISBN: 978-1-946328-60-1

AGINCOURT PRESS
P.O. Box 1039
Cooper Station
New York, NY 10003
www.agincourtpress.org

© 2016 by Agincourt Press

Savage Words:
Invectives as a literary genre

Edited by
Massimo Ciavolella and Gianluca Rizzo

Agincourt Press
New York, 2016

Table of Contents

- 9   Gianluca Rizzo
  Introduction

- 19   Luigi Ballerini
  The World Is Not a Horse: A Few Remarks on the Inadequacy of Contemporary Invective

- 46   Donald Beecher
  The Limits of Invective: Ben Jonson's Poetaster *and the Temper of the Times*

- 60   Remo Bodei
  Righteous Wrath

- 66   Thomas Conley
  Toward a Rhetoric of Insult

- 72   Paolo Fabbri
  Est iniuria in verbis

- 92   David Marsh
  The Invectives of Petrarch and his Quattrocento Successors

- 106   Kathryn Morgan
  Domesticating Invective in Plato's Laws

- 127   Paul Perron
  Swearing, Invectives and Blasphemy: A Cross-Cultural Bilingual Example in Contemporary Quebec Society

- 140   Ennio Rao
  The Humanistic Invective: Genre, Mode, or Meta-Genre?

- 153   Gianluca Rizzo
  Issues of Language and Genre in Macaronic Invectives

Gianluca Rizzo

Introduction

> OSWALD
> *Why dost thou use me thus? I know thee not.*
> KENT
> *Fellow, I know thee.*
> OSWALD
> *What dost thou know me for?*
> KENT
> *A knave; a rascal; an eater of broken meats; a base, proud, shallow, beggarly, three-suited, hundred-pound, filthy, worsted-stocking knave; a lily-livered, action-taking knave, a whoreson, glass-gazing, super-serviceable finical rogue; one-trunk-inheriting slave; one that wouldst be a bawd, in way of good service, and art nothing but the composition of a knave, beggar, coward, pandar, and the son and heir of a mongrel bitch: one whom I will beat into clamorous whining, if thou deniest the least syllable of thy addition.*
> KING LEAR, Act II, Scene 2

Laurence Sterne's *The Life and Opinions of Tristram Shandy, Gentleman* is one of those few texts (together with Dante's *Divine Comedy* and the *Oxford English Dictionary*) one can turn to for advice under nearly any circumstance. The issue of how one should best swear, curse, or otherwise verbally abuse a fellow human being, a situation or an idea is no exception to this rule.

For example, one could easily turn to the OED in order to establish the somewhat elusive difference in meaning between contiguous terms such as invective, vituperation, insult, irony, sarcasm, and satire, only to mention a few of the many words found within this rich and mystifying semantic field.

Alternatively, one could peruse Canto XXXIII of *Inferno* to see a master in the art of vilification at work. Dante is approaching the end of his underground journey; he is at the bottom of hell's pit, surrounded by the scum of the earth. As he and Virgil are strolling through the frozen lake of tears, tripping over the half-submerged heads of the betrayers' souls, they run into Friar Alberigo, a contemporary of Dante's who was actually still alive as the Poet was writing his masterpiece. How could somebody who is still alive be already in hell, you might ask. Well, it turns out this happens, sometimes, to the worst sinners: Dante explains that a devil takes control of their body and lives out the remainder of their natural life, while their soul is cast into Cocytus, to be tormented for all eternity. Now, that's a man you don't want to cross: he'll count you among the infernal dwellers, denouncing you to all posterity, even if you are still alive. And then he will close the episode by saying something like: *cortesia fu lui esser villano*!

However, those who find their inclinations to be of a more speculative nature, those who favor the abstraction of philosophy, will greatly benefit from consulting Sterne's novel, and in particular a passage that is so crucial for the present investigation that we feel compelled to transcribe it in full. In the second volume, chapter 2, Mrs. Shandy has gone into labor. Dr. Slop is there to help, but he doesn't have his bag with him. The servant Obadiah is sent to fetch it. He goes to the doctor's house as fast as he can, picks it up, and before rushing back to his mistress, he thinks it best to tie it with some twine, so as not to spill the doctor's precious tools all over the English countryside. The bag is successfully delivered, but the knots are so tight Dr. Slop must cut the twine, and in doing so he cuts his own thumb, all the way to the bone. He proceeds to curse the poor servant in a rather joyless and uninventive manner. It is at this point that Mr. Shandy, Tristram's father, after "condoling with him [...] upon the accident" begins to expound his ideas on the subject of cursing:

> Small curses, Dr. Slop, upon great occasions, [...] are but so much waste of our strength and soul's health to no manner of purpose. [...] They serve [...] to stir the humours—but carry off none of their acrimony: —for my own part, I seldom swear or curse at all—I hold it bad—but if I fall into it by surprize, I generally retain so much presence of mind [...] as to make it answer my purpose—that is, I swear on till I find myself easy. A wife and a just man however would always endeavour to proportion the vent given to these humours, not only to the degree of them stirring within himself—but to the size and ill intent of the offence upon which they are to fall. [...] For this reason [...] I have the greatest veneration in the world for that gentleman, who, in distrust of his own discretion in this point, sat down and composed (that is at his leisure) fit forms of swearing suitable to all cases, from the lowest to the highest provocation which could possibly happen to him—which forms being well considered by him, and such moreover as he could stand to, he kept them ever by him on the chimney-piece, within his reach, ready for use[1].

I find this passage remarkable for at least 4 reasons:

1. The purpose of cursing, it would seem, is to free oneself of those humors that are stirred by anger and that, left circulating within the body, would cause harm to the organism. This is a wonderfully enlightened way of looking at the whole issue: far from being an antisocial behavior, cursing is a matter of physical and psychological health, something a doctor might recommend a patient do, provided he or she follows the appropriate prescriptions. The first of such prescriptions is that cursing must be carried out for as long as necessary in order to purge the body of its bad humors.

2. The second prescription is proportionality. And here we can appreciate the lasting impression Aristotle's *Nicomachean Ethics* left on Sterne, his father, and the 18th century man in general. There must be a strict correlation between the offense and the vituperation, the cause and the effect. After all, "small curses upon great occasions are but a waste."

3. The only way of achieving the right duration and the right proportion is to deliberately set about the task of composing curses while perfectly calm, when one is in complete control of his faculties, and can match each possible offense with its proper vilification. The beauty in this way of reasoning is that it displays a disproportionate and perhaps unjustified faith in human ingenuity: as if all possible circumstances requiring one to curse could be clearly envisioned by a reasonable man, working at his table, in his study. Again, there is something wonderfully optimistic and exquisitely enlightened in this assumption.

4. Finally, the proper place to store the product of such a thorough exploration of the universe through the lens of cursing, this encyclopedia of verbal abuse, is the "chimney-piece." The implication being that the armchair by the fireplace, preferably in one's study, surrounded by books and papers, is the rightful post from which a gentleman is supposed to look at and interact with the world. A contemporary of ours would have certainly envisioned a pocket-size paperback (or, even better, an app) as the most useful form for this swearing vade mecum: that way one can carry it around at all times. But Sterne's world is different. His philosophers are gentlemen, and they can think of no reason why they should abandon their armchairs (desert their posts, as it were) and go out into the world. Their place is by the fire, and the chimney-piece is where they store everything they might need at a moment's notice.

Reading on, one finds that not only such a book—such a collection of maledictions, swears, and insults—is possible, but that it actually already exists, composed by a certain Bishop Ernulphus quite some time ago. Naturally, Mr.

Sterne owns a copy, and he is more than happy to lend it to Dr. Slop, provided he agrees to read the whole thing out loud.

> My father, who generally look'd upon every thing in a light very different from all mankind, would, after all, never allow this to be an original. —He considered rather Ernulphus's anathema, as an institute of swearing, in which, as he suspected, upon the decline of swearing in some milder pontificate, Ernulphus, by order of the succeeding pope, had with great learning and diligence collected together all the laws of it; —for the same reason that Justinian, in the decline of the empire, had ordered his chancellor Tribonian to collect the Roman or civil laws all together into one code or digest—lest, through the rust of time—and the fatality of all things committed to oral tradition—they should be lost to the world for ever.
> For this reason my father would oft-times affirm, there was not an oath from the great and tremendous oath of William the conqueror (By the splendour of God) down to the lowest oath of a scavenger (Damn your eyes) which was not to be found in Ernulphus. —In short, he would add—I defy a man to swear out of it[2].

The thought that a book exists such that no aspect of a given facet of reality—no matter how small—could escape its pages is strikingly modern. One can't help but think of Borges' unlimited and periodic library.

A similar assumption was at the core of a conference Massimo Ciavolella and I organized in February of 2009, entitled "Savage Words: Invective as a Literary Genre," and it is from that conference that this volume stems. As we were preparing the call for papers, we were looking mostly at humanist invectives, a genre that displays a remarkable regularity and predictability. Most of these texts presented the same general structure, and even some of the insults directed at adversaries, their works, character and lineage, kept returning over and over again.

Also, one does not need to be a sociolinguist to notice the monotony of the epithets we routinely hurl at our fellow humans in places such as a busy street during rush hour traffic, a stadium, or in front of the TV. Keeping all these considerations in mind, we wrote a description of what we thought our conference would be about, only to be soon taken to task by our guests, who disagreed with our view of invectives and pleasantly surprised us by producing a remarkable variety of texts and opinions. Here is the description we had written:

> Together with the insult and the verbal attack, invective inhabits the most antisocial sphere of language—a sphere one might expect to be ungoverned by any rules or conventions of genre, where scathing ridicule is unleashed with the same heated anarchy that animates its devoted practitioners.
> And yet, upon closer examination, invectives reveal themselves to be the most tightly

regulated of literary genres, in which genealogies and norms have been strictly codified since the time of Cicero and Sallust. In fact, manuals of rhetoric, meant for students at all levels, formalize its every aspect—even determining, with clinical precision, the kind of shortcomings to be excoriated in one's colleagues. Notwithstanding the ironclad regulations to which it is subjected, or possibly because of them, invectives have enjoyed a consistent favor throughout European circles, always rediscovered, revisited, and rekindled.

This conference will bring together an international array of scholars to delineate the rules of the invective genre, showing its evolution and expressive ductility, analyzing the vast corpus of texts that, over the centuries, individuals of every provenance (civil and ecclesiastic) have discharged in an effort to vilify either the ideas or the character of their colleagues, to demonstrate their superiority in the art of rhetoric, or, perhaps, simply to vent their genuine loathing for those same colleagues.

The essays collected in this volume will show how these expectations were in part wrong, and in part just the generalization of a rather limited sub-segment of texts. In fact, as we mentioned, there seems to be a sort of general rule, a rather prescriptive model at work in most of the humanistic invectives. But as soon as we go outside humanists' circles and the timeframe within which they were most active, things change quite dramatically, and the predictability therein is replaced by a whirlwind of creativity and verbal inventiveness. This is not to say, however, that any reliable constants do not exist. There might not be "ironclad rules" to this type of discourse, but all these texts certainly share many commonalities. Here are the three that seem to be the most important:

1. The meaning these texts are intended to convey is rather monotonous; they all say, in one form or another, "I don't like you." Hence, the whole point of producing them is to communicate this age-old message in new and unprecedented ways. We might be rather unimaginative in our day-to-day interactions, but when we sit down to write, a certain degree of novelty is imperative. In fact, one would say that in order to work, no two *orationes invectivae* can be exactly alike (not even humanistic ones). At the same time, however, one doesn't want to be so inventive that the audience fails to recognize the text for what it actually is. This double constraint (creativity and transparency) produces an endless quantity of variations, and is the real engine of that verbal inventiveness we see at play; ultimately, this is the reason why we find these texts so interesting to study and to write.

2. If we look at all the different textual strategies mentioned so far (invectives, insults, satire, irony, sarcasm, etc.), we will see they all have one ba-

sic, crucial rhetorical device in common: they all pit one group (or individual) against another. They are all, to different degrees, divisive[3]. This divisiveness can be, and usually is, used for different purposes, and it comes in different forms. It can be a *"me vs. you"* type of opposition; although this is not necessarily the most common one, I must confess it is my favorite, for the author goes *mano a mano* with another author, engaging in a battle of wits. Its negative effects are usually contained to the two individuals who are involved in the fight, while the rest of us, the audience, can sit back and enjoy the show.

Another form this divisiveness can take is the *"me vs. you plural (y'all)"* type, which is the rhetorical stance of the censor. The author imagines (or believes, or pretends) he or she is endowed with higher morals than the rest of society, and can mete out judgments and punishments. Sometimes this kind of text can be interesting; it is usually historically and anthropologically revealing, but it also gets old rather quickly.

Then there is a third possible outcome, a rather unpleasant and useless one: the *"we vs. them"* kind. This is a divisive strategy routinely used to unify one group against an outsider (or another group), thus being a staple of political discourse. Such a rhetorical device might have been useful and even justified at some point in the past, when there might have been substantial differences between groups such as, say, Venetians and Genoese, Protestant and Popist, or Tramecksan and Slamecksan; in our contemporary world, however, where the actions of one group inevitably affect all other groups, such a discourse is not only short-sighted, but positively and criminally misguided. Given the magnitude of the issues our generation is facing (population growth, depletion of natural resources, climate change, etc.) this is one of those past-times from which we should probably refrain.

And this is where we find ourselves in a bit of a paradox: the more we are interconnected, the more we are exposed to each other's speech (through ever-evolving and ever-increasing means of communication), the more the right to speak freely, the right to insult and offend one's opponents and the right to feel offended by someone else's speech become difficult to reconcile. And this is especially true whenever power is not distributed equally among different groups (that is to say, this is nearly always true). The group with more power will inevitably claim that their offensive speech is within the confines of "protected, free speech;" the less powerful group will inevitably interpret these verbal outbursts like so many other manifestations of the general injustice that is endemic to society. If the situation is inverted, and it is the less powerful group that initiates the invective, their words will be characterized as class hatred and routinely censored, resulting in yet more injustice, and thus fueling the vicious cycle.

3. The brand of divisive speech we have been describing can cause even more damage by tricking people into thinking of the world in terms of dichotomies, as if there were only two alternative and mutually exclusive possible outcomes to any given situation or argument. By framing all issues in terms of dichotomies, the influence of powerful groups can be even more constricting: once there is a general consensus that all issues are a matter of choice between two and only two alternatives, all that remains to be done is to shape those alternatives and make sure that neither of them interferes with the established power structure. Thus the choice is rendered meaningless, effectively invalidating freedom and self-determination. It is the same difference between asking someone what they would like to drink, and asking them if they would prefer pepsi or coke. The first scenario allows for a real choice. The latter is only an exercise in futility. And this, I think, is the most dangerous distortion of all. Real issues rarely come in the form of an either/or proposition, as it will be made clear by the essays here collected. We organized them alphabetically, according to their author's last name, and here is a brief summary of each.

Luigi Ballerini's contribution investigates epigrams, a form of invective carried out in verse. In particular, he looks at the epigrams written by Pasolini at the end of the '50s, and likens them to those by Jacopone da Todi. Both poets, he says, belong to a similar anarchist culture typical of peasants and intolerant of all authority. Jacopone is the *terminus a quo* of this culture, Pasolini the *terminus ad quem*, even though, in his time, the peasants have turned into the urban sub-proletarian class. The problem, Ballerini argues, is that while Jacopone still has an audience receptive to his outbursts (and capable, to a certain extent, of protecting the intellectual that had produced them), Pasolini is left completely alone and has to bear the brunt of the retaliation mounted by the powerful people his invectives irked. His case is emblematic of our times: epigrams seem to be utterly ineffective in the modern political arena, pervaded and sedated by neo-capitalism. Is there any way poetry can return to invectives? Ballerini believes there is, finding a possible solution in Pagliarani's poems of the 80s and early 90s.

Donald Beecher takes us back to the beginning of the 17th century, to a play Ben Jonson had written attacking John Marston. Jonson sets it in a fantastical version of Augustus' court, where all the great poets of antiquity are present. He casts himself in the role of Horace, and his enemy as Crispinus, who is repeatedly verbally abused by the other characters. Eventually, a makeshift tribunal is instituted and Crispinus is condemned to ingest an emetic. This remedy is supposed to bring out all the neologisms and stylistic improprieties his works contained, so that he may be purged of them once and for all. In spite of the imaginative fiction, this is still a frontal assault to the reputation of Marston, and thus just the latest installment in a long tradition of invectives that can be traced back to classical antiquity. Beecher frames these texts within the context of society at large and the social behavior that regulates human interactions. In particular he is interested in the way invectives and gossip are used to shape social hierarchies: here words are used to procure genuine harm. He writes: "it is an instance in which *le mot* becomes *la chose*, when the power of the imagination becomes omnipotent, making defamatory naming tantamount to physical injury." Both victim and perpetrator of verbal assaults can suffer the real-world effects of language. And this is why, Beecher concludes, Jonson sets his tale in the remote past of Ancient Rome, in an attempt to deflect some of the collateral damage.

Remo Bodei's article focuses on wrath, the precursor, in a sense, of all invectives. This passion is often seen in contradictory terms: it can be considered a noble sentiment, but also a temporary blindness of reason. He proceeds to analyze it by looking for its philosophical roots and justifications. When is wrath not only acceptable, but the proper response to an injury or an offence? How can we reconcile this righteous wrath with the Christian commandment to love and forgive? In addition to answering these questions, Bodei offers a way of understanding passions and their logic. He argues that passions are not the opposite, the negation of logic, but rather they are the expression of a different kind of logic, an "anomalous" one. In the case of wrath, for instance, we might observe that often the reaction of the wrathful is disproportionate to the episode that caused it. And yet, Bodei argues, the wrathful's reaction is not a response to the individual episode that triggered the emotion, but rather "it is all the frustrations of […] life, all the betrayed expectations, all the unrealized or poorly compensated hopes, that collapse at that point, that explode because they reached a critical mass. Therefore, the element of excess exists, but it becomes understandable, because this single episode conveys and attracts all the analogous episodes. The logic of the passions is, therefore, an agglutinative, synthetic logic, one that makes a sheaf out of every blade of grass." Then Bodei moves on to the role wrath plays in the political arena, and concludes by looking at the way Machiavelli describes Savonarola's speeches and sermons, and their use of the Bible (Exodus in particular).

Thomas Conley approaches the issue of verbal abuse from a rhetorical perspective, focusing on insults rather than invectives. In a sense, Conely's approach is similar to Beecher's, in that both scholars regard invectives and insults as expressions of human behavior that implicitly presuppose a social environment: "Yet invective, surely, is not just a matter of verbal skill or of mastering a genre (whether verbal or not) but above all a matter of human relations conducted by means of symbolic action." He shows how the ultimate goal of anyone who utters insults is "to consolidate their audience's 'us against them' stance by 'repeating' what 'everybody knows': that the Pope is a pervert, and that priests steal and are little more than pernicious beasts." There is an inescapable political dimension to verbal assault that can be used not only to create unity by aggregating people against a common enemy, but can also serve as a way of enforcing or challenging social hierarchy: "That is to say, there is a vertical dimension to insults. Often overlooked, however, is the fact that that dimension works both downward and upward. Some insulting behavior seems designed to maintain established hierarchies [...] and others seem designed to interrogate the established hierarchy." Conley ends his essay on a positive note, inviting his readers to develop an aesthetic appreciation for insults: "By attending to the aesthetic angle, we gain some distance that allows us to see an insult not just as verbal abuse but as a performance before an audience, a performance intended not just to divide, but to unite. [...] There is, in short, a benign as well as a malign side to insults, just as there is a malign as well as a benign side to persuasion. We ought to keep that in mind."

Paolo Fabbri attempts to create an atlas (both a map and a catalogue) as well as a typology of insults and swear words, while registering the invasion of obscene speech into the public sphere. He goes beyond the rhetorical analysis of the phenomenon and tries to uncover the complex cultural assumptions that are hidden under the surface of insults, considering them as signs and therefore as bearers of a "semio-physics of [their] own: a form endowed with a gradient of intensity and with vectors of meaning." He focuses on the more adversarial, agonistic and almost war-like aspects of verbal confrontation, a realm in which using words equals causing wounds, and the last man standing will be declared the winner. He also shows the commonalities between insults, verbal abuse and poetry. The long lists of epithets, taken from newspapers and online media, that complete his article are a truly marvelous window into the Italian soul, and have been a veritable challenge for the translator, who had to render them in English.

David Marsh begins his overview of humanistic invectives by looking at their classical, Latin predecessors, discussing, in particular, the insults Cicero uses in his writings. Then he talks about Petrarch, who revived the genre in early modern times but who left out "the elements essential to Quintilian's conception–the open confrontation and direct address to his adversary." Then Marsh moves to Leonardo Bruni who, like Petrarch, does not name his targets: his *Oratio in hypocritas* (1417), for instance, is directed against three unnamed foes. Poggio Bracciolini, instead, adopts the opposite strategy: his writings are clearly addressed to someone in particular, with no pretense of anonymity. "The combative Lorenzo Valla (1407-1457) naturally aroused the enmity of rival scholars, and engaged in a series of invectives [...] The richness and complexity of Valla's invectives defy brief characterization, and much of his argument is conducted along philological rather than rhetorical lines." This is, according to Marsh, a turning point in the evolution of the genre: "with the invectives exchanged by Poggio and Valla, we move from personal and anecdotal abuse into a different sphere toward which Petrarch pointed the way–the debate on texts and their authority." The remaining part of his essay is dedicated to a close analysis of the invectives exchanged by Antonio da Rho and Antonio Panormita.

In her article, **Kathryn Morgan** investigates the way in which Plato frames the problem of verbal abuse in his philosophical works: "In the body of this paper I shall sketch the way Plato has his characters formulate the problem of abuse, comic and otherwise. This will generate a familiar result: comedy and abuse call forth a kind of emotional indulgence and representation that pander to the lowest parts of the human soul. They must be regulated because they are psychically damaging. More specifically, however, I shall concentrate on the society portrayed in the *Laws*, using one lengthy and important passage as a tool to ponder why invective and the persona adopted by the speaker of invective poses a particular problem for the quasi-utopian city whose design is the central task of the dialogue." Is there any room left for invective and mockery in Plato's ideal state? Morgan's reading of Plato's text reveals a surprising answer to this question.

Paul Perron's article investigates the possibility of creating a "hypothetico-deductive descriptive method of studying invective from a socio-semiotic perspective," by analyzing a court case that occurred in Montreal in 2008 and that was subsequently covered by Canada's national newspaper, the *Globe and Mail*. The principal tools for his analysis are derived from the theories and methodologies of the Paris School of Semiotics, which developed under the tutelage of Algirdas Greimas in the 1960s and is still going strong today. The conclusion

Perron reaches is that for an invective to be successfully exchanged between two individuals, they have to share a remarkably large set of assumptions, conversational rules, and behavioral patterns: "knowledge of values constituting a norm as well as deviance from the norm —a common encyclopedia, for example— has to be shared both by the inveigher or the inveighed for invective to occur. If there is a largely asymmetrical relationship in their respective awareness, or, if either or both subjects are not culturally sensitized to their interlocutor's value system, then invective misfires."

Ennio Rao begins his contribution by contrasting Petrarch's brief invective (written in 1352 against a papal physician) with the invectives exchanged between Poggio Bracciolini and Lorenzo Valla about one hundred years later. He highlights the transformation that the invective underwent during the Quattrocento, particularly between 1440 and 1453, when it evolved from a simple oration or open letter into a composition that borrowed from the philosophical treatise, the philosophical dialogue, Lucian's satire, Aristophanes' slapstick humor, and Martial's caustic epigram. Despite this evolution, he argues, the humanistic invective conserved features that were identified by Cicero and the author of the "Rhetorica ad Herennium." Rao then offers an overview of the definitions of invective from ancient times to the 15th century, and concludes by addressing the question of whether or not humanistic invectives could be considered a literary genre.

Finally, in my essay, I look at the role played by invectives in the fabric of Folengo's macaronic masterpiece, *Baldus*. Here, the narration of events is often suspended and the author intervenes directly to lash out against a wide variety of human vices. Being a mixture of many different languages, however, the macaronic style lends a comic undertone that helps Folengo avoid the most common faults of verbal abuse: that of pitting censor against censored, absolute good against absolute evil. Throughout the *Baldus* he refuses to align himself with any categorical position (be it linguistic, political or religious), thus rendering his mock epic poem a remarkable exercise in intellectual independence and proving how productive and entertaining macaronic invectives can be.

In sending this volume to press, the editors would like to thank Gianpiero (William) Doebler and Dominic Siracusa, for helping in translating and proofreading some of these essays. We would also like to express our gratitude to the UCLA Center for Medieval and Renaissance Studies and the Franklin D. Murphy Chair in Italian Renaissance Studies for their generous support.

Notes

[1] Laurence Sterne, *The Life and Opinions of Tristram Shandy, Gentlemen*, Volume II, Chapter 2-II.
[2] Laurence Sterne, *The Life and Opinions of Tristram Shandy, Gentlemen*, Volume II, Chapter 2-V.
[3] For a more in depth discussion of these issues, see Thomas Conley's article in this volume, as well as his monograph *Toward a Rhetoric of Insults* (Chicago: Chicago UP, 2010).

Luigi Ballerini

The World Is Not a Horse: A Few Remarks on the Inadequacy of Contemporary Invective

> exeo tamquam / mancus et extinctae corpus non utile dextrae
> Juvenal, III, 47-48

On November 7, 1958, Pier Paolo Pasolini wrote his Bolognese friend Roberto Roversi, who alongside Francesco Leonetti, and Pasolini himself, had been editing and independently producing the first series of the journal *Officina*, a letter containing the following remark: "... sto mettendo a posto anche i miei brutti epigrammi, cercando di renderli meno brutti." (I am putting the final touches on my ugly epigrams, trying to make them less ugly than they actually are).[1]

A few days later, on November 22nd, he informs Franco Fortini, who was supposed to join the editorial board for the second series of the journal, and whose tormented exchange with our author is documented in the rather transparent book Fortini compiled a good number of years after Pasolini's death, entitled *Attraverso Pasolini*[2] (Through Pasolini), that he has forwarded to "i nostri bolognesi una bellissima poesia di Bertolucci" (I have sent our Bolognese friends a beautiful poem by Bertolucci), adding: "i miei epigrammi sono ancora qui, in un momento di forte odio dell'autore verso di loro." (I haven't yet sent off my epigrams; right now their author hates them with all his heart).

Finally on Dec. 4 he takes courage. "... Vi mando, tremebondo, il pacchetto degli epigrammi." (With trepidation, I am sending you the batch of my epigrams) he writes to both Leonetti and Roversi, subsumed under the appellation of "Redattori di (editors of) *Officina*."

The reaction on the part of the recipients is one of great enthusiasm. On behalf of both, Leonetti writes back: "Non tardiamo neanche un giorno a dirti che gli epigrammi sono molto piaciuti a Roversi e a me. Sono carichi della tua passione, che io, letteralmente, amo. Roversi a una prima lettura penserebbe di togliere "A un figlio non nato," insomma condensare un poco la raccolta, o forse togliendo "A un monte"; ma non credo te lo consiglierà." (Without letting a single day go by, we want you to know that both Roversi and I are very happy with your epigrams. They are filled with the passion in you which I love, literally. Roversi, upon a first reading, would seem inclined to exclude "To an Unborn

Child," so as to tighten up a bit the whole, and perhaps also "To a Mountain," but I do no think he'll come forward with that suggestion).

Let us note in passing that this letter by the high spirited Leonetti, and the slightly more sedate Roversi, is dated Dec. 5, a fact that should make us reflect, if not on the literary merits of Pasolini's denunciatory poems, at least on the efficiency of the much maligned Italian Postal System in the late Fifties: 1 day from Rome to Bologna, as opposed to the 5 or 6 that it takes now, and only if you pay for the extra postage of *Posta prioritaria*.[3]

Be that as it may, and whether or not Roversi gave voice to his reservation, Pasolini, in a letter to the *redattori* written 4 days later, concurs with it: "Accetto la soppressione di 'A un monte'" (I accept the elimination of "To a Mountain"). No punitive action is decreed for "To an Unborn Child" which, in the meantime, has received, the enthusiastic endorsement of Fortini. In a letter dated Dec. 14, the latter wrote to Pasolini: "Ho letto i tuoi epigrammi, che mi han fatta una forte impressione e che trovo molto belli e giusti, fra le cose migliori tue, e che 'ti stanno bene addosso'." (I have read your epigrams and I am really impressed: I find them beautiful and necessary, to be numbered among the very best things you have written. 'They fit you like a glove.') And further down, in the same missive, "Negli epigrammi (quello a un figlio non nato è molto "giusto" ed è una cifra esatta per leggere molte cose tue) sei davvero felice [...] Hai fatto bene a scriverli. *Bellissimo* quello per la Francia" (These epigrams of yours are indeed felicitous. An air of necessity runs through the piece to an unborn child, which, furthermore, is a very convincing key to read much of what you write. [...] Right you were to write them. *Beautiful* the piece on France.)

Generous as he certainly is in his appreciation of his correspondent's epigrams, Fortini feels uncomfortable, however, about the composition addressed to the literati whom Pasolini attacks "*nominatim*" and are, all of them, except Bárberi Squarotti, says Fortini, "di quart'ordine" (fourth rate). "Eleganza vorrebbe che ce ne fosse di più temibili o che quelli mòrsi fossero anonimi." (Elegance would require that you took on more formidable enemies, leaving to their anonymity those you have chosen to reproach).

It is not a major indictment, but a relevant one just the same, as it confirms an inclination in which Pasolini indulges, and not infrequently, I am afraid, in his polemical writings. "In morte del realismo" (The Death of Realism), of 1961, is a case in point. In a parody of the celebrated speech by Marc Anthony in Shakespeare's *Julius Caesar*:

Friends, Romans, countrymen, lend me your ears;
I come to bury Caesar, not to praise him.
The evil that men do lives after them;
The good is oft interred with their bones;
So let it be with Caesar. The noble Brutus
Hath told you Caesar was ambitious.
If it were so, it was a grievous fault,
And grievously hath Caesar answer'd it.
Here, under leave of Brutus and the rest -
For Brutus is an honourable man;

Pasolini replaces Caesar with *Realistic Style* and *Brutus* with *Cassola*, in those days a fairly prominent, as well as fairly harmless, author whom Pasolini accuses of having stabbed to death the realistic style to resuscitate the discarded (and irrelevant) form of writing, generically referred to as literature for literature's sake, or Belles Lettres, or, specifically by Pasolini, as reactionary Purism:

Friends, Romans, countrymen, lend me your ears!
Sono qui a seppellire il realismo italiano
non a farne l'elogio. Il male di uno stile
gli sopravvive, spesso, ma il bene resta,
spesso, sepolto insieme al suo ricordo.
E così sarà dello stile realistico.
L'eletto Cassola vivacemente attesta
ch'esso era ambizioso: se così fosse
sarebbe, questo, un gran demerito, ed equa
quindi, la sua fine. S'egli lo concede
– e Cassola è un rispettabile scrittore:
tutti i neo-puristi son rispettabili scrittori –
son venuto qui io a parlare della morte
del realismo italiano...

(I come to bury Italian Realism, not to praise it.
The evil a style does lives after it;
The good is oft interred with the memory of it;
So let it be with the Realistic Style. The noble
Cassola hath told you Realism was ambitious.
If it were so, it was a grievous fault,
And grievously hath Realism answer'd it.
Here, under leave of Cassola and the rest -
For Cassola is a honourable man;
And all neo-purist writers are honourable men –
I have come to speak of the death of
Italian Realism...)

It is, no doubt, a very clever joke, a bitter Shakespearean *scherzo*, devoutly to be wished, if only to ward off the possibility that the situation it depicts might be true, as Pasolini himself writes at the close of his text: a *cauda*, deprived of *venenum*. The only problem is that in those years, the foundations of the so called realistic writing (which Pasolini stretches to include such diverse practitioners as Calvino and Gadda) were not being shaken by Cassola's "regressive" fiction, bur rather by the turbulent, chaotic, willfully incongruent, linguistically motivated poetry and prose, in one word, by the then hotly debated experimental writings of the neo-avant-garde whom Pasolini largely ignores, showing a marked interest only for the neo-epic poetry of Elio Pagliarani, whose position within the movement many have regarded as eccentric.

Enough said, however, for the moment. We shall reopen this wound later. Let us return now to his 1958 epigrams. Curiously, none of Pasolini's correspondents who had read the epigrams prior to their appearance in print in the March-April 1959 issue of *Officina*, mentions epigram number XII, entitled *To a Pope*, which, as we shall see, was to cost Pasolini and Co. the benevolence of Valentino Bompiani, the well established Milanese publisher who, having accepted to undertake the publication of the journal, refused to continue, after the second issue of the second series, frightened or enraged by Pasolini's text. Which goes to show that "*To a Pope*," though not a tragedy, induced fear and piety on at least one member of the audience, without however producing cathartic results.

We shall come back, to this crucial silence. Not a word about it, not even from Fortini who, as we have seen, gives his preferences in details, and from whose critique, in a letter dated Dec. 20, Pasolini acknowledges to have drawn "un grande piacere [...] per l'acutezza del giudizio sugli epigrammi" (great pleasure for the acumen [...] you displayed in your analysis of my epigrams).

It is a very peculiar letter written, in response to two letters by Fortini, under the most unusual circumstances. "Ieri notte è morto mio padre: ti scrivo dunque due righe: il suo corpo è ancora qui in casa, partiamo domani per Casarsa per il suo funerale, e puoi quindi immaginare lo stato d'animo in cui mi trovo." (My father died last night: can only write you a few lines: his body is still in the apartment, we leave tomorrow for Casarsa, for the funeral, you can imagine how I feel).

The "few lines," actually, are not so few. After an explosion of grateful enthusiasm caused by Fortini's positive appreciation of his texts, Pasolini declares himself to be utterly dismayed and irate at the complications surfacing from his idea of enlarging the editorial board of the projected new series of *Officina*.

In a letter to Leonetti the following days, the day of the *translatio cadaveris* to Casarsa, Pasolini becomes a little more compassionate, describes the agonizing experience of his father's fatal illness, admits to the difficulties he and his beloved mother encountered in their relationship with him, and the sense of guilt he now experiences, but cannot renounce his "pensiero dominante" which is the future of *Officina*, for which he proposes an official return to the old formula (the three original editors) with the understanding that he will personally handle the transaction with the "external," and unofficial editor as it were, namely Franco Fortini.

Please forgive this downpour of detailed information. It is meant to bring out the flavor of a literary culture marked by an intensity of purpose that might be viewed, by some, as verging on the obsessional, while people of my generation are likely to fully identify with it, or at least reflect on it with shamelessly un-repenting nostalgia. It is also intended to shed some light on Pasolini's *disperata vitalità*, on his relentless and tragic vitality, a *joie de vivre* in the face of doom, which prompted from him a somewhat confessional poem by the same title. In it we have access to such excruciatingly beautiful and very poignant lines, as

> È per l'istinto di Conservazione
> che sono comunista
>
> (It is my Survival instinct
> that makes me a communist)

and

> avrai un'infinita capacità di obbedire
> e un'infinita capacità di ribellarti
>
> (your propensity to obey will be boundless
> boundless your propensity to rebel)[4]

It is, I believe, in this frame of reference that the invectival epigram "To a Pope" may be best devoured and metabolized. Here's the text:

> Pochi giorni prima che tu morissi, la morte
>   aveva messo gli occhi su un tuo coetaneo:
> a vent'anni, tu eri studente, lui manovale,
>   tu nobile, ricco, lui un ragazzaccio plebeo:
> ma gli stessi giorni hanno dorato su voi

la vecchia Roma che stava tornando così nuova.
Ho veduto le sue spoglie, povero Zucchetto.
  Girava di notte ubriaco intorno ai Mercati,
e un tram che veniva da San Paolo, l'ha travolto
  e trascinato un pezzo pei binari tra i platani:
per qualche ora restò li, sotto le ruote:
  un po' di gente si radunò intorno a guardarlo,
in silenzio: era tardi, c'erano pochi passanti.
  Uno degli uomini che esistono perché esisti tu,
un vecchio poliziotto sbracato come un guappo,
  a chi s'accostava troppo gridava: «Fuori dai coglioni».
Poi venne l'automobile d'un ospedale a caricarlo:
  la gente se ne andò, restò qualche brandello qua e là,
e la padrona di un bar notturno, più avanti,
  che lo conosceva, disse a un nuovo venuto
che Zucchetto era andato sotto un tram, era finito.
  Pochi giorni dopo finivi tu: Zucchetto era uno
della tua grande greggia romana ed umana,
  un povero ubriacone, senza famiglia e senza letto,
che girava di notte, vivendo chissà come.
  Tu non ne sapevi niente: come non sapevi niente
di altri mille e mille cristi come lui.
  Forse io sono feroce a chiedermi per che ragione
la gente come Zucchetto fosse indegna del tuo amore.
  Ci sono posti infami, dove madri e bambini
vivono in una polvere antica, in un fango d'altre epoche.
  Proprio non lontano da dove tu sei vissuto,
in vista della bella cupola di San Pietro,
  c'è uno di questi posti, il Gelsomino...
Un monte tagliato a metà da una cava, e sotto,
  tra una marana e una fila di nuovi palazzi,
un mucchio di misere costruzioni, non case ma porcili.
  Bastava soltanto un tuo gesto, una tua parola,
perché quei tuoi figli avessero una casa:
  tu non hai fatto un gesto, non hai detto una parola.
Non ti si chiedeva di perdonare Marx! Un'onda
  immensa che si rifrange da millenni di vita
ti separava da lui, dalla sua religione:
  ma nella tua religione non si parla di pietà?
Migliaia di uomini sotto il tuo pontificato,
  davanti ai tuoi occhi, son vissuti in stabbi e porcili.
Lo sapevi, peccare non significa fare il male:
  non fare il bene, questo significa peccare.
  Quanto bene tu potevi fare! E non l'hai fatto:
    non c'è stato un peccatore più grande di te.[5]

(A few days before you died, death had begun
   to shadow one who was your age: at twenty,
you were a student and he a manual worker,
   you with lineage and wealth, and he was nothing
but a bad plebeian boy: yet days identical have dusted
   both of you with the gold of Rome, ancient and renovated.
I saw his corpse, poor old Zucchetto. Drunken, at night,
   he'd roam the streets around the Mercati and
a streetcar coming from San Paolo ran him over
   and dragged him for a stretch along the tracks
between the rows of plane trees: for a few hours
   he remained there under the wheels. A small,
silent crowd gathered around to look at him:
   it was late, few were the passers by. One
of those men whose existence is justified by yours,
   an old flat-foot, noisy and coarse like a thug, shouted
"keep off my ass" at those who came too close. Then
   came the hospital van and took him away. People left;
only a few shreds stayed behind and the woman
   who owns a night bar further down the street,
who knew him; she told a newcomer Zucchetto
   was gone, run over by a street car. A few days later
you too were gone: Zucchetto was one in your
   immense flock, Roman and human, a poor old drunkard,
without a family, without a bed, one who stayed
   up nights, living who knows how. He meant nothing
to you: thousand and thousand of poor devils like him
   meant nothing to you. Perhaps I am too harsh with you
when I ask why people like Zucchetto were unworthy
   of your love. There are horrible districts where mothers
and children live in a cloud of ancient dust,
   in a mud of by-gone times. Not too far from where
you lived, in view of beautiful Saint Peter's dome.
   One of these district, called Gelsomino...
a hill, really, half of it carved out by a quarry, and right
   below it between a ticket and a row of new buildings,
a heap of miserable constructions, not homes, but pigsties.
   One word from you, one gesture, and those children
of yours could have had a home: you chose not to do it,
   you did not say the word. It wasn't like asking you
to get along with Carl Marx! No, an immense and millenary
   wave forever breaking on the shore of life, divided
you from him, from his religion: and then again compassion
   isn't it part of your religion? Thousands of people,
during your pontificate, and right before

> your eyes, have lived in veritable stables and pigsties. You
> were fully cognizant of this; sinning is not, doing things
>   that are bad; sinning is, not doing things that are good.
> You could have done so much good! And you did not
>   You are the worst sinner of them all.)

Within the first batch of epigrams, this is the only one that can be properly termed an invective. The I-YOU relationship, or rather the distance separating them, is fully respected. Sarcasm abounds ("It wasn't like asking you to get along with Carl Marx!"). Indignation is explicit ("You could have done so much good! And you did not.") The condemnation of the addressee at the end of the poem is unambiguous and predicated on the equation of social negligence and ethical misconduct. Furthermore, the existence of a sympathetic readership is assumed as plausible.

Let us not forget, also, that Pasolini is writing his epigrams at a time when Italy seemed to be awakening from the moral lethargy of acquired privileges and, fifteen years after the fall of Mussolini (thirteen since the end of WWII), beginning to discard the fascist legacy that had continued to pervade its institutions, the schools, the judiciary, the military etc.: a frustrating situation Pasolini had blamed, in part, on the hesitation tactics of the Communist Party (see his "Polemica in Versi"). These are the years of Fellini's *Dolce Vita*. And this is Rome, the seat of one the most cynical superstructures western history has known. Italian civil life was grossly interfered with, by the obscurantism of the Catholic Church, to a degree that would be judged preposterous even by to-day's rather novocained standards. No divorce. No abortion. No legal status for common-law partners, etc. And to top it all a judiciary system that would mete out its justice, sentencing to a maximum of three years of imprisonment a husband who bumped off his wife on account of her having stained his honor through adultery. (See Pietro Germi's *Divorce Italian Style*.) Pasolini's text, however, addresses ills that are even more fundamental, such as the lack of acceptable dwellings ("not homes, but pigsties") for the vast sub-proletarian portion of the Roman population (The Pope's flock) whom he was particularly attracted to, for various and often neurotic reasons.

Paying close attention to what Pasolini's has to say about the political governance of the city, and the ethical implications of Popes retaining temporal power ("There are horrible districts where mothers / and children live in a cloud of ancient dust, / in a mud of by-gone times. Not too far from where / you lived, in view of beautiful Saint Peter's dome."), nothing much seems to have changed, in Rome (except for the dome, of course, which was not there), since the time of Boniface the VIII, so vehemently targeted by Jacopone da Todi's XIII century invective: the third of the rhymed letters the rebellious Franciscan Friar aimed, from the dungeon in Palestrina where he was kept, at the occupant of the Holy See, who had not only jailed him, but also excommunicated him. It is, as everyone knows, the same Boniface for whom Dante reserves a seat in hell. Writes Jacopone:

> O papa Bonifazio, molt'ài iocato al mondo;
> pensome che iocondo non te 'n porrai partire!
>
> Lo mondo non n'à usato lassar li sui serventi,
> ched a la scivirita se 'n partano gaudenti.
> Non farà lege nova de farnete essente,
> che non te dìa presente, che dona al suo servire[6]
>
> (Pope Boniface, you have had a good deal of fun in this world;
> You'll not be very lighthearted, I suspect, as you leave it.
>
> The world does not usually let its servants
> Take their leave joyfully;
> No special privilege will exempt you from this rule,
> Allow you to turn down the gift you have coming)

Setting from the start the vehemently sarcastic tone of the whole composition, Jacopone proceeds to detail the numerous sins that have blackened the soul of the pope, chief among them nepotism and simony, both of them inscribed under the general aegis of shamelessness:

> Pare che la vergogna dereto agi gettata
> l'alma e lo corpo ài posto a llevar to casata;
> omo ch'en rena mobele fa grann'edificata,
> subito è 'n ruinata, e no li pò fallire.
>
> Como la salamandra sempre vive nel foco,
> cusì par che llo scandalo te sia solazzo e ioco;
> dell'aneme redente par che ne curi poco!
> à 've t'accunci 'l loco, saperàilo al partire.
>
> (Body and soul, sweeping aside all sense of shame,
> You've given yourself to advancing your family's fortunes.
> You have built your house upon sand,
> And there's never any future in that.

Just as fire renews the salamander,
So scandals give you new life, confidence and boldness.
The care of souls doesn't seem to interest you much:
When you die you'll see the abode you've prepared for yourself.)

Dangerous as it might be, the proposed analogy I am about to suggest, between Pasolini's and Jacopone's texts, may be measured by the churlish attitude that both display, and, much more to the point, by the fact that such an attitude could be the sign of a literary wisdom and courage deeply rooted, in turn, in a peasant subculture[7] of which Jacopone could embody the *terminus a quo* and Pasolini the *terminus ad quem*. This ancient insulated culture, and the more recent sub-proletarian culture to which many of its values are to be traced (altered and manipulated as they may have been) began to perish, in Italy, in the mid and late fifties and was to come to a pitiful end during and immediately after the year of the great unrest, usually epitomized as the '68. Fossils of the erstwhile existence of such culture and the preposterous hope of its return, may also be found in some of Zanzotto's poetry: in *Filò*, for example. But we shall address this issue at some other time.

A mixture of critical gruffness, and referential coarseness, the Jacoponean- strategy to bring about social justice, is characterized, in Pasolini, by a mystical reliance on the enactment and celebration of the wild, the restless, and the instinctual. Such are the behavioral attitudes our author intends to revamp and offer as epistemologically justified and energizing aporiae. These he invests with a tenacious and consciously *counter-current* dialectical function.

It is not surprising, indeed, that in those years, while he himself was writing to protect what he viewed as the natural anarchy of the sub-proletarian masses and thought of himself as the most daring explorer of genuine oppositional drives (and their hindrances), Pasolini was often accused of being a reactionary by the officialdom of the protesting movement (whose members were for the most part the offspring of well-to-do professionals).

Burdened by the pressing desire to provide a lyrical exaltation to his personal anxieties, while injecting revolutionary significance into the repressed values of his half buried ethnicity, Pasolini resorted to invectival solutions when it was still possible (for him, at any rate) to imagine not merely the existence of an audience motivated by the political values he saw embedded in them, but a readership that would expect those messages to be made manifest through the deployment of an established literary genre. This however proved to be illusory. If not immediately, soon after.

The protesting voice which, it was assumed, would be heard by the oppressed as well as by the oppressor – a necessary condition for invectives to effectuate some kind of change –, fell actually on the deaf ears of the former, and did not at all "amuse" the latter who fueled a campaign of retaliation against an author whose power of vituperation, sharp and sophisticated as it might have sounded, was not, at any rate, capable of envisioning the radically new approach to literary theory and praxis the times and the evolution of a fairly large section of Italian society had been waiting for. Pasolini's message was received (and implicitly rejected) by the authorities of the institution (the organized church) it was hoping to shake up through a recommended return to such evangelical values as charity, and love for one's neighbor, while those who shared the author's appreciation for rhetorical exercises, stuck their heads in the sands of obsolescence. The late arrival of Pasolini's invective on the scene of the crime was furthermore coincidental with the disappearance of a popular audience interested in being exposed to, let alone sharing in, the author's political enthusiasm.

Doubtless no one was more aware or would eventually acknowledge the dramatic situation more forcefully than Pasolini himself and in his *Scritti Corsari* (dated 1973-74) – notably in such pieces as "Acculturazione e acculturazione" and again in "Vuoto di carità vuoto di cultura" – indicated in no uncertain terms how a new and very powerful epidemic was devastating the psychological landscape of the late fifties and early sixties, it's principal name: Consumers' Capitalism, although the average Italian preferred to call it "Economic Miracle" (once a Catholic always a Catholic?):

> Nessun centralismo fascista è riuscito a fare ciò che ha fatto il centralismo della civiltà dei consumi. Il fascismo proponeva un modello, reazionario e monumentale, che però restava lettera morta. Le varie culture particolari (contadine, sottoproletarie, operaie) continuavano imperturbabili a uniformarsi ai loro antichi modelli: la repressione si limitava a ottenere la loro adesione a parole. Oggi, al contrario, l'adesione ai modelli imposti dal Centro, è totale e incondizionata. I modelli culturali reali sono rinnegati. L'abiura è compiuta. Si può dunque affermare che la tolleranza della ideologia edonistica voluta dal nuovo potere, è la peggiore delle repressioni della storia umana.[8]

> (No fascist centralism has managed to do what the centralism of the consumerist society has done. Fascism proposed a reactionary and monumental model that remained mostly on paper. The different, localized cultures (peasants, sub-proletariat, laborers) kept their own ancient models: repression could only force them to a formal, superficial conformity. Today, on the contrary, the acceptance of models imposed by the Cen-

ter is complete and unconditional. The real cultural models are rejected. The abjuration has been completed. Thus, one could argue, the tolerance for an hedonistic ideology put in place by the new power is the worst kind of repression in human history.)

Within its parameters, thinking was equated to prepackaged thought and recast as a commodity democratically available to all. These were the years when Italian newspapers made room for art but the appreciation of it they divulged was no longer predicated on an active participation in the shaping of its aim, structure and exchange. It was then, and it continues to this day to be served, cold or hot or re-heated, on the plate of *loisir*, of *leisure*, of entertainment.

The audience Pasolini had been hoping to attract had begun its process of self-annihilation. Whether this process has reached its "final phase" and whether or not, in subsequent years, Pasolini intervened in it with more powerful and more successful instruments (with such films as *Uccellacci uccellini*, *Salò* etc.) lies outside the limits of the present investigation, and we shall refrain from indulging in more or less educated guesses. Instead we shall resume our journey to invective, by re-assessing the alleged proximity of the medieval and the modern texts before us.

Doubtless a contextual difference between the situations depicted by Jacopone and Pasolini can easily be pointed out. In the frame of reference of the present discourse they can both be viewed as examples of the antithesis that good and evil create in the fields of pure ethics and applied morality. A shift has occurred however in the definition of evil: Jacopone has compiled for us a long list of deplorable actions perpetrated by the object of his execration, while Pasolini has simply affirmed "that sinning is not, doing things that are bad; sinning is, not doing things that are good." The temptation of conjuring up the specter of another Pope, Celestino V, whom Dante, as it is known to all, vilifies in the Ante-Inferno, for having made the "great refusal", for not having done, that is, the good he had been chosen to carry out, is rather strong, but would not prove very fruitful. When it comes to "doing" or "not doing," Pasolini seems to feel very much like Ezra Pound who, in his *Canto* number 81 gave voice to the ethics of *poiein* by declaring:

> Thou art a beaten dog beneath the hail,
> A swollen magpie in a fitful sun,
> Half black half white
> Nor knowst'ou wing from tail

> Pull down thy vanity
> > How mean thy hates
> Fostered in falsity,
> > Pull down thy vanity,
> Rathe to destroy, niggard in charity,
> Pull down thy vanity,
> > I say pull down.
>
> But to have done instead of not doing
> > this is not vanity
> To have, with decency, knocked
> That a Blunt should open
> > To have gathered from the air a live tradition
> or from a fine old eye the unconquered flame
> This is not vanity.
> > Here error is all in the not done,
> all in the diffidence that faltered . . . [9]

Negligence in the welfare of others and the relentless pursuit of evil deeds against others may not seem to weigh equally in the scales of abstract justice, but they find a common denominator in the agonizing and agonistic philosophy of activism, where *omissions* count as sins, on a par with transgressions through *words* and through *works*. Not doing, in other words, translates into a disregard for the precept of charity ("and then again compassion / isn't it part of your religion?"). Not doing is tantamount to claiming the world must be preserved in whatever state one finds it if, keeping it that way is the only historical possibility to enjoy the comfort of one's privileges. And this, in turn, would suggest the world is a horse, a creature that can be bridled and mounted at one's pleasure, the sarcastic contrary of what Jacopone affirms in his own invective:

> El mondo non n'è cavallo che sse lass'enfrenare,
> che 'l pòzzi cavalcare secondo tuo volere!
>
> (The world is not a horse you can bridle,
> To be mounted and ridden at your pleasure.)

While the target of the invective can be assumed to occupy the same position in both Pasolini's and Jacopone's texts, the circumstances of their respective authors vary however, a great deal. Opposing the more sedate and by far less evangelically inclined Conventualists, Jacopone belongs to both the Spiritual faction of the Franciscan Order, and to the Party of the Colonna who are actively fighting the Pope, a member of the rival Roman clan of the Caetani: their confrontation cost Jacopone not merely imprisonment, but excommunication as well. Jacopone's oppositional stance could not be clearer. Vis a vis power, Pasolini occupies instead a strangely ambiguous position.

The very text of his invective is placed, or seeks to be placed, under the protection, indirect as it might have been, of the enemy, here represented by publisher Valentino Bompiani, a Catholic aristocrat, one who, if he didn't see eye to eye with the Pope, certainly would never have done anything to displease him. In this respect he is not very different from today's card-carrying members of the former Communist Party whose propensity to be photographed with His Holiness has reached alarming proportions.

In a moment of unexplainable enthusiasm, or confusion, Signor Bompiani had accepted to take on the publication, and what really matters, the distribution, of *Officina*. The outcome of this decision proved to be a major source of chagrin for Pasolini and friends. Their travails began when the situation had, at long last, begun to look very promising. Bompiani seemed to offer a solution to the financial difficulties that was stifling the production of the journal and the enthusiasm of its redactors. So, when the first issue of the new series appeared and all worries seemed to be memories of the past, Bompiani learns that his "noble" Roman friends are quite displeased with what he, wittingly or unwittingly, had allowed to slip through his own press.

To have a sense of the "thousand decisions and revisions which a minute will reverse," and the demoralizing sentiments that must have accompanied them, let us once again resort to a letter Pasolini wrote on March 9th, 1959 to the usual suspects, the editors of *Officina*: "Carissimi, è rientrato il pericolo. Bompiani ha parlato con un suo avvocato (cattolicissimo) che l'ha completamente rassicurato" (Dearest friends, danger has been averted. Bompiani spoke with one of his lawyers – a super-catholic – who has put his mind at ease, completely). Realism may have been Pasolini's forte, but reality often escaped him. The invective against the Pope had in fact done more than raising an eyebrow with Prince Barberini and the Aristocratic (*maneat iniuria verbis*) Members of The Roman Hunting Club to which Signor Bompiani was seeking admission. Surely not endowed with "un cuor di leone" (a lion's heart), as Manzoni would have said, and not at all reassured by his super-catholic lawyer, he removed his support, technical and editorial, from *Officina*. Pasolini, Leonetti and Roversi managed to assemble and publish one more issue. In it, mixed with others Pasolinian epigrams, we can read the following three that deal directly with the circumstances at hand:

Al principe Barberini (To Prince Barberini) (xii)

Non sei mai esistito: ora, a un tratto risorto,
fai, parli, minacci: ma sei cadavere di morto.

(You have never been alive: now, suddenly resurrected, you do things,
you speak, you threaten: you are the corpse of a dead man.)

Ai nobili membri del Circolo della Caccia (To the noble members of the Hunting Club) (xiii)

Non siete mai esistiti, vecchi pecoroni papalini
ora un po' esistete perche' un po' esiste Pasolini.

(A life of your own you never had, you spineless, popist nerds:
now you manage to have a little of it, siphoning it from Pasolini's.)

A Bompiani [To Bompiani] (xiv)

Tutto ciò che essi difendono è il puro male.
 sono così ciechi e avidi che non sanno speranza.
Il fascismo è la vera, l'ultima novità, l'autentica
 luce di questa nazione, nel mondo che pure avanza.

(All they stand for is evil in its purest essence. Their greed
 and blindness are such that hope to them is an unknown.
Fascism, that is truly the last novelty, the authentic light
 of this nation, in a world that moves forward no matter what.)

There is ample reason to suspect, however, that while the Celestinian great refusal vicariously performed by Bompiani, ought to be viewed as the epicenter of the tremor, the true hypocenter of the phenomenon, literary chronicles frequently refer to as the "Demise of *Officina*," must be sought among the tensions and conflicts that exacerbated the relationship of the *redattori*, both the original ones and those who Pasolini would have wanted to add, writing for instance, in the previously quoted letter of Dec. 20 to Fortini, that it was impossible for the journal to continue "senza la tua disperata intelligenza critica, la tua acuminata angoscia" (without yours fierce critical intelligence and piercing angst).

This is clearly and convincingly argued by Enzo Siciliano in his *Life of Pasolini* published in 1978: "L'illusione di Pasolini, la sua 'umiliante ingenuità' fu di ritenere acquisita una volta per tutte la propria *leadership* letteraria. L'‛umiliante ingenuità' aveva radice nel narcisismo." ("Pasolini's delusion, his ‛humiliating naïvete' was his belief that he could retain once and for all his literary leadership. The ‛humiliating naiveté' had its roots in narcissism"). Telegraphic and perhaps overly simplified as it may sound, this opinion reverberates also in a letter, quoted by Siciliano, written by Roberto Roversi to Fortini, on Nov. 11th 1959, while the crisis of *Officina* was brewing and in fact reaching its climax. It throws a completely different light on the comings and goings, on the ups and downs of *Officina* as well as on the different levels of awareness reached by its editors:

> Liberati dal complesso Pasolini e dalla sua fortuna. È sua non tua; non nostra. Cerca la tua; che sarà tua, non sua, non nostra. ... Capisco bene [...] che brucino a te (soldato delle Termopili) le delusioni passate e gli anni, in apparenza, perduti; che tu veda alcuni giovani (o vecchi) leoni correrti avanti a dimenar la coda. Ma in passato l'engagement era una forma di paranoia politica, un rivoluzionarismo velleitario e statico, una autentica arretratezza. Oggi superati gli schemi neo-capitalistici, e bruciate le torbe delle esperienze di questi ultimi anni, possiamo veramente avere e cercare la chiarezza per agire. Per collocare le proprie idee *al luogo giusto* e per verificarle e comunicarle. Rifiutando Gorgia e cercando Socrate.[10]

> (Free yourself from the Pasolini complex and his fortunes. They're his, non yours, not ours. Find your own that will be yours; it will be yours, not his, not ours... I'm well aware (and I love you and understand you) that you (soldier of Termopylae) rankle the disappointments of the past and the seemingly lost years; that you see certain young (or old) lions running ahead of you and waving their tails. But ion the past, commitment was a form of political paranoia, a fanciful and static radicalism, a genuine backwardness. Today, with neo-capitalistic patterns overcome, and the peat pf experiments of recent years burned, we can really have and seek out the clarity to act. To arrange our own ideas *in the right place* and to verify and communicate them. Rejecting Gorgias to seek Socrates.)

I must confess that even to-day the idea of equating Pasolini to Gorgias, and to all the negative reflections the sophist's name brought about at the time when the letter was written, is something one does not do without experiencing a more or less explicit sense of embarrassment. Yet nothing could be more helpful, if we are to lift anchor and get poetry to start navigating again, mostly in uncharted waters. Along with Enzo Siciliano, I too marvel at the notion that neo-capitalistic paradigms, whatever Roversi meant by them, may have been then, or may be now, for that matter, behind us. Yet in his letter I sense the presence of a curiosity that may in turn promote the creation of open models, the formation of a discourse that picks up strength as it proceeds, elaborating its own premises into unprecedented and ever surprising effects of sense, a discourse that seeks its truth not in the stolid obedience to its own premises but rather constructs and reconstructs its challenges, *buscando el levante por el poniente...* And this is something traditional invectives cannot do.

Pasolini's expostulations can be shelved, in this perspective, next to the parody of Shakespeare to which we have alluded earlier, and catalogued as a piece of perfunctory bravura, gratifying at best the amiable self-righteousness and/or the masochistic propensities of its author.

Such an impudent statement begs an unavoidable question: if invectives, formerly a quintessentially social and political type of poetry[11], have become powerless tools, what kind of poetic work should be encouraged that might regain a modicum of pervasively, if not strictly, iambic[12] relevance? In other words, is it possible for poetry to draw from invective, or at least from an invectival disposition, enough energy to enact its own reinstatement as an activity of collective interest?

Let us start by observing (again) that whereas the "intentional" distance between Jacopone and Pasolini is clearly negligible, the difference of their stance before their respective audience is incommensurate and hardly comparable. Jacopone could assume a plaintiff's "authorial authority" that is historically denied to Pasolini, through no fault of his own, to be sure. The absence of such authority, the loss of the poet's aureole, is predicated on the very special relationship between writer and reader which has been at the center of much critical reflection since the day Baudelaire called the latter *hypocrite, semblable* and *frère*[13]. Such an epochal mutation radically affected the writing of poetry: ignoring it meant, of course, playing down the conative component of the poetic message and reaffirming the narcissistic structure of its legacy.

Pasolini's friend and biographer Enzo Siciliano, as noted above, did not hesitate to identify the poet's narcissism as the principle cause of *Officina*'s demise. Here we'd like to widen and deepen his diagnostic pronouncement to encompass Pasolini's inability to align himself with the historical responsibility of his time which was, first and foremost, linguistic.

Few, I believe, have been clearer on this issue than Alfredo Giuliani in the opening statement of the by now justly celebrated anthology *I novissimi* (1961), featuring experimental poems "for the sixties" and written, naturally, in the fifties, at the same time of Pasolini's *La religione del mio tempo* and *Poesia in forma di rosa.* It is worth reading it again and again, bearing in mind the date of its composition:

> Scopo della «vera contemporanea poesia», annotò Leopardi nel 1829, è di accrescere la vitalità; e, dopo questa osservazione disarmante, aggiungeva che a quei tempi raramente la poesia era capace di tanto. Noi, che non siamo classicisti e nemmeno crepuscolari, abbiamo della vitalità un concetto linguistico che cercheremo di spiegare. Senza dubbio, in ogni epoca la poesia non può essere «vera» se non è «contemporanea»; e se ci domandiamo: – a che cosa? – la risposta è una sola: al nostro sentimento della realtà, ovvero alla lingua che la realtà parla in noi con i suoi segni inconciliabili. Quell'*accrescimento* verrà da una apertura, da uno choc, che ci metta a portata di mano un accadere in cui possiamo ritrovarci.[14]

(The aim of "true contemporary poetry," remarked Leopardi in 1829, "is to increase vitality"; and, having made this unsettling observation, he added that in times like his own poetry was rarely capable of such a feat. Being neither classicists nor crepuscular poets, we have a linguistic concept of vitality that we shall attempt to explain. Undoubtedly in every age poetry cannot be "true" unless it is "contemporary"; and if we ask ourselves, contemporary with what?, we meet with a single response: with our sense of reality, or rather with the language that reality speaks within us by its irreconcilable signs. The said *increase* comes from an opening, a shock, which puts within our grasp an occurrence in which we may find ourselves once more.)

In the subsequent pages, as it is known, Giuliani will argue in favor of a reduction of the psychological ego, a first step, I would venture to say, towards the necessity of coming to terms with the disintegrated authority of the self, viewed as a legitimate cognitive entity. It goes without saying that such a reduction and fragmentation, and, more precisely, the transformation of its matter into energy, does not translate into renouncing the power of affirming and distinguishing. This abdication may indeed have been the historical responsibility Pasolini did not wish or could not pursue.

Times, at any rate, were running faster and faster, for the *Novissimi* and for everyone else. Not only the authorial I was being divided and subdivided and rendered into a fugue of signifiers – to quote a very pertinent and cogent expression by Andrea Zanzotto,[15] which in and of itself was a major step forward, even though at first it caused apprehension and dismay, as it is only natural – the I of the reader was being pulverized as well.

The distance from Pasolini could not be more unbridgeable. The epochal change that he declared was not followed (unless perhaps after 1971, with the publication of *Tasumanar e Organizzar*) by reflection on the necessity of placing under discussion poetry's very charter and preparing "at all costs" investigatory tools that might avoid the trap of material referentiality. The media bombardment, of which we are all victims, had further aggravated the situation with respect to what he had proclaimed, annulling to the last drops of curiosity that a prepared reader should nourish for etymological strings, for the stylistic peculiarity of every single author—in essence, in those textual openings in which it is necessary to fall if one wants in some way to compare with the sensorial (and sensual) truth hidden (revealing itself intermittently) behind and beneath the materiality of the speaker's statements.[16] The idea that in the mechanics of stating there may be more meaning than the statement itself might carry, was something did not even pass through Pasolini's mind.

In short: the audience for poetry (expert, curious, and excitable as it should be), which had been thinning out dangerously for a long time, was coming close to extinction. If the situation was not one of the most rosy for lyrical poetry (the lyricists could always read their work among themselves), for invective—chosen as the symbolic manifestation of a socially responsible poetry—it was truly catastrophic. Noise had replaced meaning (the awareness and flavor inherent in the speaking) and function as a universal anesthetic. It did not spare anyone (poet, reader, worker, housewife, handyman, or intelligent woman), rendering the search for any sort of truth of little interest and less entertaining than ever. The lie, or the repeating of statements at a zeroed-out semantic level, went in parallel with the favor that inveterate liars (the public ones in particular) enjoyed among a vast number of people and readers (and voters), and certainly cannot be explained by dragging in an improbable enthusiasm for the paradox of the liar (the famous "I lie"). It is the result of a condition that was right in front of the eyes and the ears of everyone: it became extremely difficult, when not outright impossible, to hear what was being said or read by a boy[17] or by anyone else. At this point, the psychological deafness had become epidemic. Reestablishing any sort of hope for a socially responsible revival of the poetic function seemed the same as giving water to a dried-out plant. On the one hand, poets had dismissed, through a reached awareness, the old prerogatives of authorial authority. On the other, the readers that one supposed would have given life to a rich and surprising textual dialogue had less interest for poetry that for the skin of fig.

Nevertheless, contrary to all predictions, and unbeknownst to almost all readers (both the hair-splitting academics and the vacationers who only read books written with pasteurized ink), in some narrow ravine that separated the poet's frustration from the reader's indifference, contemporary poetry—or more specifically, certain of its rare but significant practitioners—had found the courage of a new, unexpected "cunning." Nor was it excluded that—thanks to this shrewdness of poetic reason, understood precisely in the Hegelian sense of migration of an evolutionary necessity from an exhaustion to a rebirth (that is, thanks specifically to the hypercalyptic autonomy of the forms of the statement that attracted or distracted the systole and diastole of a living organism)—poetry could be the only prosthesis capable today of reactivating in the human being not just the sense of what is heard, but the desire of what is listened to, the enjoyment felt when one realizes that some illuminations of thought are connatural with the linguistic practices that do not produce information and that presage the attainment of objects.

Thus, someone who was not yet ready to bury poetry once and for all, someone who was persuaded that there cannot be great poets without great readers, could find themselves tempted by the idea of imparting a turn, a *clinamen* in the descending line of its path.

From this perspective, a small phalanx of poets (among whom I am pleased to recall with particular interest and sympathy the late Corrado Costa, who should be completely reread) and artists not desperately mute or stammering, kept alive for years the art of thinking by resorting to the most civil corrosiveness of an event-based logic, not enslaved by paradigms of some Flaubertian *idée recue*, and to which the aphorismic genre can be splendidly suitable. In his last *barrage* of anti-glossolalic lunges, the painter Claudio Olivieri invites us to reflect on this type of apophthegm:

> Per non soccombere alla mortifera equivalenza a cui ci ha condotti il delirio informativo bisognerà imparare a far tesoro di ciò di cui siamo ignari.
>
> (In order not to succumb to the lethal equivalence to which informational delirium has led us, it will be necessary to learn to bear in mind that of which we are ignorant.)

Another example:

> L'*iconoclastia* non è l'astrazione ma la bulimia di immagini che sommerge la nostra attenzione. Col rendere ogni cosa uguale all'altra si abolisce la nostalgia, proprio ciò che si faceva garante di ogni vero.[18]
>
> (*Iconoclastia* is not the abstraction but the bulimia of the images that submerge our attention. In rendering every thing equal to another, nostalgia—precisely that which was made the guarantor of every truth—is abolished.)

If the apostrophized invective was destined to failure (however honest and generous those who resorted to it might have been), then it is clear that the task of the civil poet is to get back to work making linguistic motors that would not run the risk of immediate neutralization. I believe the works of Elio Pagliarani of the 1980s and early '90s may be examples of this, inscribed as they are in a rhetorical path in which the conciseness of aphorism and the critical vehemence of invective come together in the bite of the epigram. If they do not immediately "wake the conscience of the king,"[19] they are results that nevertheless have some intrinsic possibility of awakening the reader from the somnolence into which the notoriously low cogitational level of media entertainment has cast him. I propose that this is possible thanks to two characteristics in which, in Pagliarani, the epigram finds its own answer: constructive sarcasm and transformative quotation.

The *Ferraran Epigrams* [*Epigrammi ferraresi*][20] and, generally, the rare and highly fragmentary efforts of the last two decades (including, then, the last sections of *The Ballad of Rudy* [*La ballata di Rudy*], published in its entirety by Marsilio in 1995) give ample evidence of this. If it is constructive sarcasm, it is the result of a provocative celebration of the art of the survivor and the embarrassment of survival[21] duly formulated in a style in which affirmation is exalted and debased at the same time:

> Ancora non resuscita questo Lazaro.
> Io vi dico che bisogna rompere questo sepolcro.[22]
>
> (He still does not come to life again, this Lazarus.
> I tell you that this sepulcher must be broken.)

The transformative quotation is an old technique in Pagliarini:[23]

> Li tiepidi hanno fatto congregazione a Roma.
> Item arde la camicia e non la carne.
> In caligine significa che non ne vedrete la faccia.[24]
>
> (The unenthusiastic congregated in Rome
> *item* burns the shirt and not the flesh
> in a haze means that you will not see its face.)

There is, however, a meaningful difference between these new "textual thefts" and those of poetic prehistory. If in the beginning, the quotation—though subject to new rhythmic scansions—remained lexically intact (or almost), we now find ourselves faced with fragments that are decidedly "full of gaps." The raw material of these epigrams is provided to him by the *Sermons* of Fra Girolamo Savonarola. The presence of this author who was relieved or (as Pagliarani himself likes to say) "sacked" is conspicuous, and at the same time, deprived of the logic that originally supported it. The space between the two attempts becomes the *locus* where sequentiality and concatenation are remixed according to a procedure that we will call paratactically open. The sequence just cited is an excellent example. In fact, it is tied together by perfectly coherent sensorial evocations (*unenthusiastic – burn – haze*) (*tiepidi — arde — caligine*), but the meaning of the conclusion ("you will not see its face") that ends up, according to the prevailing logic, bound to the third term of the string, is really also connected to the two previous ones, from which, in fact, comes its significant peculiarity and effect of meaning that takes away all forms of consumable knowledge.

In the essay, *Da Savonarola all'avanguardia* [*From Savonarola to the Avant-Garde*], Francesca Bernardini Napoletano carefully reconstructs the dramaturgy of the citation process:

> Il discorso delle *Prediche* procede secondo una struttura logico-argomentativa lineare, su una scena storica concreta e definita; il discorso degli *Epigrammi* si sviluppa inceppando continuamente il senso e il significato, che vanno pertanto rintracciati in una "lettura [...] a salti, in modo trasversale", allegoria della perdita di funione storica e sociale della poesia moderna.[25]

> (The discourse of the *Sermons* proceeds according to a linear logical-argumentational structure, on a concrete and defined historical scene. The discourse of the *Epigrams* develops by continually obstructing the sense and the meaning, which are then found in a "reading [...] in fits and starts, crosswise," an allegory of the loss of historical and social function of modern poetry.)

In the introduction to the book of the *Epigrams*,[26] it was brought to light, in particular by Romano Luperini, that the first person singular (the reciting voice) is systematically set against the third (the object of the indignations), while the second person implicitly holds the role of an audience favorably disposed toward listening. The *I* of the poet, in other words, is not an obstruction; it does not take advantage of the abhorrent opportunity to put itself on display. But let's read Luperini's words directly:

> La riduzione al minimo (un minimo assai vicino allo zero) della narrazione non è rinuncia alla persuasione e alla retorica (nel senso tecnico del termine, sintende).

(The reduction to a minimum (a minimum very close to zero) of the narration is not a renunciation of persuasion and rhetoric (understood in the technical sense of the term).)

And even more explicitly:

La divisione io / costoro non è dunque un'invenzione del soggetto (anzi, questo tende a sparire come soggettività e a restare unicamente come voce recitante, seppure in tensione agonistica), ma espressione di un contrasto oggettivo che è *in re*, connaturato nelle cose stesse.[27]

(Thus the distinction I / them is not an invention of the subject (actually, the subject ceases to be a subjectivity and remains exclusively a voice that is reciting, albeit in an agonistic fashion), but rather it is the expression of an objective opposition that exists *in re*, part of the very fabric of things themselves.)

To be clear, Pagliarani combines in one of his rough and harmonious embraces the necessity to reach an audience of readers (he always tirelessly asserted literature's social function) and the awareness that poetry is, first and foremost, a process of re-signification, a game that one could not only witness, but in which one must participate, and in which the fleeting appearance of a profile that is personal (and more often personalized) is a product that is incidental and, ultimately, irrelevant. It is necessary that the terrain of this epigrammatic poetry be crossed many times, in directions that are slightly moved each time from the first pass, for the simple fact that the opposition of which it bears witness is recited by words whose political value makes itself felt at the very moment in which they are removed from the insolvency of verifiable prophecies. One wanders about darkly in the linguistic architecture that renders it possible.

> Bisogna combattere contro duplice sapienza.
> Ma voglio che tu sappia che questo lume non mi fa giusto.
> Preterea è ancora
> L'abisso della scriptura[28]

(It is necessary to fight against double wisdom.
But I want you to know that this light is not right for me.
Preterea is still
The abyss of writing.)

A new logic is at work. It is a logic that is neither absurd nor *quia absurdam*, but a slippery logic, that digs while moving laterally, a "signifying transference," as Gérard Haddad proposes calling it in his *Manger le livre*,[29] in which the associative process does not depend on evidentiary proof or, put another way, in which the potential for meaningfulness is predominant with respect to the data of the meaning.

It is curious (but not more than a little) that on two different occasions, Pagliarani wanted to connect his own statements imbued with regenerative epigrammatic impulse to the work of Pier Paolo Pasolini. First in "The anguish of your cracked voice broken by a freezing wind of death," a poem from 1995 and now included in the *Poesie Disperse*[30] in which Pasolini's name, not pronounced explicitly, is evoked indirectly by a series of singularly Pasolinian *topoi* (Friuli, Piazza del Popolo, India). On the other hand, explicit is the intent to retrieve a piece of his own literary biography:

> Solo dopo aver trascritto epigrammi da Savonarola
> *La carne è un abisso che tira in mille modi*
> *Così intendi la libidine dello stato*
> mi resi conto che dialogavo ancora con te[31]

(Only after having transcribed epigrams from Savonarola
The flesh is an abyss that pulls in a thousand ways
This is the way you understand the lechery of the state
I realized that I was still conversing with you)

The second time is a note, written six years later, that accompanies the second group of Savonarolan epigrams in the edition of 2001. Here, Pasolini's name is brought fully to light:

> Dopo aver compiuto e pubblicato questa ricerca, mi accorsdi che la mia parte di lavoro potevo e dovevo definirla un omaggio a Pasolini. L'ho detto una volta o due in pubblico, ora ci tengo a vederlo stampato qui.[32]

(After having completed and published this investigation, I noticed that I could have and should have defined my part of the work as an homage to Pasolini. I said this once or twice in public, now I want to see it printed here.)

Without a doubt, it is a case of a moving revelation. It seems wise to accept it as an expression of a feeling that comes from the heart, from a desire—perhaps a regret—from a nostalgia that humanly has full right to make itself heard. On the other hand, as far as the evolution and destiny of the poetry is concerned, between the Pasolini's epigrams and Pagliarani's, there seems to pass an impartial distance as wide as the sea. "To communicate," however, does not mean to have identical views. In fact, very often (and Pasolini could be one of these cases) communicating means that one of the interlocutors exhausts every effort in keeping alive even just the possibility of a dialogue. In support of this hypothesis, and to give these pages a provisional conclusion, I suggest reading another text removed, or re-aligned, by Elio Pagliarani—this time from *Filebo*—that comes from a Platonic dialogue where it is placed in doubt that the true good, when it coincides with pleasure, is capable of guaranteeing a happy life. But here, there is no air of invective. Rather, he has left, with incredible sweetness and unknown by his own source, a lesson:

> Nel caso in cui da tutte le arti
> si tolga via quella che procede
> a misurare e a pesare, di ben poco conto risulterà
> quanto rimane della singola arte. Basterebbe soltanto una
> capacità di congettura e di esercizio sui dati del sentimento...[33]

(In the case in which from all the arts
one takes away that which proceeds
to measure and to weigh, very little will result
from what remains of the single art. Just one capacity
of conjecture and exercise on the data of the feeling would be enough...)

[Translated by Gianpiero W. Doebler]

Notes

[1] All epistolary quotations are from P.P. Pasolini, *Lettere*, 1955-75 (Turin: Einaudi, 1988).

[2] Turin: Einaudi, 1993.

[3] Something like Priority Mail. In reality, rapidity was not a commodity that came cheaply, even then. It could be achieved exclusively by mailing your item "fuori sacco" (out of the official pouch) directly "at the train" a few minutes before it left Stazione Termini.

[4] From section IV and VII of "Una disperata vitalità," in *Poesia in forma di rosa* (Milan: Garzanti, 1964), p. 735 e p. 744, respectively.

[5] Merely a working translation. Pasolini's epigrams, first published in *Officina* (March-April issue of 1959) were later reissued in *La religione del mio tempo* (Milan: Garzanti, 1961), under the dostoyevskyan title "Umiliatio e offeso" and with the addition of a second batch grouped under the title "Nuovi Epigrammi" that had seen the light in the last issue of *Officina*. In December 1959 some reappeared in *L'Almanacco del Pesce d'oro*, while others still, in 1960, in *L'Europa Letteraria*.

Significantly, neither of the two latter venues chose to include the most controversial of Pasolini's lines, chief among them those dedicated to the *Bandiera Rossa* and the invective against Pope Pious XII, who had died in 1958.

[6] See complete text and paraphrase in *Laude*, a cura di Luigi M. Reale (Perugia: Fabrizio Fabbri Editore, 2006), pp. 350-54. Translation by Serge and Elisabeth Hughes (New York: Paulist Press, 1982), pp. 180-82.

[7] This insightful observation was first advanced by Ellemire Zolla in the preface he wrote for the American edition of *The Lauds*. See previous note.

[8] *Pasolini: A Biography*, transl. by John Shepley (New York: Random House, 1982), p. 191.

[9] Pound, Ezra, *The Cantos* (New York: New Directions, 1970), pp 521-22. For Pound's invective see above all his so called "Hell Cantos," and especially Canto XIV, ibid. pp. 61-3.

[10] Quoted by Siciliano (see note 8), p. 195-96.

[11] There are two examples of effective invective that can be considered: *Le invettive contro un medico* [*Invectives against a Doctor*] and *L'invettiva contro un uomo di alta condiziona ma senza dottrina e senza virtù* [*Invective against a man of high state but without learning and without virtue*] by Francis Petrarch. The first was composed in Avignon between 1352 and 1353, against a doctor whose name has remained unknown, but who was prominent enough to be able to number himself among those in charge of the care of Clement VI— as we learn from a letter addressed to the latter by Petrarch himself (*Familiari* V, 19). The second was drafted in 1355 at his Milan residence against the apostolic protonotary Jean de Caraman, who was made a cardinal by John XXII, during the Babylonian captivity. In these cases, the effectiveness is assured not so much by the violence of the language as by the authority of the sender and by the addressee's readiness to listen. In fact, the doctor, accused of incompetence ("You think, therefore, that that it is necessary to imply the nobility of an art. It is completely the opposite. Otherwise, a peasant would be the most noble of all workers; the shoemaker, the baker, and even you, if you were to stop killing, would be held in great esteem.") responds by saying he sought a "montanus artifex" (a minor writer who came down from the mountain) and charged him with countering Petrarch's ruthless observations. The polemic would be drawn out. Both the one against the doctor and the one against the highly placed man ultimately testify to the disgust Petrarch felt for the environment of the Avignon curia. See Francis Petrarch, *Prose*, G. Martellotti et al., eds. (Milan: Ricciardi, 1955), 648-709.

[12] According to the equation, established by Horace in his *Ars poetica*, of the iambic meter and violent elocution. See verse 79: ("Of Archilocus is the iamb, which armed his rage") and vv. 251-62: ("With its brief syllable followed by one that is long and rapid is the rhythm of the iamb, / which gives name through increase to the iambic trimeter, / even if this has six lines, / from the first to the last all are equal; subsequently, / so that its rhythm reaches the ear more slowly and heavily, / it agreed to share the rights acquired with the immobility of the spondees; / available and tolerant, but not to the point of surrendering, through sociability sociability, / the second and the fourth place. In the famous trimeters of Accius / the iamb appears rarely, while it accuses / with violence the verses of Ennius, / placed on the scene like heavy boulders, / of improvisation, sloppiness, and ignorance of art. / Not everyone is a good judge in understanding the dissonance of the verses, / and to the Roman poets it was accorded an offensive indulgence. And is this the reason why my verses ramble beyond all license? / Or, in the fear that everyone may see my deficits, do I remain prudently / safe within the limits in which one hopes to arrive? In this way I would avoid error, / but I certainly would not merit praise. Leaf through the Greek models, / leaf through them day and night.")

[13] In "to the Reader," the opening poem of the *Flowers of Evil*.

[14] The latest edition of *I novissimi* (Turin: Einaudi) is dated 2003. See p. 15.
[15] See "Nei paraggi di Lacan," in *Aure e disincanti* (Milan: Mondadori, 1994), pp. 171-76.
[16] In the wake, for example, of the essays of *Linguistics and Literary History* by Leo Spitzer (Princeton, Princeton UP, 1948).
[17] As in the *incipit* of T.S Eliot's "Gerontion": "Here I am, an old man in a dry month, / Being read to by a boy, waiting for rain."
[18] Unpublished.
[19] *Hamlet*, Act II, scene II.
[20] (Lecce: Piero Manni, 1987). Re-issued in 2001 as *Epigrammi da Savonarola, Martin Lutero eccetera.*
[21] From the Title of Paul Vangelisti's Selected Poems (New York: Agincourt Press, 2001).
[22] See *Tutte le poesie*, a cura di Andrea Cortellessa (Milan: Garzanti, 2006), p. 360.
[23] For Pagliarani's first published "quotational text" (*Vicende dell'oro*) see Pasolini's *Piccola antologia sperimentale*, in *Officina*, n. 9-10 (June 1957).
[24] *Tutte le poesie, cit.,* p. 356.
[25] In *Avanguardia*, anno III, number 9 (1998), p. 19.
[26] Vedi *Epigrammmi ferraresi, cit.*, pp. 8 e 11.
[27] See *Epigrammmi ferraresi, cit.*, pp. 8 e 11.
[28] *Ibid.*, p. 49.
[29] (Paris: Grasset & Fasquelle, 1984). English version, *Eating the Book* (New York: Agincourt Press, 2013), pp. 177- 87.
[30] *Tutte le poesie, cit.,* p. 359.
[31] *Ibid.*, p. 436.
[32] Now in *Tutte le poesie, cit.* p. 368.
[33] *Ibid.*, p. 236.

Donald Beecher

The Limits of Invective: Ben Jonson's Poetaster and the Temper of the Times

In the play he called *Poetaster*, first performed in 1601, Ben Jonson indulged himself in a not so covert attack upon two of his fellow playwrights and one-time collaborators, John Marston and Thomas Dekker, coming as close to outright invective in his representation of them as those censorious times would allow[1]. Despite his feisty nature as the self-styled and sanctimonious champion of high poetic culture against the pretensions of upstarts and hacks, Jonson had to proceed with caution, for the authorities had recently clamped down on satiric libel[2], the theatre was under scrutiny, and his opponents were far from helpless, having a play of their own ready for the boards in which he was to be "untrussed." *Poetaster* represents the ultimate salvo on Jonson's side to secure his own name and reputation following a three-year exchange of theatrical badinage referred to by Dekker as the "poetomachia," and by theatre historians as "the war of the theatres," the events of which have been anatomized in considerable detail.[3] It all began, in Jonson's words, when Marston "represented him on the stage."[4] Jonson boasts in that same entry in his *Conversations with William Drummond of Hawthornden* that already he had "had many quarrels with Marston," had beaten him and taken his pistol from him, the irony of it all being that in the ostensibly offending portrait of Chrisoganus, taken for Jonson, in Marston's *Histrio-mastix* (1599), he had intended to pay his fellow writer a compliment.

In extending the feud, rival acting companies realized the commercial advantage in staging raillery that involved combatants of little interest to the state, so long as they kept the point-counter point confined to theatrical mud slinging under the guise of fictional characters. Yet with Jonson, such containment was never sure, for he had already killed an actor in a duel,[5] and in *Poetaster* itself, his reputation is called to memory by Purgus, who warns the others concerning Jonson's alter ego in the play, "take heed how you give this out, / Horace is a man of the sword" (IV.vii.16-17). This is simultaneously a reminder of how closely invective is related to honour combat and physical assault even to the death. For Jonson, satire may represent his great vision for the improvement of society, but invective, within that satiric enterprise, is never far removed from his dangerously pugnacious instincts. Jonson was touchy about his humble origins and his apprenticeship to his step-father's trade of bricklayer, a favorite topic of his enemies, and he was sensitive to the likes of Marston who had a family coat of arms and openly claimed gentry status. Jonson's deprecatory language in the play may target a poetaster whose diction smells of the inkhorn, but in proving himself the better dramatic orator, he also assaulted the personhood of the character representing Marston, including his self-esteem, physical appearance, parvenu social ambitions, pedigree, trivial ethics, and political influence. Claiming never to name persons but only to censure the vices of the age, Jonson nevertheless delivers broadside invective by sharing out the tactics of assault among the characters and ventriloquizing his own voice through the satires of the Roman poet, Horace, who, by convention, is merely himself in the play. Having used up his credit with the law, Jonson dared no more physical bullying, but claiming extreme provocation, he was prepared to stretch the conventions of the theatre to their limits, under his high classicizing strain, to wield language as a weapon in murdering at least the integrity and reputation of his opponent.

Jonson's evasive design was to disguise the society in which he embedded himself and his opponents as a humanist fantasy in which Augustan Rome is brought to the stage, a portrait of high society, including the Imperial court, in which the great writers and their famous patrons so familiar to Renaissance scholars and schoolboys alike from Ovid to Virgil are assembled and placed in their pecking order in accordance with Jonson's critical predilections and their general reputations among humanists. Just as Jonson legitimizes his own aggression by adopting the Horatian voice and persona as his own, he also realizes a fantasy in that same persona of assigning himself to the inner circle of the court, if only the Augustan court, where Caesar, as Virgil's patron, places the epic writer in a chair above his own to recite from the *Aeneid*, surrounded by the poetic luminaries of that age. At the same time, this distinguished circle is called upon by Caesar to function as a law court to sit in witty judgement upon the talentless intruders and false witnesses. Marston, meanwhile, is assigned to the character Crispinus, a despised philosopher who appears in Horace's satires. With a touch of poetic license, he is also made to serve as the boor who provokes Horace to invective after dogging him in the streets in search of the great man's critical approbation and a share in the largesse of his patron.[6] Dull, but not ultimately indifferent to Horace's withering scorn, to revenge himself he turns false informant, accusing Horace of treason. This was Jonson's greatest ploy in disguising his imprecatory purposes, for in displacing his action to the ancient world, the play takes on the ethos of an era in which poets upheld the glory of the state and Cicero's high indignation against traitors and malefactors rang out in the tribunals. His own persona was not only the Horace of the epodes and satires, but the Horace who was the excellent and true judge of poetry by an interior assurance Jonson authorizes with the words, "because he knew so."[7] As David Riggs suggests, Jonson was looking for the "license granted to classical authors."[8] He wanted to recover his own assumed entitlement to speak truth in relation to the public good. Such a play might then pretend to the highest of social purposes, which was nothing less than the reification of Roman standards in his own times, making poetry and critical discourse the choicest instruments in the maintenance of civility and the urbane life. In such an ideological order, invective was merely the acknowledged instrument whereby the ideal state was protected from the polluting effect of the envious and malicious in their failure to distinguish between true virtue and their own vanity. In this way, like Horace, he sought to defend his own necessary art, in which truth is asserted in the place of libel, even though in doing so he appeared to contravene the laws, for as he declares in the play "I will write *satyres* still in spite of fear" (III.v.100).

His noble ideology as satirist and public benefactor not withstanding, Jonson was on a barely controlled rampage in the spirit of the invective endorsed and practiced by ancient orators and rhetoricians. His own *amour propre* indubitably wounded, Jonson was out for a kind of revenge, no only in styling his principal opponent as a salon crawler and boor turned informant, but in creating dramatic confrontations in which the man is condemned to hearing himself abused to his face with a round of epithets and name calling parceled out to Horace and others, including Tucca, the bluff, braggart soldier, who abuses indiscriminately anyone he can verbally domineer. Each occasion provides Jonson with an opportunity to turn wit into injury. In the end, Crispinus finds himself arraigned by an impromptu court made up of the received poets of the age. Their notion of poetic justice for a transgressor reduced to a poetaster is to administer to him an emetic with the peculiar properties of forcing him to retch up, not the contents of his stomach, but of his pseudo-poetic mind in the form of ludicrous neologisms and pompous diction. Such a purge pretends to a cure, but it serves rather as the ultimate gesture of humiliation in which, if style is the man, the man has been reduced to vomit. In the words of the indictment read out by Tibullus, "You are, before this time, jointly and severally indited, and here presently to be arraigned, upon the statute of Calumny, or Lex Remmia," Crispinus as "Poetaster and plagiary," Demetrius as "play-dresser, and plagiary" (V.iii.214-20). Of the 34 terms disgorged, only 15 may today be found in Marston's works, confirming still that Marston alone was intended by the portrait. Moreover, theory holds that the remaining 19 were expunged during the revision for subsequent publication of such plays as *What You Will*, the originals of which have been lost.[9] Presumably Marston learned something from this harsh experience. Among the hard words were "glibbery, lubricall, defunct, magnificate, snotteries, turgidous, ventositous, prorumpted, and obstupefact," words we may rejoice to have been eliminated by Jonson's censorious ear. The administrators of the purge, poets all, emphasized the egregiousness of such verbal confections by repeating them and commenting upon how hard it was to get them up. Such was the dramatic climax to a play that promised a knock-out blow to those who had gotten under Jonson's skin, thereby provoking his most vitriolic muse. It was perhaps as much as a troop of boy actors could be brought to play after so many acts of name calling and vituperation. But while for some it may seem too timid and too late, for others it was altogether juvenile and excessive. For John Enck, it was little more than "horseplay that offends by its pseudo delicacy," a "grim business, which extends to sadistic lengths," like "the bullying humility of a fifth-former beating his fag into conformity."[10] But even as "horseplay," its intent is clear, which is, through the strategies of invective, to demolish Marston's reputation as a poet, gentleman, and intellectual through an assault upon his verbal judgement. Drama demanded a dramatic solution, an enactment, an emblematic transaction such as the purge scene that serves in the place of pure verbal assault. But the power of invective remains because the audience, in tune with his *comedie-à-clef*, saw the historical man in the character hailed before a court, not only as a reprobate and enemy to the state, but as a poet of puff paste intelligence.

 That Jonson was building consciously and cogently upon the tradition of humanist invective is substantiated by his disclaimers in the apologetic dialogue appended to the play as an address "To the Reader." This was a wound-licking exercise following the production of Dekker's *Satiromastix*, in which, for one last time, Jonson was abused in a stage portrait. The dialogue was given one airing in the theatre before it was suppressed by the authorities, although it was surreptitiously reinserted at the time of the publication of his plays in 1616. Jonson profiles himself as the pouting but defiant "Author" of *Poetaster*, the innocent victim of three-years of libel and abuse which had at last stung him into action. In the dual attitude characteristic of the maker and receiver of invective, he professes himself above the malice of their "blacke vomit," yet hears from his interlocutors how he had been veritably hit and injured. He returns to name-calling, referring to the makers of *Satiromastix* as "the barking students of Beares-Colledge, / To swallow up the garbadge of the time / With greedy gullets" (45-47). He professes to the truth in all he said of them in taxing their crimes, while for their part, they merely indulged in plagiarism, filth, and excrement. But the war was clearly over, because Jonson had no heart to try to outdo his own performance or theirs; he was reconciled to the fact that Virgil and Horace had their detractors, and that as Horace redivivus in the play he could go no further. Yet in the spirit of pure invective he boasts of what he might have done if "Arm'd with Archilochus fury," writing such iambics that "Should make the desperate lashers hang themselves," or how he might "Rime 'hem to death, as they doe *Irish* rats / In drumming tunes" (161-64), before leaving them to the whips of their own guilty consciences. This is Horace still of the imprecatory satires and epodes, one of those epodes about a former slave, another about a libeler who had attacked one of his friends, and the last about Maevius the poetaster cursed to die at sea. Archilochus is, of course, the celebrated seventh-century B.C. Greek satirist who put his withering iambics upon Lycambes when he refused him his daughter in marriage. So terrible was the force of his words that after they were read out at the festival of Demeter, both father and daughter hanged themselves.[11] More will be said of the power of words over things as though imbued with magic, and of the imprecatory curse that is self-fulfilling in the imaginations of those targeted. Jonson displays such weapons, together with a clear knowledge of their traditions, uses, and efficacy in relation to a play that had been calculated to kill as well as to purge, for as John Enck concludes, "With Jonson, in whom nothing is proportionally life-sized, the attack on poetasters carried more invective than usual."[12]

In a further allusion he places himself at the very heart of the classical invective tradition in refusing to waste more time "With these vile *Ibides*, these uncleane birds, / That make their mouthes their clysters, and still purge / From their hot entrails" (219-21). Ibides, without doubt, refers to the literary quarrel from Alexandria involving Callimachus who cursed his enemy, Apollonius of Rhodes, under the name of Ibis, not only because the bird ate garbage around the Egyptian markets, just as Apollonius was said to feed off the scraps of Homer, but more scatologically because the bird possessed the remarkable ability to purge itself by shoving its water-filled beak up its own fundament.[13] In the play, Jonson reduces this to an emetic, taking his cue from the *Lexiphanes* of Lucian in which a rhetorician's surfeit of words is cured with a vomit administered by the physician Sopolis.[14] Nevertheless, the Ibis allusion ties Jonson's thoughts to a literary feud of classical standing having features resembling his own situation. Ovid, too, wrote an "Ibis" poem, an exercise in erudite invective, in which he speaks of the verbal savagery of the Thracians, who went so far as to murder their guests.[15] In these poems, as with the Jonson-Marston feud, the injuries redressed were often trivial, but the intent of the words was brutal. Such disputes were, simultaneously, occasions for rhetorical display of a highly entertaining nature, confirming Northorp Frye's astute observation that "invective is one of the most readable forms of literary art, just as panegyric is one of the dullest."[16] We enjoy hearing people denounced and fools exposed as part of our own pleasure-seeking natures, provided there is a modicum of wit and invention. We enjoy them as finer expressions of our own complex social instincts for managing the survival of the self within groups through the adverse verbal construction of the conduct of rivals and threats. These tactics are never practiced without risk, and hence the particular delight we take in watching the writer of invective establish his own integrity and security as he makes the case against his opponent.

To the extent *Poetaster* really is about poetry, it assumes a place in the humanist tradition of invective against those deemed to be abusers of the art. Callimachus had a falling out with a former associate, leading to common complaints concerning borrowing and plagiarism, matters of influence, and the failure to achieve a noble and independent social vision. The themes are redeveloped at length by Antonio da Rho in his *Philippic against Antonio Panormita*, a feud which, as with Jonson and Marston, arose between two men backing rival professional positions that lead by degrees from misunderstanding to blatant verbal assault. By 1429, Rho had Latin poems in circulation denouncing Panormita, followed by letters, leading to an all-out literary war. In the *Philippic* he then denied writing any preliminary provocations. Rho, like Jonson, stood up for his personal values and standards, styling himself the modest, humble, sincere man, esteemed by his friends, the innocent victim of the other's malignity. The similarities need not be evidence of influence, but a testimony of the *sui generis* defense tactics of the rhetorical mind preoccupied with similar professional circumstances.[17] Correct Latin style and the "oratio inepta" were constantly under scrutiny amid the accusations. Rho's target was, elsewhere, Lorenzo Valla who began in a light-hearted way to point out the Latin errors of the other until feuding broke out through insult and invective. Again, rivalry and professional envy played a part as one looked askance at the *succès d'estime* of the other, accompanied by accusations of plagiarism, leading Rho to a peroration in the form of a beast fable in which he assigns himself the role of the lion while relegating his opponent to that of the ass.[18] The degree to which Jonson's engagement in the war of the theatres was conducted as an active and conscious production in Renaissance literary invective is a moot point. But that the profiles of those feuds all seem to follow a common course and psychology is reason enough to urge comparison, not so much at the level of literary genre as at the level of generic human strategizing within competitive verbal environments.

One scene in the play that epitomizes Jonson's skills at invective is the first of Act III. It is a dramatized re-enactment of Horace's Satire I.ix through which Jonson taxes Crispinus as a tedious and pedantic poet, not only for his solecisms and "worded trash," but for his sartorial foolishness and affected manners, while professing to his own "tame modestie." As a character in the play, Horace's sober disdain highlights the enacted portrait of Crispinus as a prating poet, singer, and idle talker, indifferent even to the death of his own father, who concludes by demanding that Horace share his patron Mecoenas (III.i.253). The exchange allows Jonson to include such epithets as "base govelling minds," styling his assailant as a "Land-Remora," the fish described by Pliny for its sucking mouth by which it attaches itself to the bottoms of boats in great numbers, slowing their progress. Trebatius, the lawyer and Horace's friend, joins in the execration, while the dullness of Crispinus, meanwhile, incites the satirist to ratchet up his attack. It is a clever exercise in humanist poetics and Renaissance *imitatio*, a way of declining to speak in his own voice while performing an act of appropriation that serves in its stead, having behind it all the authority of classical invective.

Crispinus boasts of being a gentleman born (II.i.88), which sets him up for ridicule. Chloe makes mention of his shortness of stature, stating that true gentlemen have little legs. Meanwhile, in a mock description of his family coat of arms, Crispinus draws further attention to his class pretensions (II.i.95). Thus by spontaneous discovery, or by design, the play touches upon the received categories of classical invective set out by Cicero and the rhetoricians. Under the category of *res externa* such matters as a man's birth, education, citizenship, ancestry, status, manners, names, friends and associates, and occupation come under attack. Under the heading *res corpus* there follows the denigration of a man's health, stature, deformities, debauchery, immorality, affected dress, and eccentric personal tastes. Finally, *res anima* covers his intrinsic character, corrupt or diminished intelligence, judgement, motives, and such traits as avarice, cowardice, vanity, shamelessness, cruelty, or superficiality, so that by degrees, the unfavourable description of the parts constitutes a thoroughly depraved portrait. The final effect is a kind of hermeneutic loop in which nature, style, and temperament explain the inevitability of criminal, antisocial, or debauched conduct, just as the conduct reveals the essence of the person. A favoured method for bringing truth to the portrait is to turn a man's own words against him through quotation. Such apparent truths are difficult to gainsay and work to devastating effect. Not surprisingly, Jonson hits Marston under all these headings, discrediting his judgement as a poet by discrediting his judgement as a person in several aspects of his social life, while having his own words witness against him in the purge scene. Always, we are mindful of the slights of rhetoric, the ambiguity of words, the tendency to hyperbole, the excesses of libel, the animus of the maker, the license taken with dramatic portraits, and the faint of make believe in the creation of such invectives. Without wit they are nothing, but if overly witty they become merely artistic creations and exercises in the resources of language. In his *Poetaster*, Jonson employs the conventions of the theatre to displace the properties of direct invective, but his purpose remains all along to profile an obnoxious and misguided socialite and poetizer with all the force of Cicero's demolition of traitors in the name of the state. His own smug sense of superiority might have brought him to decline invective altogether, or so he would have us believe, until the outrageous lies put upon him necessitated the counter-attack. But even that ploy is part of the posture of the mode. He would urge that right poetry, if true and perfect, moulds the state, making men brave and ready to fight and die for the patria (V.i.17). It is a brilliant deployment of the myth of the Augustan age in justifying his own self-representation as Horace and his assault upon a Roman poetaster and corrupter of manners. Yet all along, it was pure spleen, as it was on the other side. Dekker's *Satiromastix* was still to come, perhaps written with Marston's collaboration, and Jonson knew it. Dekker professes to his own right to the law of talion in the sense that those who offend in language should be punished in kind.[19] Not surprising, Jonson is anatomized in an equally comprehensive and unflattering way for his manners, arrogance, and ambition, his envious and scrapping nature, his corpulence and his pock-marked face, described as the lid of a warming pan full of holes for the escaping heat. Pretend as Jonson might to reticence through historicizing his setting and fictionalizing his portraits, the intended victims confirm their identities in their acts of retaliation. Read without these identifications, the play maintains a modicum of interest as a representation of Augustan Rome interpreted by a humanist scholar interested in the regulation of the social life of the state through a culture of high poetry. As a barely disguised invective, however, the play's hold upon readers vacillates between academic drama and epigrammatic assault, that assault itself divided between humours performed, exposed and ridiculed, and language tending toward the curse.

The economy of invective including its power as a weapon of attack and self defense is the invention of man the speaking animal who, through language, regulates social politics and pecking orders. It is a component of gossip, which is the quintessential activity whereby, through verbal communication, members of the collectivity protect themselves through an exchange of information from all individuals suspected or selectively proven to hold hidden agendas deemed detrimental to the survival of the group. Gossip is the counterpart to reputation, for reputation is the abstract quantification of the working esteem of the individual in relation to collective standards and expectations. All individuals must therefore seek to maintain a positive response from others and a sense of self esteem.[20] Because that esteem is established essentially through gossip, individuals within groups seek to assert positive information about themselves and run constant damage control through the micro-management of opinion. The contortions of invective writers pertain to just such exercises on a larger and more combative scale of name clearing and counter-attack. Invective thereby seeks to do unto others what one most dreads to have done unto oneself, for it seeks to assassinate through language in order to reconfirm one's own social entitlements as a person of received integrity and worth.

The cause of the criminal lawyer, in mastering the art of invective, is to diminish the entitlements of a man presumed not only guilty of a specific crime, but more broadly demonstrated to be corrupt to the core, untrustworthy, a repeat offender, a perverted mind, a psychopath. Through a notion of correspondences, it was thought that a man's nature was as readily interpreted out of his physiognomy as from the report of his deeds. Hence the assessment of character down to physical traits in the demonstration of crimes. That two playwrights should vie with one another for the place of prestige in the competitive environment created by rival theatrical companies would appear to be of an entirely different order, yet the verbal tactics were much the same. Perhaps to these men their places in the playwright's pecking order seemed like a matter of survival, one that depended not only upon their comparative talents, but upon their reputations and moral integrity. The "poetomachia" was more than a talent match; it was a form of gossip in which the measure of talent was made to depend upon the full measure of the man—a little piece of the humanist mind set run wild. Or it may simply be a law of society that where there is equality among men a process will arise whereby echelons and hierarchies will be constructed through which the bullying alpha male is simultaneously the alpha dramatist.[21] This is in keeping with Northrop Frye's assessment of invective as "militant irony," a mode which, in fact, has little irony about it. Invective purports to be fact, assaulting the target directly, often with the risk of being too concise and direct, in an effort to make that person mutually loathed. An acquiescent audience joins in collusion with the calumniator, as in gossip clatches, in mutually descending an individual deemed a nuisance to the public or common good.[22] As with gossip, there must be an audience, as well as a speaker and an intended victim. Invective is the most aggressive form of news whereby, in the name of the group, the reporter-as-prosecutor seeks to expose all that is hypocritical, parasitic, or undisclosed in the intentional states of the targeted individual through clear, forceful, rhetorical profiling. But the economy is a dangerous one, because wit itself may be a devious means for gaining cruel advantage by playing upon the vulnerable imaginations of auditors, despite its careful appeal to truth and objectivity. Jonson's *Poetaster* works its measures in precisely this ambiguous economy.

What then of the power of words themselves to kill with all the efficiency of a verbal firing squad in the vein of Archilocus or the rhyming of Irish rats? This has to do with the power of invective not only over the imaginations of auditors, but over the imaginations of the victims themselves, insofar as each individual, in a sense, calibrates social currency according to a psychological Fort Knox of self esteem. If invective guts the Federal Reserve, for those so sensitively inclined, despair may seem the only option. Invective takes its toll upon those carefully attuned to their own dependency upon social approbation. It may constitute an art of portraiture so powerful that a sense of comprehensive worthlessness appears beyond all countermanding. It is an instance in which *le mot* becomes *la chose*, when the power of the imagination becomes omnipotent, making defamatory naming tantamount to physical injury.[23] Honour is a vital compulsion, a by-product of our gregarious natures and survival strategies. Insofar as language has achieved the power to create provisional versions of reality capable of invoking the most powerful of emotions and fears, language itself takes on the qualities of ritual magic, given the close alignment between signs, intentional states, and belief and the unfolding of the material world. Invective seeks mastery over others as opposed to inclusiveness, working as it does through public opinion to exclude, placing the destructive force not in the words but in the power of groups to ostracize, yet it shares in intent with the curse through which language is granted ritual power over the forces of chance and destiny, to the extent that victims believe superstitiously in the power of imprecation to harness and control destiny. That interplay between invective and cursing is seen in Horace's Epode 5, in which the victim vows that his tormentors will in turn be visited by the nightmare and suffocated, pelted to death by stones, then eaten by dogs and carrion birds. It may well be said that sticks and stones can alone break bones while words are inoffensive. Yet the social dynamics of self-esteem and ritual fear of the magical power of words argues otherwise. Just as sorcerers might invoke devils by conjuring with words and signs, or priests might pronounce the magic words whereby wafers and wine are transubstantiated, so the writer of invective may study the imprecatory effect of words upon the imagination of the victim not only as insults but as spells in control of the forces shaping the future.

In his *Poetaster*, Jonson indulges his voice of invective as in no other play, oriented as it is in the traditions of ancient Rome, displacing his own rancorous voice as he might in adopting the vocabulary of Horatian satire—the vocabulary of a man who, in his own times, had confronted envy and verbal assault. Formally, Jonson declines the role by adapting the conventions of the theatre to his ends, in a sense reducing invective to satire through the dissimulation of identities, the displacement of slanderous voices, and the transposition of setting. Moreover, he knew only too well that invective is dialogic, and that unless he could disguise his intentions, if not sting his victims into silence, the combat would continue until wits ran dry or the audience lost interest. Ironically, too, despite his outcry against cowardly or opportunistic informers, anonymous complaints over this very play were lodged with Chief Justice Popham, which might have led to very real corporal punishment, given that Jonson had already exhausted the patience of the law with his truculence and verbal brinkmanship.[24] To decline invective was the greater part of valour. Jonson studied to have it both ways, yet he was never certain that he had avoided subsequent wrath or that he had seized the final word in his play. His apprehension is made clear in the "apologeticall dialogue" "To the Reader" in which Polyporus reports of him, "O, vex'd, vex'd, I warrant you." Jonson's worry was not that he was guilty of all that he had been accused of in Dekker's *Satiromastix*, but that the world was only too ready to believe it of him. Dekker was not without his power to hit, and now Jonson's own imagination worked upon him in a way that spelled defeat in his own mind, making him, curiously, the biter bitten, despite his own blustering self righteousness. Clearly by then he had lost his taste for invective, for when his friends in this dramatic postlude ask if he will answer the libels, he declines, whereupon they declare him to be undone with the world. It is then that he boasts of what he might have done but would not do, cursing them like Archilocus, rhyming them like rats, or purging them in the manner of the ibis, preferring rather to withdraw from society in defeat to devote himself to historical tragedy "high, and aloofe, / Safe from the wolves black jaw, and the dull asses hoofe" (238-39) in hopes that time and a different muse might restore where invective against his enemies had been deemed to fail.

Notes

[1] The play was entered into the Stationers' Register on December 21, 1601 by Matthew Lownes. Jonson was no doubt looking for early publication to confirm his position in the feud and to further induce readers to his side, recognizing, perhaps, that print is the more natural medium for invective.

[2] Following a spate of cankerous satires in the 1590s, the Privy Council, in the spring of 1599, decreed that such writings were a menace to the state. On June 1, John Whitgift, Archbishop of Canterbury, and Richard Bancroft, Bishop of London, issued a list of scurrilous books to be publicly burned, titles that included writings by Thomas Lodge and John Marston.

[3] A concise history may be found in D. Heyward Brock's *A Ben Jonson Companion* (Bloomington: Indiana University Press, 1983), pp. 292-93. But the history of "the war" can be said to begin with Josiah H. Penniman's *The War of the Theatres* (Boston: Ginn, 1897), and to continue with Roscoe A. Small's, *The Stage-Quarrel Between Ben Jonson and the So-Called Poetasters* (Breslau: M. & M. Marcus, 1899), and to arrive at documentary exhaustion in Stuart Omans's "The War of the Theatres: An Approach to its Origins, Development and Meaning," Ph.D. thesis, Northwestern University, 1969. The subject is treated by Herford and Simpson in their monumental edition of Jonson's works, and by all of his biographers, such as Anne Barton's *Ben Jonson, Dramatist* (Cambridge: Cambridge UP. 1984), pp. 58-91 passim. Noteworthy is that most of the plays were presented by child actors: Marston wrote for Paul's Children and Jonson for the Children of the Chapel at Blackfriars.

[4] *Ben Jonson's Conversations with Drummond of Hawthornden*, ed. R.F. Patterson (London: Blackie and Son Ltd., 1923), p. 27.

[5] The victim was Gabriel Spencer, an actor in the company of Phillip Henslowe. The duel took place in Hoxton Fields in September of 1598, thus about the time the "War of the Theatres" began. The cause of the feud is unknown. Jonson was imprisoned in October, tried, confessed, but managed to escape hanging by pleading benefit of clergy. His goods were confiscated and he was branded as a malefactor on his thumb. Jonson says he was also wounded during the quarrel, and that Spencer's

sword was 10 inches longer than his. D. Heyward Brock, *A Ben Jonson Companion* (Bloomington: Indiana University Press, 1983), p. 259.

[6] The "blear eyed" Crispinus is mentioned by the scholiasts as an "aretalogus," one who babbles of virtue and writes trivial verse, a stoic despised by Horace; see Satire I.i.120; I.iii.139; I.iv.14; and II.vii.45. He is combined with Maevius the poetaster of Epode 10 cursed to die of shipwreck. Dekker's character, Demetrius, is derived from Satire I.x.78-80 where he tortures Horace by carping at him behind his back.

[7] *Discoveries* (2594), in *Ben Jonson*, ed. C.H. Herford, Percy and Evelyn Simpson, 11 vols. (Oxford: at the Clarendon Press, 1925-54), vol. VIII, p. 642.

[8] David Riggs, *Ben Jonson: A Life* (Cambridge, Mass.: Harvard UP, 1989), p. 58.

[9] Herford and Simpson, *Ben Jonson*, vol. IX, pp. 578-79.

[10] John Enck, *Jonson and the Comic Truth* (Madison: U of Wisconsin P, 1957), p. 80.

[11] Robert C. Elliott, *The Power of Satire: Magic, Ritual, Art* (Princeton: Princeton UP, 1960), p. 7.

[12] John, Enck, *Jonson and the Comic Truth*, p. 70.

[13] See Lindsay Watson, *Arae: The Curse Poetry of Antiquity* (Leeds: Francis Cairns, 1991), p. 123.

[14] This reference was first noted by James Upton in his pamphlet *Remarks on Three Plays of Benjamin Johnson* (London: G. Hawkins, 1749), p. 3; see Herford and Simpson, *Ben Jonson*, vol. IX, pp. 577-78.

[15] Ovid, "Ibis," ll. 381-82, 401-02.

[16] *Anatomy of Criticism* (Princeton: Princeton UP, 1967) (fifth ed.), p. 224.

[17] David Rutherford, ed., *Early Renaissance Invective and the Controversies of Antonio da Rho* (Tempe, AZ: Medieval & Renaissance Texts & Studies, 2005), passim.

[18] *The Apology of Antonio da Rho. . .Against A Certain Archdeacon and his Loathsome Sycophant Accomplices*, in *Early Renaissance Invective*, p. 241.

[19] Thomas Dekker, "Preface," *Satiromastix*, *The Dramatic Works of Thomas Dekker*, ed. Fredson Bowers (Cambridge: Cambridge UP, 1953-61,) Vol. I, p. 309.

[20] Charles Flynn, *Insult and Society: Patterns of Comparative Interaction* (Port Washington, N.Y.: Kennikat Press, 1977), p. 10.

[21] David Riggs, *Ben Jonson: A Life*, p. 79.

[22] Northrop Frye, *Anatomy of Criticism*, p. 223.

[23] Jerome Neu, *Sticks and Stones: The Philosophy of Insults* (Oxford: Oxford UP, 2008), p. 124.

[24] Herford and Simpson, *Ben Jonson*, vol. IV, p. 201. The reference in the Preface is to the Chief Justice, to whom Jonson boldly dedicates the play in an effort to solicit his acquiescence to the play's necessary strategy by a man more sinned against than sinning, abetted by the representation within the play of Horace's own friendship with a leading Roman lawyer.

Bibliograhy

Barton, Anne. *Ben Jonson, Dramatist*. Cambridge: Cambridge UP, 1984.

Ben Jonson. Eds. C.H. Herford, Percy & Evelyn Simpson. 11 vols. Oxford: Clarendon Press, 1925-54.

Ben Jonson's Conversations with Drummond of Hawthornden. Ed R.F. Patterson. London: Blackie and Son Ltd., 1923.

Brock, D. Heyward. *A Ben Jonson Companion*. Bloomington: Indiana UP, 1983.
Dekker, Thomas. *The Dramatic Works*. Ed. Fredson Bowers. Cambridge: Cambridge UP, 1953-61.
Elliott, Robert C. *The Power of Satire: Magic, Ritual, Art*. Princeton: Princeton UP, 1960.
Enck, John. *Jonson and the Comic Truth*. Madison: U of Wisconsin P, 1957.
Flynn, Charles. *Insult and Society: Patterns of Comparative Interaction*. Port Washington, N.Y.: Kennikat Press, 1977.
Frye, Northrop. *Anatomy of Criticism*. Princeton: Princeton UP, 1967.
Neu, Jerome. *Sticks and Stones: The Philosophy of Insults*. Oxford: Oxford UP, 2008.
Omans, Stuart. "The War of the Theatres: An Approach to its Origins, Development and Meaning." Ph.D. thesis. Northwestern University, 1969.
Ovid. "Ibis." Ed. Robinson Ellis. Exeter: Bristol Phoenix Press, 2007.
Penniman, Josiah H. *The War of the Theatres*. Boston: Ginn, 1897.
Small, Roscoe A. *The Stage-Quarrel Between Ben Jonson and the So-Called Poetasters*. Breslau, M. & M. Marcus, 1899.
Rho, Antonio da. *The Apology of Antonia da Rho ... Against a Certain Archdeacon and his Loathsome Sycophant Accomplices*. In *Early Renaissance Invective*. Ed. David Rutherford. Tempe: Medieval & Renaissance Texts & Studies, 2005.
Riggs, David. *Ben Jonson: A Life*. Cambridge Mass.: Harvard UP, 1989.
Rutherford, David, ed. *Early Renaissance Invective and the Controversies of Antonio da Rho*. Tempe: Medieval & Renaissance Texts & Studies, 2005.
Upton, James. *Remarks on Three Plays of Benjamin Johnson*. London: G. Hawkins, 1749.
Watson, Lindsay. *Arae: The Curse Poetry of Antiquity*. Leeds: Francis Cairns, 1991.

Remo Bodei

Righteous Wrath

1. In the philosophical and literary culture of the West, the image of wrath (of which invective is one aspect) has traditionally had two faces: on one side it is considered a noble passion of revolt against offenses and injustices endured, on the other, a type of madness or temporary blindness, a feared loss of self-control and, therefore, of freedom.

In the first case, we are set against the (real or presumed) lion-like attempts of others to belittle us and subject us with impunity to their will. In the second, we are exposed to the danger of not being present to ourselves, to say things and to complete acts that we may later regret, to become slaves to the opinion of others or to the worst part of ourselves and, consequently, the easy prey of adversaries.

The alternative is between the "ruinous wrath" of Achilles and the patience of Odysseus until his revenge upon the Pretenders, between Aristotle and the Stoics, between giving in to wrath or restraining it, between being sensitive to the way in which others treat us, jealous of our reputation and of our "rights," and rendering ourselves—temporarily or definitively—insensitive or impassive in the face of the others' offenses; the feeling, the acute sense of being subjected to a wrong and forcing ourselves not to pay attention to it, because wrath poisons the mind. This last path is the one advised by Seneca, who sees wrath in its most degrading aspects[1] and conjures up "cures" for it that consist particularly—for Seneca, as later for Descartes—of an increase in magnanimity and benevolence.[2]

If, therefore, in the Stoic tradition there can be neither wrath nor invective, we must look to the Aristotelian tradition. There, someone incapable of becoming angry—because it is as if the "nerves of the soul" have been cut—also does not know how to defend himself and, with the attitude of a slave, allows himself and those dear to him to be trampled.[3] Nonetheless, wrath can be controlled; it is a virtue only if it attains the right mean, the *mesotes*, between surrendering to it easily and freely and not surrendering at all. In fact, "in the domain of wrath there exist an excess, a defect and a middle path, and these dispositions being essentially nameless, and since we call someone who has the right mean gentle, we will call gentleness the middle ground."[4]

More generally, we could say that wrath is an indicator of the degree of one's own vulnerability and, sometimes, the exceeding of the legitimate defenses of one's system of values. In this sense, it is a matter of protecting personal identity and the self-esteem to which it is connected. In not consenting or consenting to wrath, we choose between the forgetting and the strengthening of the self, between forgiveness and punishment of the other, between acquiescence in the face of offense to oneself or to something that one holds dear (family, homeland, moral and religious convictions) and rebellion.

2. In this latter case, we can look at wrath with sympathy and admiration, as in the episode of Elie Wiesel who, as a child in a Nazi concentration camp, sees an American official of color who, as soon as he arrived in this inferno, began to shout, curse and rail, thus showing that—through this indignation—humanity had returned.[5]

If, as I said, invective can clearly be seen in the Aristotelian model of indignation, of righteous wrath, Dante—who had the *Nicomachean Ethics* as a constant point of reference—uses this sense of invective often against Florentines, Genovese, Pisans, etc. And spares no one! But it is this, tinged with bitterness, that can be noted, particularly, in Canto Six of *Purgatorio*, when he thinks of the state of Italy: "Ah Italy enslaved, abode of misery" [*"O serva Italia, di dolor ostello..."*].

Yet there can exist invectives born from wrongful wrath: from envy, desire for revenge, unrestrained ambition. Only then does wrath become unrestrained or excessive in the Aristotelian sense or, in Christian terms, a capital vice. To clarify this point, it is necessary to introduce a fundamental distinction between the ancient lack of restraint and Christian vices.

In Aristotle, for example, the ideal of ethical behavior consists of "acting in friendship with oneself," while in Christianity, it consists of acting in harmony with the Divine commandments, often against one's own inclinations and desires. In the first case, it is a matter of developing one's own potentialities according to the precept: "Become that which you are!" (but not more than that, in order to avoid overwhelming or surpassing the limits of human nature). In Christianity, on the other hand, there is the supreme challenge, the impossible mission, to surpass oneself ("Be perfect, therefore, as your heavenly Father is perfect." *Matthew* 5:48), a tendency to excess in drawing nearer to God, sacrificing oneself.

In ancient philosophy, vices are somaticized habits of behaving in a certain way, the crystallizing or rooting deeply of erroneous behaviors that good upbringing, if there were any, did not succeed in correcting. Again, one can fall into a particular vice through excess or through defect, through weakness or through intention. Wrath is a vice of excess determined by *akrasia*, by the lack of strength to resist impulses, while its opposite is sloth, the incapacity to react to incidental offenses, and carelessness.[6] Beyond vices owing to the incapacity to control oneself, there are others born of the "mad brutishness," of committing evil not through weakness or ignorance, but through will.

After some fluctuation in their number, in the Christian tradition, with Cassian and Gregory the Great, the capital vices, the *deadly sins*, became seven—one of which is wrath. As in the case of invective, the pleasure of surpassing limits, of letting oneself go, always contains a dose of bitterness, or as Plutarch says in *De cohibenda ira, On the Inhibition of Wrath*, "an extract of pain, pleasure and insolence" (452F-464D).

To be precise, it may be thought that all the so-called capital vices have their foundation in the desire to reach, through transverse (or perverse) pathways, something that one desires and cannot have. Vices are compensation for human beings who have an infinite desire of self-fulfillment but cannot succeed in satisfying it, and, therefore, they react by over-compensating or under-compensating for their frustrated expectations.

In the wrath for the destruction of something we desire, for the loss of a good or of an expected advantage, the frustrations and delusions accumulated through the unpleasant surprises that life has held for us—and that we fear still holds for us— discharge themselves instantly in an aggressive manner.

Let's take an example drawn from daily life. Suppose that I have a friend of whom I ask a favor. I say to him, "At noon tomorrow I need some documents and you should bring them to me." The documents that I want from him are important, but not particularly so. I wait for my friend, who arrives for the appointment, but who forgot to bring what was promised. In a type of emotional storm, I rail against him, I complain, I insult him. At the time, such excess aggressiveness seems disproportionate, incommensurate with the cause that provoked it.

It is precisely from such experiences that an irrational character has come to be attributed to wrath (and to passions in general), because we do not understand that this excess has its own logic, however anomalous, one that I would define as cumulative. That is, in the instant of wrath, it is not the single episode—the fact that the friend did not bring me the documents—that upsets me. Rather, it is all the frustrations of my life, all the betrayed expectations, all the unrealized or poorly compensated hopes, that collapse at that point, that explode because they reached a critical mass. Therefore, the element of excess exists, but it becomes understandable, because this single episode conveys and attracts all the analogous episodes. The logic of the passions is, therefore, an agglutinative, synthetic logic, one that makes a sheaf out of every blade of grass.

3. But what happens in the field of politics? I will limit myself to considering briefly one example: the wrath (strewn with invective) of Savonarola as witnessed by Machiavelli.

I picture, sneering behind a column of the Church of San Marco, the Machiavelli who, in March of 1498, had gone to listen to Girolamo Savonarola. He was thus able to observe, with no "little admiration"—the sermon begun by the Friar with the bold move of dismaying his enemies and consolidating his friends: "He began with great frights, reasoning with the most effective discourse, demonstrating his excellence to both his followers and his most wicked adversaries, touching upon all those points that might weaken a contrary position and fortify his own." Machiavelli then continues, citing *Exodus* and affirming that "'when it was time to go into a fury, we did so as on the day of the Assumption [in which the Compagnacci tried to murder Savonarola], because that is what the honor of God and the times required. Now that the honor of God desires that we surrender to wrath, we have surrendered it.' And having made this brief speech, he made two ranks [*"dua stiere"*]: one that supported God, and this was he and his followers, and the other that supported the devil, who were his adversaries."[7]

In the following sermon, Savonarola specified what surrendering to wrath would mean, alluding to the necessity of getting rid of one of his adversaries, who wanted to play "the tyrant [...], hunting the friar, excommunicating the friar, persecuting the friar." Then he illustrates his subject by resorting again to an episode related in *Exodus* (2:11-12): "Then, the other morning, explaining Exodus and coming to that part where it is that Moses killed an Egyptian, he said that the Egyptians were the captive men, and Moses, the preacher that killed him, revealed their vices; and he said, 'O Egypt, I want to stab you'."[8] Christian love, the *diligite inimicos vestros* (private enemies, not public—that is, the *in-*

imici, not the *hostes*) and the precept of offering the other cheek and substituting forgiveness for wrath makes room not only for the attitude of Christ among the merchants in the temple or for the Pauline precept of not permitting wrath to know the sunset, but also the explicit justification of the "stabbing" of Moses and the not-so-veiled incitement to political violence in religious garb.

Savonarola can be taken as an example of the confluence of two traditions that do not shun wrath: that of the Thomist Aristotelianism often adopted by the Domenican order and that of the tradition of the "wrath of God" (the expression appears fully 325 times in the Bible) that, in this case, refers to the example of Moses in the Old Testament, who, having descended from Mount Sinai and seen the Jews dancing around the Golden calf and regretting Egypt, "stood in the gate of the camp and said, 'Who is on the Lord's side? Come to me!' " [thus he too, in Machiavellian language, formed "two ranks"]. "And all the sons of Levi gathered around him. He said to them: 'Thus says the Lord, the God of Israel: "Put your sword on your side, each of you! Go back and forth from gate to gate throughout the camp, and each of you kill your brother, your friend, and your neighbor." ' The sons of Levi did as Moses commanded, and about three thousand people fell on that day." (*Ex.* 32:26-28). As Michael Walzer has shown in his book *Exodus and Revolution*[9], the model of Moses as emancipator of his people is the basis for our image of revolution in which, in the journey leading from slavery to freedom, from Egypt to the Promised Land, one need not have any hesitation to punish he who lags behind or he who looks with nostalgia toward the old ideas and the old ways of life. The bitter medicine of liberation consists of the inexorable punishment of those who look back, in the wrathful pushing of others toward the Promised Land, even if one is not destined to see it himself. Machiavelli shared this terrible requirement, as did Savonarola—for whom there remained, however, (not having power and being an "unarmed prophet") only the repudiations and invectives. His wrath is ineffective, his threats blunted.[10]

Unlike Savonarola, Pope Julius II Della Rovere was not an unarmed prophet. He knew about necessity, about how to don armor and fight. He was one who gave in—boldly—to wrath and impulsivity. Again as Machiavelli said, when there came "times in which it was necessary to break with patience and humility," this combative pope "proceeded in all the time of his pontificate with force and with fury; and because the times favored him" he succeeded in all his undertakings."[11] Not for nothing, on his (Julius') tomb in San Pietro in Vincoli, Michelangelo had powerfully placed his Moses at the center, at the moment in which he was about to give in to wrath and break the tablets of the commandments. Michelangelo knew the character of this pope. After all, even Dante had represented Saint Peter, red with indignation (and with him, all of Heaven) against Boniface VIII, as he recalls, almost with a shout, "my place, my place, my place" [*"Il luogo mio, il luogo mio, il luogo mio"*], his throne occupied by someone unworthy and, therefore, empty in the eyes of God (*Paradiso*, XXVII, 21-27).

Today, is it once again time for noble invectives born of indignation?

Notes

[1] See *De ira*, I, 1, 3, where he describes the distortions of the face and voice of someone who is enraged.

[2] See the *Colamus humanitatem* and the end of *De ira* or the *Culpa est totam persequi cumpam* of *De clementia*, 2, 7, fr.; and see Descartes, *Les passions de l'âme*, art. 203)

[3] See *Eth. Nic.*, 1126 a.

[4] Ibid., 1108a.

[5] See M. Nussbaum, *The Therapy of Desire. Theory and Practice in Hellenistic Ethics*, (Princeton: Princeton UP, 1996), p. 403.

[6] Dante, in the swamp of Styx, puts the slothful beneath the wrathful, cf. *Inferno* VII, 112-130.

[7] *Niccolò Machiavelli a Ricciardo Becchi*, Firenze, 9 marzo 1498, in N. Machiavelli, *Lettere*, ed., F. Gaeta, in *Opere complete*, vol. VI (Milan: Feltrinelli, 1961), pp. 30, 31.

[8] Ibid., p. 32.

[9] Michael Walzer, *Exodus and Revolution* (New York: Basic Books, 1985).

[10] See Machiavelli, *Il principe*, VI.

[11] *Discorsi*, III, 9 and see also *Il principe*, XXV.

Thomas Conley

Toward a Rhetoric of Insult[1]

I read the call for papers for "Savage Words" with great interest, as I am a long-time aficionado of insults; and I have a book on the subject, published in the Spring of 2010. But I was struck by the emphasis on studying a "literary genre" and on "the ironclad regulations to which it is subjected". I want to argue today that to approach insult, or invective, as a literary genre is probably wrong-headed. It may be true that most of what we count as invectives are "literary" texts, but that is no good reason to reduce invective to some set of rules governing texts. And I want here to talk not about invective but about insult, which I think is a better place to start. "Insult" is in one way narrower than invective, as not all invective is insult; and it is in another way broader, as it covers behavior that goes beyond the merely discursive—and even farther beyond "literary" discourse. And if we are going to look at "insult", I propose we do so from a rhetorical angle, not from a "literary" point of view.

When I say "rhetorical," I am not talking about a set of rules governing a genre, with its requirements and stock of commonplaces. And I am not about to try to survey the figures and semantic resources found in discourse generally understood as having as its aim ridicule or excoriation. After all, not all insults are literary—or even verbal. Rather, the rhetorical angle I am promoting here is the sort taken half a century ago by Kenneth Burke in *A Rhetoric of Motives*, which sees rhetoric not restricted to modes of discourse but as a pervasive feature of human relations.

It might seem strange to drag in a thinker who defines rhetoric in that book as "the use of language as a symbolic means of inducing cooperation in beings that by nature respond to symbols.[2]" Insults are scarcely intended to induce cooperation, it might be argued; and unless you understand "language" to cover more than verbal language, it is hard to see how non-verbal insults—the many gestures in the repertoire of the effective insulter—fall under Burke's formulation. Yet invective, surely, is not just a matter of verbal skill or of mastering a genre (whether verbal or not) but above all a matter of human relations conducted by means of symbolic action. So the important thing to look for is what those symbolic actions are meant to accomplish in the particular situation in which they are performed, whether on the page or on the street. The first scene of *Romeo and Juliet* is "literary," to be sure, on the page. But contrast the depiction of that scene in, e.g., Franco Zeffirelli's 1968 movie version: the livery and the arrogant strutting of the Capulet faction. These are symbolic actions we cannot see in the script, but they are undoubtedly the ones that motivate the fighting that ensues.

But getting back to Burke, how can we invoke a writer who has said that "persuasive communication (that is, persuasion by identification) is the abstract paradigm of courtship"[3] and "by the principle of courtship in rhetoric we mean the use of suasive devices for the transcending of social estrangement."[4] "Courtship", after all, connotes a sort of ingratiation and an "upward" appeal; whereas insults are typically understood as "put-downs." And insults don't seem to transcend social estrangement, but to reinforce it by making an "Other" of their targets. But some of Burke's key notions are nevertheless not only pertinent to understanding insults, but essential.

I recently spent considerable time surveying a wide assortment of explicit or otherwise obvious insults, both verbal and non-verbal, ranging from places in Cicero and Martial to some in Shakespeare and Aristophanes to those to be found in sixteenth-century *Flugschriften* illustrations, in anti-Semitic editorials in Henry Ford's *Dearborn Independent*, and in the performances of Eminem and J-Z—to name just a few. And what I found is that, one way or another, and despite the fact that insults are radically situational, two Burkeian themes emerge time after time: identification and hierarchy.

To understand how "identification" is pertinent, consider why it was that Mark Anthony was insulted when Cicero charged him with being a drunkard and a catamite in the Philippics. Might we not say that, perhaps paradoxically, Cicero and Anthony shared the same opinion of drunkards and catamites; and that beneath their enmity there is a substratum of agreement? What then about racial or ethnic slurs? What sort of identification plays out when one person calls another a "nigger" or a "kike"? It's hard to see how such language is not meant only to injure. But in such cases both the insulter and the insulted share the knowledge of what associations such terms of abuse are intended to call up: "lowly, servile, dirty, uneducated, physically and sexually threatening less-than-human beings", for instance; and both parties probably share the same feelings toward such beings—which is to say that there is an intimate sharing of both beliefs and values.

In this respect, insults share a great deal with two other kinds of social interaction: jokes and irony. Like insults, they invite us to ask not what is the relation between what is said and what is meant, but who "means" it, and where and when, which are rhetorical questions, not philological or grammatical questions. So, with jokes, it is said, "You had to be there"; and the reason is that (and I have borrowed this from Ted Cohen) telling a joke is a transaction that can "work" only when the teller and the listener share an implicit acknowledgement of a shared background that teller and listener are already in possession of and can bring to the joke. Likewise, I am contending, with insults. And as for irony, here is what Wayne Booth wrote thirty-odd years ago:

> Irony, when perceived and appreciated, completes a more astonishing communal achievement than most accounts have recognized. Its complexities are, after all, shared: the whole thing cannot work unless both parties to the exchange have confidence that they are moving together in identical patterns... [E]ven the most simple-minded irony, when it succeeds, reveals in both participants a kind of meeting with other minds that contradicts a great deal that gets said about who we are and whether we can know each other.[5]

The ability of an insulter to enlist the support of an audience works in a similar fashion. As in jokes and irony, insulting effectively requires you to know your audience—and there is no handbook or set of ironclad rules that can teach us to do that. But it is clear, for instance, that Martial articulates, even in the most obscene of his epigrams, the public morality of the Roman upper class and points it at "someone" (as most of the objects of Martial's scorn turn out to be fictional characters) who fails to measure up to those ethical norms. The authors and distributors of *Flugschriften* seek to consolidate their audience's "us against them" stance by "repeating" what "everybody knows": that the Pope is a pervert, and that priests steal and are little more than pernicious beasts. As Burke would put it, this is "yea-saying by nay-saying," not a modality of opposition and division, but of "identification." In the case of Martial, his readers were invited to identify with him—as both moral authority and skillful poet—so as to get them to identify with the basis of his moral authority, traditional Roman virtues. Now except in a few cases, as I mentioned, the targets of Martial's epigrams were not real people, but fictions representing "the worst" sort of human. So in Martial's case, it might be said that identification was prior to the ranking of the targets' position in the moral hierarchy. In the case of the sixteenth-century *Flugschriften*, the producers of those pamphlets were not merely trying to consolidate their supporters; they were also trying to persuade them that they were morally superior to the other side by, for instance, portraying Catholics as various animals. And we must remember that the audiences of the religious pamphlets often included members of the lower social classes; whereas the opposition—at least in the Reformation literature—was seen as rotten with luxury.

In thus talking about identification, we are also, it seems, talking about status, something in short supply and something implicit in the characterization of insults as "put downs." That is to say, there is a vertical dimension to insults. Often overlooked, however, is the fact that that dimension works both downward and upward. Some insulting behavior seems designed to maintain established hierarchies—e.g., the editorials in Henry Ford's *Dearborn Independent*, such as the famous "Angles of Jewish Influence," or the similarly anti-Semitic speeches of Julius Streicher that he published in the 1930's in *Die Stürmer*; and others seem designed to interrogate the established hierarchy— the insults in Aristophanes' *Knights*, for instance. Insults can be a vehicle for upward social mobility— consider the aims of the *Oratio contra Erasmum* of Julius Caesar Scaliger in 1531 (unsuccessful, a *tour de force en excédent*) or the insult competitions at the dinner table in the 1997 movie by Patrice Leconte, *Ridicule*, where it is shown that shortcomings in one's lineage can be overcome by an ability to generate, in the company of one's purported superiors, exquisite insults.

There is a sense in which the insults meant to maintain hierarchy may be instances also of insults interrogating hierarchy. The anti-Semitic insults of Ford and Streicher are defended by the conviction that Jews exercise enormous influence on and control, in ways almost unimaginable, our daily lives. So they must, it seems, be despised; but they must also be feared. Hence, the rhetoric of denigration is an indirect means of questioning the legitimacy—in both the legalistic and psychological senses—of the implied hierarchy that puts the Jews in a superior position. In a similar fashion, the anti-Catholic *Flugschriften* depict Catholics as morally corrupt and less-than-human; yet they are represented by the Pope and bishops and the nobility.

This paradox may be resolved if we bear in mind who the audiences are for this sort of tactical use of insults. The audience for Ford's hacks—the writers he hired never revealed their names— is clearly not the Jews they attack, but the "Nordic" or "Anglo-Saxon-Celtic" readers who bought the *Dearborn Independent*; and Streicher's audience is, likewise, Germans who were already inclined to accept as real the as real plots detailed in *The Protocols of the Elders of Zion*. The audience for Aristophanes' insulting references in *Knights* to Kleon was not Kleon himself (although he was probably present in the theatre); just as the primary audience of Scaliger's attack on Erasmus was not Erasmus, but the "*optimi adolescentes*" whom he occasionally addresses. In the end, by the way, Scaliger's attack was poorly received, mainly because he misread his audience—his real audience—and so failed to get it on his side.

All of this tells us that insults—or invectives, if you will—have two audiences: the insultee and the community of witnesses (who need not actually be there) who identify with the insulter. And that, in turn, reveals another paradox: that, like jokes and irony, insults—or invectives—are both divisive and aggregative. This suggests that the dynamics of a harmonious society may be shaped not by politeness but by the rejection of it, much as social status among the Native Americans of the Pacific Northwest is determined not by who has the most goods, but by who gives the most away. Insults can be seen, in short, as an engine of community cohesion, and thus as a crucial component of human relations.

When we don't know enough about our audience, we can't tell a good joke or be recognized as being ironic. When we don't know what one needs to know to come up with, or to recognize, an effective insult, we tend to go formalist and attend only to the discursive shapes insults take in theory. But what theory do we need to perceive the intention behind a remark H.L. Mencken once made about Warren G. Harding:

> He writes the worst English that I have ever encountered. It reminds me of a string of wet sponges; it reminds me of tattered washing on the line; it reminds me of stale bean soup, of dogs barking through endless nights. It is so bad that a sort of grandeur creeps into it. It drags itself out of the dark abyss of pish and crawls insanely up to the topmost pinnacle of posh. It is flap and doodle. It is balder and dash.

Now there is a lot going on here aesthetically. The general shape of Mencken's observations is governed by what we might call "accumulation by repetition," an inventory of different respects in which Harding's writing is both boring and irritating. The first part is an extended anaphoric triplet: three "It reminds me. . ."'s, with a fourth understood before "of dogs barking." This is balanced by another four sentence unit in the second part, all beginning with "It. . ." Mencken's similes are striking: "wet sponges," "tattered washing," "stale bean soup", and "dogs barking". Harding's style becomes "active", as "grandeur creeps," the style "drags" and "crawls insanely"; and, as a result it is judged to be "pishposh" and "flapdoodle" and "balderdash." There is, in short, considerable formal elegance.

But that is not what makes Mencken's insult work. We "get it" not because of its literary qualities, but because we share Mencken's aversion to wet sponges, stale bean soup, and barking dogs; we agree that such things are as disgusting as Mencken thinks. And that brings us back to the "intimacy" I spoke of earlier.

On the other hand, cultivation of an awareness of the aesthetics of insults might be a first step toward a much-needed social skill, what we might call "insult appreciation." Insults, whether real or not, will always be with us, just as hierarchy and identification will always be with us. What is called for is not a Code of Civil Conduct, but a change of perspective and a consequent change of attitude. By attending to the aesthetic angle, we gain some distance that allows us to see an insult not just as verbal abuse but as a performance before an audience, a performance intended not just to divide, but to unite. If we'd care to notice that insult is not simply a means of encouraging enmity and disdain, we'd be able to regard it as an interesting and important aspect of human relations as viewed from a rhetorical perspective, not as a social or moral failing, as it is commonly held to be.

There is, in short, a benign as well as a malign side to insults, just as there is a malign as well as a benign side to persuasion. We ought to keep that in mind. I very much hope the lessons we learn over the next couple of days will constitute an accelerated mini-course on insult appreciation.

Notes

[1] The first presentation at the conference "Savage Words: Invective as a Literary Genre", at UCLA, February, 2009.

[2] Kenneth Burke, *Rhetoric of Motives*, (Berkeley: U of California P, 1969), p. 43.

[3] Kenneth Burke, *Rhetoric of Motives*, p. 177.

[4] Kenneth Burke, *Rhetoric of Motives*, p. 208.

[5] Wayne Booth, *Rhetoric of Irony* (Chicago: U of Chicago P, 1975), p. 13.

Paolo Fabbri

Est iniuria in verbis

> "We all feel offended, irritated by something... Then, the open argument, the diatribe, the shout, and the insult are preferable to the pseudo-narrative terms of a supposed objectivity"
>
> (C.E. Gadda, *On Neorealism*, 1950)

1. Elements of Gossip[1]

> "Quicker than I could close my eyes, he had called me a prick."
>
> (E. Montale, "Il Pirla," *Diario del '71 e del '72*)

In the real piazzas and on the virtual highways of politics, insults, filth, and swearwords, fly. This is no surprise. Swearwords, legitimized for a long time now, have come from linguistic shoals and have extended beyond traffic and sports stadiums to land, emphatically and imperatively, on all forms of life. There is a pandemic of "secularized" scurrilous language. Popular songs (where Fabri Fibra soars) and film soundtracks are by now swearwords and music. In parliamentary chambers and in condominiums, Swearwords are asked for; in the courts, the Swearword will be given in defense; in public offices, a good Swearword will find its place. When we are in a hurry, we will exchange two or four Swearwords. In essence, we will live through crossed Swearwords, and the bigwigs will die with their famous final Swearwords. Listen and they will come: obscene, vulgar, dirty, extreme, crude, indecorous, scurrilous, impious, cowardly, trivial, and so on. The epithet in particular, which originally had the sense of a linguistic "additive," has become, par excellence, the insult given a name. The anti-ceremonial, formerly a parasite of good rules, has by now become a codified formula in the turbulent semantic universe of Bad Speech.[2]

It is a list that is at first juicy (in terms of coprolalia), then ever more redundant, and finally depressing, a list of complete vulgarity that reserves some surprises for us, as we will see. Attesting to this, for example, is the fact (or near-fact or factoid) that employment of the swearword—long a masculine monopoly—has reached parity between the sexes. Colloquial terms like *cazzate* [bullshit] and *figate* [nonsense][3] have had an inverse career and signal, in a post-macho society, the opposition between coarse obtuseness and brilliant result.[4]

And to think that only recently we were complaining of PO.CO—POlitical COrrectness—in the post-Victorian period of good feelings, the respectful realm of the euphemism and the litote. It was a distant time when written obscenities were replaced by ellipses, often of the same length as the word, and oral obscenities were muffled by a beep. Swearwords were not hidden, they were just neither pronounced nor heard. Regarding genitals and orifices, coitus and the entire spectrum of corporeal secretions, regarding illness, death, and particularly roles and ways of collective life (genders, communities, and professions), there hovered an unctuous atmosphere of taboo, indirect acts, oblique definitions, hypocritical allusions, and colorless hints. Escorts and sanitation workers were previously prostitutes and garbage men. Mental illness became alteration, disorder, disturbance, and discomfort. The minority of yesteryear was first called disadvantaged, then handicapped, the bearer of a handicap, and subsequently, disabled (even "intellectually and interpersonally") or differently able. English went beyond "mentally challenged," responding, in cases of dwarfism, with the sarcastic "vertically challenged." In university guidelines, so clever and proper, it was impossible to write a pronoun without double mention of gender. Particularly reprobate and taboo were the racial nicknames by which Italian emigrants were made a race: from the Argentine *Tano* to the French *Rital*, from the American *Wop* to the German *Itaker* and so on. One government minister, an Italian of Ghanaian origin, reacted not to the epithets of "orangutan" and "Congolese ape" or to the invitation to rape her, but to those who defined her as being "of color," claiming to be "really black"![5] Meanwhile, in the course of a demonstration against gay marriage, French children offered the Franco-African minister, Christiane Taubire, "a banana for her macaque."

The expurgated lexicon was a conservative reaction. Jacques Derrida called it the "armed slogan"—in the licentious language of the 1960s, when language was politically libertarian and sexually libertine. He turned all of its motifs into curses. The relativist avant-garde laid claim to the value of the neologism and, *horribile dictu*, the equal literary value of every word in the dictionary. And for sexual relations, they chose the use of crude transitive verbs (*chiavare* [nail], *fottere* [screw], *scopare* [fuck], *trombare* [bang], etc.), while those of the politically correct, the *Pochisti*, expressed themselves with verbs that were intransitive and delicately reciprocal: *fare l'amore* [make love], *fare sesso* [have sex], etc… (Speaking of sex, we are all ill-mannered: the lexical choice is between nursery school, anatomy, and the blog!).

From understatement to overstatement. How can we explain the ill-intentioned inversion of this inversion? With the evidence that the sign is maniacal (Bataille) and that language is not a window onto the individual mind but a view of the collective culture, its hierarchies, and its margins. It is not the tautological reference—*to call a spade a spade*—of the colorless world of logic, but the effective action of values and their conflicts and transformations. The insult as a semio-physics of its own: a form endowed with a gradient of intensity and with vectors of meaning—a heading, a direction, and a point of application. It can become a complete political program. In France, it is proposed: "The Blacks in the trees, the Arabs in the Sea, the Homosexuals in the Seine, and the Jews in the ovens."

With its opposite, the laud, the insult has been part of the large rhetoric of the epideictic since Aristotle. But it not just a case of processes of valuation. One must defend against offenses, because the insult is a reproach, and the Latin etymon of "insult" is "jump upon." It is a disparaging aggression that leads to values and their transitive and reflexive recognition—that is, to trust, esteem of oneself and other—and it places in crisis true and false solidarities (Honneth). In the insult, which etymologically anticipates juridical relevance and possible judicial sanctions, language is askew. For semiotic research is no longer a cabinet of curiosities or a "teratology of knowledge" (Foucault), but a renewal of the (im)pulsive dimension of communication. In language, there are no neutral expressions except in official, purposefully constructed registers.

One famous precedent can be found in a classic that never ceases to tell us that it knows very well how to be unbecoming. Rabelais had previously given literary sublimation to picturesque colorful dialogues full of obscenities that today we would find to be "signifying" in the local jargon of young black Americans. Without adhering to the thesis of the original ambivalence between praise and blame and their illogical somersaults in the town square (Bakhtin), in the great *Gargantua* we find the most original forms of the "figurative negation" of the other: the imprecation that is attached to the inferior and posterior parts of the body. In the speech of Asskiss and Fartsmell, in Chapter 25, and particularly in the parodic litany of the third book. Here, Panurge addresses Brother John, repeating 153 times *couillon* [turd], associated by rhyme and assonance with other epithets drawn from the literary and figurative arts. And the interlocutor replies with 150 epithets of equal tone. From the affectionate and the mocking, the imploring and the disdainful, the word *couillon*—a two-toned and two-sided term of "universal and cosmic meaning" (Bakhtin)—is repeated 303 times.[6]

2. Insulting Each Other is the Order of the Day

> "I want him to gasp for breath under the insults."
> (Céline, *Mort à crédit*)

In their intensive quality, emphatic expressions of informality, machismo, impudence, and coprolalia incite, provoke, and offend, but they quickly lose their bite and sulfurous odor. One thinks of words that were formerly defamatory like *buggerone* [bugger] and *becco* [cuckold], *briccone* [rascal], *bagascia* [trollop], and *manigoldo* [scoundrel]. Or the Christian-Democratic *forchettone* [profiteer]. The redundant expletive lightens its own mark: from verbal imposition it becomes an interjection and ends up, discharged like an empty casing, interpolated into the conversational string. Like the affectionate *bastardo* [bastard] and the relaxed *Vaffa* [fuck]. Semantic satiety that is a sign of the reversible game of blasphemy through euphemism. Through the double law of Gresham, bad words drive away good-natured ones, but these then chase out the former, arriving at an affected priggishness. In the long run, among accomplices and acquaintances, they can become signs of complicity and even of ironic compliments—a figure of speech that rhetoric provides for under the cryptic name of asteism. One can even profess that those who speak badly flaunt meanings without referring to the bad things they are saying; in so doing, they would not, therefore, bear the responsibility for it. There must be some truth to this—pleonasms are one of the strongest threads in the rhetorical tissue of demagoguery.[7]

The same thing happens in the preferred linguistic act of the political divide: the insult, with its depraved variants of invective, calumny, execration, abuse, injury, pestering, offense, sneering, vilification, rudeness, and vituperation that carry over from presence to tele-presence, from the live audience to new media and vice-versa—pillories in the media where spite and shame circulate. Formerly limited to oratorical tournaments in parliamentary chambers, today the sharpest language is flung in every mediascape: the screen lends itself to scorn, and the digital to derision. Leaving aside the semiotic variants—multiple nasty gestures (even in the language of deaf-mutes), spitting, shoving, and tossing of coins—linguists ask each other about the specious syntax of the offense. They point out two movements in these "axiological lexemes" or names of negative "qualities." First, there is a de-semanticizing and then an intensive increase of meaning. It is a case of short-circuiting sentences and of emotive syncretism, and they even make the hypotheses that insults, in their very excess, may end up protecting the linguistic norm through verbal deformities like the improbable Anglo-Saxon imperative "fuck you"!, the strange genitive *quello stronzo di* ___ [that bastard of (proper name)], the indeclinable plural of the Italian *cazzi acidi* and *amari*.[8]

The most accredited hypothesis remains "familiarity"—that is, the similarities of family with the interjection, those particles to which linguistics has long entrusted the thankless task of cataloguing the forms of passion and the expression of inter-subjective emotions and/or of private feelings. Within what the Enlightenment called "language of action" (Condorcet), interjections, with their characteristic morphology—brevity, punctuality, tonal intensity, excess, equivalence to entire sentences, non-marked placement, etc.—can be easily prolonged into invectives and insults. Semiotic, verbal, gestural, and written acts, like the characters and graphs that involve evaluative modalities, aesthetic and somatic transformations, they thus place in play the various passions of the semantic value. The injurious act, euphemistic heir to ancient blasphemy (one could say "swearing"), gives strength and rhythm to speech, sensitizes to axiologies, reawakens emulsified and drowsy relationships. It chooses some signs, made sacred by their association with other sacred signs that circularly confirm their value; then it translates them in a text or a context populated by more despicable and trivial signs that bear upon secretive and excretive somatic functions of the body, their sexual and reproductive interactions, and various taboos of the animal kingdom. "Tommaso Munzter said he shit upon that God who was not talking to him "(E. Pagliarani). All are terms that lose their "referential" value—a woman can demand *non le si rompano i coglioni* [don't bust my balls]—but they maintain their prohibition on being stated.

It is the vast world of "phatic" language (Jakobson), in which contact counts more than content, the haptic more than the semantic. Locus of co-enunciation—that is, co-involvement with others and with oneself as others (*self-talk*, Goffman)—the insult is inter-agential; one insults like a man, not in the third person! A fierce baptism that introjects shared or divided values beyond emitting emotion, cathartically. The end should not surprise us; one does not respond to the interlocutor but replies, polemically challenging his assumptions or shutting him up with an insult. We are beyond the "weak spell of good manners" (Simmel) that prescribed reverence and irreverence. On the other hand, it is difficult to say *ma non mi dica!* [don't tell me!] if there are books entitled *Rancor* or *I curse you.*

Insulting one another is the order of the day. Toxic expressions, like financial derivatives, come from depositors in the banks of rage—that is, politicians and parties. The clinical and critical case of Beppe Grillo bears witness of the political permeability to infiltration of other discursive genres, such as the comic, in the semiotic environment of show business society.[9] Here, Grillo was already practiced in verbal lambasting: Fazio had been labeled *stuoino* [doormat], Jovanotti *curreggina* [fart], P. Daniele *monnezzaro* [*trashman*], V. Rossi *menomato mentale* [*mentally damaged*]. Whence, with resolute continuity: Andreotti *mela marcia* [rotten apple]; Berlusconi *cavaliere dell'apocalisse* [knight of the apocalypse], *puttaniere* [whoremonger]; Fornero, *Vispa Teresa* [Lively Theresa]; Tronchetti Provera, *il tronchetto della felicita* [Dracaena fragrans—i.e., "potted plant"]; Veronesi, *uomo sandwich* [sandwich man], etc. The barker from Genoa specialized in distortion of those rigid indicators that are, as logical soloists, proper names: Alemanno becomes *Aledanno*; Brunetta, *Brunettolo*; Formigioni, *Forminchioni;* Fornero, *Frignero*; Marchionne, *Marpionne*; Pisapia, *Pisapippa*; Veronesi, *Cancronesi*, etc. And in the use of nicknames: *Big Jim* or *Truffolo* (Berlusconi); *Baffino* (D'Alema); *Gargamella* (Bersani); *Merdoch* (Murdoch), *Mortadella* (Prodi); *Morfeo* (Napolitano); *Topo Gigio* (Veltroni); *Tutankhamoun* (U. Agnelli), etc. Less obvious than these denominations are some definite descriptions: *Ebetino di Firenze* [Little Fool of Florence] (Renzi); *Figlia di Fantozzi* [Daughter of Stooges] (Lupi). Remaining to be explored is the rich harvest of the general figures of speech and metaphors that transfer to the person being compared, the coarse semantic manners of the comparer: *Larve ben pagate* [Well-paid maggots] (Parlamentari); *Buco senza ciambella* [Hole without a donut] (Vendola); *Container of liquid shit* [*Container di merda liquida*] (Ferrara); *Mountain of shit* [*Montagna di merda*] (TAV); *Ovetto Kinder senza sorpresa* [Kinder egg without a surprise] (Passera), *Il signor Pendola* [Mister Pendulum] (Vendola); *Scoreggia nello spazio* [Fart in Space] (Miglio) o *Paved Head* [Testa asfaltata], *Torero Camomillo* [Camomille Toreador] (Berlusconi), etc.

Beyond the unsophisticated categories in the United States (*hate speech*, *fighting words*, and stalking) a simplified typology distinguished invectives into descriptive, idiomatic, emphatic, and cathartic—but there are numerous others. In the string of insults, we can distinguish various linguistic acts: vulgar interpellations ("At salut busòn, in Bolognese dialect, Grillo), scornful observations ("D'Alema would like to have me by the balls, like he has Berlusconi by the nuts, but he doesn't have mine in his hands," Bossi), invitations (to kill, to rape, to pass on to a better life, etc.), threats ("I piss on your head," Sgarbi), and pseudo-advice ("Call the nuthouse, there's someone who thinks he's a minister," Grillo).

As far as content, we know that the extremists of the right and the center (read: the Northern League) favor Interpellations/Observations with animal metaphors—*topo di fogna* [sewer rat], *pidocchi* [ticks], *vermi* [worms], *parassiti* [parasites], *capponi* [capons], etc. and Advice: "*Vaffa*" is their byword and "*Fanculo*" the banner of a new political movement that prefers affronting to confronting. With the language of respect forgotten, with the signs and ways of recognizing value removed, contemporary society can thus reflect on why—and with regard to whom—dignity and respect are systematically transgressed. Might the insults directed toward mom be a lay form of prayers? Might the old curses hurled by victims now be replaced by media pardons functioning as exorcisms? Has the curse become "cursed"? Why do Italians, more than other vulgar communities, use the word "culo," while the French stuff their utterances with *merde*—daily and sometimes heroically (see Cambronne at Waterloo)? And why do southern Europeans, in heavy traffic, prefer to insult out loud, while protesters in the north prefer nasty gestures? Where are the places of collective elaboration of insolence? (In England, for example, anti-Argentine insults that emerged during the Falklands War propagated in the stadiums, with a wealth of variants). We shall see. And we have the time and the means to do so because insults, like swearwords, are born and die, but in the meantime they make themselves heard and known. They are, at this point, the meter of the political speech and emphatic writings of so many xenophobic and racist sites on the internet (Rastier).

And they are even asked for, if not exactly desired. In the alphabetic scientific lexicon (sic!) to which he dedicated himself, Casalengo, called *coreografo nazi* [Nazi choreographer], and *distruttore dell'universo* [destroyer of the universe], *fallito* [failed], *peloso* [hairy], *Telespalla Bob* [Sideshow Bob], etc. hopes for an insult that is still missing: one that begins with the letter Z. May he be satisfied—there is an embarrassment of choices!

3. A Noble Art

> "'Swine,' he shouted, 'swine.' Amazed,
> the people looked at him.
> He was saying it to Italy.'"
> (V. Sereni, "Saba", *Gli strumenti umani*)

Let us speak generally. We are no longer at the level of dispute—that is, grammaticalized, ritual, and respectable debate. We are in the boiling public realm of polemic and virulent diatribe. It is that *vis polemica* that Gadda defined as "salivary supplies of verbal inanity." We are not aiming, as in the Elysian fields of Habermas, at persuasion and consent, but at argument and dissent. Even the impartial have their side. We are beyond satire that is a sermon and parody that is a game. Here, you do not joke and do not give lessons—you cause wounds. Let us put off the parliamentary use of objects of symbolic value (mortadella, fennel, etc.) and of threats: *"je sputo in testa"* [I spit on his head]. Limiting ourselves to the firmly documented lexicon: *Analfabeti* [illiterates], *animali* [animals], *arroganti* [the arrogant], *assassini* [assassins], *banditi* [bandits], *boia* [executioner], *bonga bonga*, *buffoni* [buffoons], *burattini* [puppets], *caimani* [crocodiles], *cadaveri* [cadavers], *carampane* [old hags], *carognette* [little bastards], *checche* [queens], *cialtroni* [slatterns], *cessi* [shitholes], *cloache* [cesspools], *coglionazzi* [assholes], *corrotti* [corrupt], *coscione (svergongate)* [(shameless) haunch], *culattoni* [fags], *delinquenti* [delinquents], *abituali e recidivi* [habitual and relapsed (criminal)], *ebeti[ni]* [(little) idiots], *falliti* [failures], *farabutti* [crooks], *fattuchiere* [sorcerer], *fifoni* [scaredy-cats], *furbetti* [sneaky ones], *(utili) idioti* [*(useful) idiots*], *impresentabili* [unpresentables], *incapaci* [incapables], *indecenti* [indecent], *intrallazzini* [shady dealers], *ipocriti* [hypocrites], *larve* [maggots], *ladri* [thieves], *markette* [streetwalkers], *merda secca* [dried shit], *miserabili* [wretches], *morti (che parlano)* [(talking) dead], *mostri* [monsters], *musulmani di merda* [shitty Muslims], *(vecchi) maschi rimbabmiti* [(old) infantilized men], ominicchi [tiny men], *palle di velluto* [(velvety) balls], *prendiculo* [ass-fuckers], *psico-nani* [psycho-dwarves], *vecchia puttana* [old whore], *(padri) puttanieri* [whoremonger (fathers)], *qualunquisti* [cynics], *salme* [corpses], *sfigati* [losers], *sodomiti* [sodomites], *streghe* [witches], *supercazzolari* [super-bullshitters], *traditori* [traitors], *troie* [sluts], *vajasse* [sluts] (just admitted into the latest edition of Zanichelli), *vermiciattoli* [insignificant worms], *vigliacchi* [cowards], *zombi* [zombies], *zozzoni* [dirtbags], *etc.* Those who you might expect say them: Berlusconi, author of *culona inscop-*

abile [big unfuckable ass]. A (linguistically) rare ejection defined Ugo Bossi as a whole: *Ladro (di voti)* [Thief (of votes)], *ricettatore* [fencer (of goods)], *truffatore* [swindler], *doppia, tipla, quadrupla personalità* [double-, triple-, quadruple-personality], *pataccaro* [conman]. And we can't forget the rare circumlocution—the harmful affront to the dignity, "honor and decorum" of those who receive it but also of those who emit it. Then there are those who collect abuse. They are hurt by it and they give it back with a steely law of escalation, reacting angrily and making oneself heard, returning the other's mark. As in an old duel, the law does not recognize the right of forgetting an offense, and it authorizes revenge. It does not aim at the ridiculous; it seeks the degrading offense—infamy when possible or at least ill omen. The sarcastic Voltaire knew something about it, "the imbecilic and disgusting Voltaire, like an ape, old and pissing" (P. Calusel).

In this target shooting of reputation and decorum, it is impossible to measure words and writing—in fact, exclamation points and capital letters are wasted!!! In fact, there is nothing more spontaneous; if provoked, we react immediately with the epithets of our native tongue. Given the difficulty of suitable translation of insults even into similar languages, with the result of euphemism or amplification, it is preferable to offend in one's own language. I would not exclude invectives in exotic languages and eventually in dead languages.[10] This can have morphologically innovative effects, like the gesture of the *quenelle*, the oblong starchy meatball that gives its name to a gesture of the anti-Semitic right in France. A politicized third-rate actor (as usual), Dieudonné has given a variant of the gesture of the umbrella—with the arm and the left hand open and stretched, supported by the back of the right arm bent at the elbow. The movement of somatic placement and the opening of the hand avoid the codified meaning of "energetic and full penetration of the rectum of others" and suggest the double meaning of the inverted Hitlerian salute (the extended arm) and of national devotions (the palm to the chest). The insulting posture has gained wide traction for the allusion to the euphemized gesture, thanks also to the culinary code on which it is modeled, and at this point it figures in the gestural dictionary of popular France with a vague connotation of offending provocation. A level that is rather pedestrian and incomparable to the expressive heights of our own unsophisticated [Italian] *pernacchio* [raspberry].[11]

The insult, then, is a "rational" performance or at least adjusted to diatribes in the most varied number of contexts. This is demonstrated by its broad and cogent use in places privileged by vehicular traffic and in cheering sections.[12] For this, turn also to the dignity of the media. The Court of Cassation that has drawn up an "insult meter," defined by the right of satire, a semiotic genre not subjected to criteria of truth, but of moderation or of contextual parameters. Thus, the insult pronounced in a reality show is not offensive because it is part of an environment "whose characteristic [is] to elicit the verbal conflict between the participants."[13] In essence, it is a question of frame—or discursive format, as the semiologist would say—that recalls, in the classification of tropes by Cicero and Quintilian, the rhetorical figure of the curse. It is an *ad hominem* apostrophe, attacking the subject of the interlocution in the absence of arguments to respond to statements, tacitly useful in the same measure as its opposites—the encomium, the euphemism—in uttering "suitable" speech.[14] An assassinating eloquence that can also be practiced through antiphrasis and litote: like the murderous question: "Who?"; the scorn of a sarcastic *signore!*;[15] or *inintelligente* [*unintelligent*]—which to Calvino was more offensive than *stronzo* [*asshole*]. This is a double-edged sword, however, to be handled with care, so as not to risk the misfortune accident of the president of the French republic, who had thusly apostrophized (23 Feb 2008) a citizen who rejected his greeting: *"Casse toi, alors, pauv' con"* ["Well then refuse it, asshole"]. The same phrase was subsequently found, returned to sender, on the signs at demonstrations against him. A most correct tactic: it is good manners, in the case of insult, to make use of the expressions of your interlocutor.

That insulting is not empty words, a mere verbal sewer, but a move in the noble art of epithet and defense, was understood by Schopenhauer. He was a theorist—particularly against the hated Hegel, Fiche, and Schelling—of the gradual defensive escalation and particularly of the disarming insult à coté of the subject—that is, outside the target, to which it is impossible to respond in kind. (How could Hegel, summarily accused of being "disgusting," have responded—or Spinoza, execrated as "indifferent to dogs"?) A stratagem shared also by eastern thought (see *marendeyisho*, L. Shiqui), in which the offense is a move in the martial art of speaking, the timely exercise of which is done in a gymnasium of verbal blows (*"Insult is reminiscent of hand-to-hand combat"*). Chinese insult must be marked in a calibrated way. A game with exposed cards, it is indirect, allusive, disguised, oblique—directing the insulted person to offend himself. It works like the cuttlefish, the sophist animal of the ancient Greeks, with circumspect cunning and prudence, mixing words of blame with praise. In these cases, even "the honored tradition of the dung metaphor seems to give wings to fantasy" (Calvino).

Staying above the lines of the statement may be not time lost but theoretically relevant, as demonstrated and disclosed by recent philosophers like J. Butler (devoted to the unpublished hybrid of Austin and Althusser), *On Bullshit* by H. Frankfurt, and *Asshole* by A. James, works reasonably translated into Italian as *Stronzate* and *Stronzi*. Theoretically assured, the part-time intellectuals of the blogosphere have thus taken from the mud the baton of the proletarian idiom of truck-drivers, garbage workers, sailors, soldiers, politicians, and sports fans.

It is carte blanche, then, for insults and their expressive *vis*, if and when they are calibrated insults and not "pertinacious contraband of necessarily confused subjects," when they might require a "high level of resoluteness and profound mental ability," associated with a good/bad mood, but with a principle of caution. The current insult—like blasphemy, reinvigorated and duly euphemized by the return of the sacred[16]—is hackneyed. It is expletive for the linguists or pleonasm for the rhetoricians, full of the voids of speech and the defects of the imagination. And if said when there is nothing to say, it is emptied of force and doomed to the most ceremonial inefficacy. It survives without the proper "musical rhythm and chromatic relief" (Calvino). Its false audacity prevents even the possibility of a well-calibrated reply; it is a simple trap for figures of speech. In essence, there is nothing with which to enrich the lexicon of Italian slander which, for Calvino, was "the great civilization of the insult, of verbal aggression," formerly very rich in epithets of every sort. And yet the figures of insult are, like poetry, possible misfits with respect to common language. They have poetic characteristics: parallelism, alliteration, assonance—remember how the Duke of San Simon respond to Mazarino, who accused him of being a traitor (*Traitre*)? Priest (*pretre*) seemed to him the most appropriate insult. A verbal magic that seemed to him to start from the low (see pieces of bravura like the recent *nano nazi* [dwarf Nazi], *psiconano* [psycho-dwarf], *energumeno tascabile* [pocket-sized madman]) but can reach the summits of the epigram (in which the Italians excel[17] and of satire, in which we are poor, with the memorable exception of C.E. Gadda's *Eros and Priapus*. For Gadda, the insult was the proper literary form to escape from a "dark mood" and was resentful of neorealism: "...*the open polemic, the diatribe, the shout, the insult are preferable to pseudo-narrative terms of a supposed objectivity*"...

The best affront or good insult is certainly the shortest—*Infame!* [Vile!] seems to me a good candidate, while cultured utterances such as "drunkard who clings to figures as if to raspberries"[18] are inadvisable. But there is no need to disallow oneself an elevated stile. There can be greatness in wickedness, as Napoleon saw in Tallyrand: "a piece of shit in a silk stocking." We can remember here the calm observations regarding Fiche: "a man for whom the fact of having taught never left the time to learn" (Schopenhauer) or regarding Thatcher's political conduct: "When she thinks she does not speak, and when she speaks she does not think"? Or the expectoration regarding M. Duras: "Senile apologists of rural infanticides"? The surrealist: "You are the methane that remains in the intestine of a dead cow," regarding S. Dalì? And the metaphysical, "Nobodaddy" with which Blake pronounced the name not to be taken in vain, if not secretly? And finally, there is the prophetic quip with which S. Johnson pointed to a demonized politician of his and of our time: "He will die in his bed without dirtying the gallows"? (Borges)

We need more effort, fellow cursers. A minor art, the insult is not at all easy. The sophisms and jokes that express insult must be memorable, however briefly, as L. Bloy, "jeweler of maledictions" held. Let us reread the neologisms of Rabelais, the nicknames and labels for Mussolini in Gadda's masterpiece.[19] I say without offense: to raise one's voice in satire, it is not necessary to use poor words (Fallaci).[20] Let us learn to curse well, and let us create personalized handbooks with polished reserves of admired insults.[21] A panoply that will end up useful to us even in the case of those fictional aggressions that are marks of true solidarity.

More inventiveness in invective!

Notes

[1] An Italian version of this essay has been published in *Il Verri*, nr. 35 (Milan: Edizioni del Verri, Milano, 2014). I thank, for their contribution, the students of the course, *La diatriba politica*, in the semiotics of specialized languages, LUISS, Rome, Academic year 2013-14.

[2] The employment of a rough terminology leads to official recognition: "Parlamento, ecco i *trombati* eccellenti" ["Parliament, here are the excellent *fuck-ups*"], 25 Feb 2013, is an official Twitter account of the Presidency of the Consul on the results of political elections. The link points to a photo-gallery with the honorable Di Pietro, Fini, Ingoria and other *esclusi eccellenti* [excellent excluded].

[3] Translator's note: The Italian terms here are based on *cazzo* [dick] and *figa* [cunt], respectively. Throughout this essay, because the original Italian forms are central to the author's discussion, they have been retained in the translation. To assist the reader in understanding the intensity, variety, and at times inventiveness of the terms discussed, a close (American) English *semantic* equivalent is provided. At times, these necessarily stray from the etymology of the Italian. For example, the Italian

coglioni would translate most literally as *balls*, but as an epithet hurled against a group of people, it is closer to the American English *assholes*. In several cases, no English equivalent is provided.

[4] "Alain felt the pain of a strong blow to his shoulder. 'Pay attention, imbecile!' He turned and saw beside him the face of a girl passing him on the sidewalk with a rapid and energetic step. 'Excuse me,' he shouted at her (with a weak voice). 'Asshole!' responded the girl (in a loud voice), without turning." (M. Kundera, *La festa dell'insignificanza*, Milan: Adelphi, 2013). In other times, a virile reprimand was possible for the protagonist of *ADA o ardore* by V. Nabokov (Milan: Adelphi, 2000) To the "*Puah!*" of Lucette: "I beg you to not use that expletive participle."

A river of words flowed from G. Boccaccio's dystopian *Corbaccio*, a text of sharp-eyed faithfulness to the anti-feminine genre of the time. Generic Faithfulness: "the perverse multitude of women must be classified as jealous, unwilling, ambitious, envious, imperious, boring, simpering, nauseating, annoying"; the odious feminine sex would be composed of "presumptuous and tiresome [women] so proud, so base, so horrible, so disrespectful, as to be treated plainly as *pigs*." And specific faithfulness: the target of the satire is a "rasping old woman, withered, unhealthy, already nauseating and bothersome to look at," "a meal more for dogs than for men."

[5] The same thing happened to a French minister, a representative of the Front National preferred her among the branches of the trees rather than as minister. If Sparta cries, Messenia does not laugh, even if France criticizes our political style. On the other hand, interesting for the semantics is the threat of the leader of the Front National, M.me Le Pen, accusing anyone who might silence her as being of the "extreme right."

[6] "…they load them with insults, calling them *villanzoni* [boors], *camorra sdentati* [toothless Camorra], *rossacci della malora* [accursed commies], *disutili* [useless], *piscialetto* [bedwetter], *barabba* [scoundrel], *lime sorde* [deaf files], *fannulloni ghiottonacci* [gluttonous slackers], *panzoni* [big-bellies], *fanfaroni* [blowhards], *buonianulla* [good-for-nothings], *mascalzoni* [bastards], *sbruffoni* [braggarts], *scrocconi* [freeloaders], *pertichini* [lampposts], *leggere* [lightweights], *addormentati* [sleepers], *tangheri* [louts], *ciondoloni* [loafers], *allocchi* [fools], *deficienti* [morons], *gabbamondo* [swindler], *balenghi* [idiots], *straccioni* [tramps], *sacchi di stronzi* [sacks of shit], *pastori de merda* [shepherds of shit], and other similar defamatory epithets." Beyond those listed in the inscription of the abbey of Thélème, in the *Monologue des sots* there are about a hundred offensive epithets addressed to fools and in the *Nouveau monologue*, at least 150.

[7] With Rableisian taste, U. Eco has provided a portable hodgepodge of 139 insults in a "Bustina di Minerva" (*Espresso*) that we suggest to representatives of the Northern League to better their discursive, rather entropic borrowings. At least for the part in which he invites finding the art of periphrasis of the affront and offers acrobatic exemplifications. "Quiet, you, whose face could have been defined by a well-known marshal of the Empire in the last hours of the battle of Waterloo?"; "She has a skull that would be more apt for reproduction than for speculation."; "I invite you to go there where you could wisely qualify as the passive partner of a relationship between two consenting male adults!"; "Stop, O spindle-shaped segment of the final product of a complex metabolic process!"; "He who, on the day of his birth, was united by an umbilical cord to a woman who had known how to lead the poliandry to almost frenetic demonstrations."; "Sicilian rod, what a great big portion of Bartolino's glands and fallopian tubes!"; "That guy? He is ready to secrete, unintentionally, from fear (and without having first abandoned his own clothes), cellular, keratin, bilious remnants, mucus, flaking epithelial cells, leucocytes and assorted bacteria!"; "Gustavo is only a fifty percent swooning of the senses, obtained manually."; "Silence, don't imitate the place in which one

buys those pleasures we owe to the weaker sex!"; "Wretched misery, I received it in an undeserved pot"; I beg you, do not spoil for me those that Latin etymology wants as witnesses!"; "As Dante says, he used the terminal part of the rectal intestine as an instrument for military signals."; "You guys, what a doors-and-windows operation!"; "The baroness? Well she is dedicated to the gathering and accumulation of tokens that testify to her diligence and from which she will receive monetary consideration at the conclusion of the second week of activity!"; "Look, regarding you and your opinion, I subject to repeated shaking the only skin bag provided to me by nature, with all that it contains!"; "But stop adulating me! Your are a subject whose taste buds have lost all familiarity with food before it has undergone all the transformations to which it is subjected by our organism so as to cope with the general curve of entropy!"; "If you don't stop, I am ready to interface the lower part of my Timberlands with your perineum, giving your entire body a propulsive force capable of making you travel a long way without your being able to resort to the usual means of ambulation!"; "You have my full censure, oh person whose inferior posterior part of the torso would need plastic surgery to restore it!"; "External organ of the male genito-urinary apparatus in the form of a cylindrical appendix inserted in the anterior part of the perineum! I lost my wallet!" Eco took his cue from the book by K. Vonnegut, *Hocus pocus*, whose protagonist decides to abstain from bad words and limit himself to circumlocutions such as: "what a piece of excrement!"; "what a head of a penis!"; "we are in a fine house of tolerance!"

[8] According to S. Fischer, it is enough to erase the requested determinative from the construction of the injunctions, and one passes to exclaim insults: *specie di scemo* [type of fool]. In Italian, starting from this structure of *N of N*, one moves to the shout of onomatopoeia, from the derogatory name to the structure of nominal type—and finally to the gesture.

The linguist of grammatical training (that is, of discursive incompetence) gives to the insult—with respect to onomatopoeia and to the interjection—a mitigated definition: the attribution to an "allocutive" of "a nominal group isolated from the axiologial genitive constant," on the part of a "locutor that merges into one form and one purpose." The (pragmatic) rhetorical movement of a taboo term to an insult that maintains its negative value, while modifying its reference, is reinserted into the category of "delocutives."

[9] Goffman would call this porosity of discursive genres, "lamination of frame." In the 1970s, a sociologist could still assert that show business personalities were celebrities but not presentable politically (F. Alberoni). Since then, the lamination of the electoral frame and its communication has accelerated its pace. Now, the unpresentability is internal and central to the frame. This is demonstrated by the joint initiative of a group of journalists who read aloud the battery of insults directed toward sympathizers (and antagonists) of the Five Star Movement to a colleague, a critic of the Grillini. It is a parade of linguistic poverty, a vast majority of it excrement-related variants—*merdaccia* [rotten shit] and *cessi* [shitholes] linked not by documented reading, but by "lombrosian" observations on the photographic "signals." In the digital spittoon, one comes across expressions of such (meager) originality as: *allucinata* [dazed], *alterazione ormonale* [hormonal change], *brigatista* [Red Brigade terrorist], *befana del nuovo millennio* [witch of the new millennium], *brutta di lingua* [foul-mouthed], *ergastolana* [lifer], *esodata* [laid-off], *galeotta* [galiot], *gemella albina di Kienge* [albino twin of Minister C. Kyenge], *martello sui denti* [hammer to the teeth], *non signora* [non-woman], *sguardo di trota pescata con la bomba* [gaze of a trout fished with a bomb], *scolapasta scassato* [broken colander], *stampo per fare i cessi nelle stazioni ferroviarie* [mold for making rail station toilets], *ruzzola* [stumbler], *satana* (or *figlia del demonio*) [she-devil (or daughter of the

devil)], *sgorbia* [gouger], *vomito in fotografia* [the picture of vomit], *turca* [Turkish woman]. Frequent are the animal-related lexemes that notoriously characterize the websites of the extreme right: *batterio fecale scaduto* [expired fecal bacterium], *bertuccia* [macaque], *civetta con occhiali* [bespectacled owl], *cozza* [ugly dog], *gufa* [owl], *larva addormentata* [sleeping maggot], *lucertola* [lizard], *oca* [goose], *pantegana infoiata* [horny sewer rat], *pappagallo ammaestrato* [trained parrot], *parassita* [parasite], *pidocchiosa* [louse-ridden], *pipistrello* [bat], *pulce* [flea], *rospo* [toad], *scorfano* [scorpion fish], *scrofa* [sow], *troia* [sow], *topa* [pussy], *vacca* [cow], *verme* [worm], *zecca* [tick].

Worrisome are the reflexive invitations: *muori merda* [die, you piece of shit], *crepa* [die], *datti fuoco* [set yourself on fire], *fatti fottere da un somaro* [get fucked by a donkey], *impiccati* [hang yourself], *sparati merda nelle vene* [shoot shit in your veins], *vai a lavorare* [get to work], *a zappare* [get digging] and the transitive instructions of two types. Type 1 is specific: *ammazziamola* [let's kill her], *diamole fuoco* [let's set her on fire], *impicchiamola* [let's hang her], *sopprimiamola* [let's get rid of her], *tagliamola a pezzi* [let's cut her to pieces]. Type 2 is generic: *da eliminare* [to be eliminated], *da lapidare* [to be stoned to death], *ai lavori forzati* [to forced labor], *al patibolo* [to the gallows], *a pulire i cessi* [to cleaning toilets], *al rogo* [to the fire], *alla sedia elettrica subito* [to the electric chair now], *un metro di corda* [a meter of rope], *ospizio subito* [to an institution now], *pena di morte* [death penalty].

[10] Here is a single example in the dubbing of Almodovar's film *All about my mother*: one of the protagonists (Nina) covers the other (Manuela) with invectives, in an affectionate and joking way of friendship and solidarity. But the translation into Italian renders *cubrona* as *animale* [animal] or *caprona* and *bruta* in *somara* [ass]. The interjection *joder* becomes *accidenti* [damn] and the construction *por cojones* is transformed into *per forza* [of course]; *un poco putón* is translated as *un po' troia* [a little slutty]; "*hacer la carrera*," which means "to beat," becomes "*fare carriera*" [to work one's way up]! There are some films that deserve an Oscar for swearwords: *The Wolf of Wall Street* (directed by Martin Scorsese and winner of a Golden Globe) holds a temporary and beatable record; it contains 687 in the course of 180 minutes—almost four per minute.

[11] By express request we would suggest the *pernacchio* [raspberry], a resonant grimace—an arrow directed toward the face of others—that allows executions from the B flat major to high G, to F sharp, with a frequency that oscillates between 61 and 1568 Hertz. It is rich in variants that render it: *classico* [classic], *corto* [short], *lungo* [long], *secco* [dry], *di petto* [energetic], *a curva* [bent], *a singhiozzo* [fitful], *strozzato* [choked], *di testa* [of the head], *a tromba* [trumpet-like], *a sega* [saw-like], etc. It is the phonic signifier of a vigorous illocutionary act. Eduardo De Filippo specified it: "The *pernacchio* is the voice of the people who have no voice. The *pernacchio* is a kick in the ass to all powerful people"; "the *pernacchio* is a revolution, it is freedom." Far from being a synonym *pernacchio* [in the masculine] is the semantic alternative to the *pernacchia* [in the feminine]: "The first can be strong or weak, long or short, massive or meager, aquiline or snub-nosed, but is always masculine, it is constructive and industrious, and all told, it works. The second is soft and lazy; tumid, white, languid, it is like an odalisque on the carpet: feminine…" V.G. Marotta, in *L'oro di Napoli*, penetrated its cultural complexity: "a complete sneer, from the chest, shaking violently, that cut the air, casting itself on earth and sea; [and] similarly the subtle and variegated sneer, from the head, the sneer that you could write about like the song of the nightingale 'It was a motif of three notes…' and continue for two pages. In addition, there was the affirmative sneer and the negative one, the tragic sneer and the comic. There was the sneer performed with just the lips, more interior and more lyrical, remote and thick, that liberated like a fluid its charge of emotivity and of the unspoken. There was

the sneer that declares and the sneer that alludes; the sneer that speaks for high heads and that which speaks in great detail. There were substantive sneers and adjectival sneers. There was the sneer like one has genius—without limits of will and of representation." The receiving model for this artistic performance, far superior to swearwords is, for De Fillippo, *'a schifezza, d'a schifezza, d'a schifezza 'e ll'uommene!* [the scum of scum of scum of all humanity!]. We can only lament its progressive disappearance and hope for a noisy, collective, well-deserved return.

[12] In the cheering sections, beyond the noted ill-approved racist slogans, they sing largely of *bastardi* [bastards], *merda* [shit], *puttane* [whores] *e troia* [sluts]. The adversaries of the Mezzogiorno or obviously *puzzoni* [stinkers], *zingari* [gypsies], *colerosi* [cholerics], *terremotati* [earthquaked], *sporchi africani* [dirty Africans], etc. But there is no lack of inventive moments: for Verona *Giulietta zoccola e Romeo frocio* [Whore Juliet and Faggot Romeo] and some politically-oriented positions, as foreseen by the epic novel by N. Balestrini, *I Furiosi* (Milan: Bompiani, 1994): "Mondays what humiliation / to go to the factory and serve your master, ' oh Juventus cocksucker / /of the entire Agnelli family... / Shit Juve, Juve, shit Juve..." Or: "Mondays what true joy / to clean your ass with the *rossonera* [red and black—i.e., A.C. Milan] shirt / O Berlusconi, Gianni Rivera, / Channel 5 and the shitty *rossonera* / and shitty Milan Milan shitty Milan."

These are collective texts that belong to politically relevant lifestyles: they dictate the everyday forms of demonstrations and of conflicts in the piazza.

[13] See, among other things, the fifth penal section of the Cassation, judgment 30956 of 2010. And as an indication, in other judgments: *Battona* [hooker], *Frocio* [faggot], *Faccia di cavallo* [horse face], *Gay, Imbecille* [imbecile], *Italiano* (or *meridionale* [southerner] or *negro* [black]) *di merda* [of shit], *Matto* [crazy], *Puttana* [whore], *Scioccherellino* (!) [little fool], *Sporco negro* [dirty black], (*Italiano di merda* [shitty Italian], however, is not there!), *Stronzo* [asshole], *Vaffa!* [fuck off]... The court confirms here its role as *arbiter* in the last application of the Italian book of manners. In particular, when it is a case of deciding if an offense in any semiotic register—writing, cartoon, photograph, etc.—is or is not to be ascribed to the so-called "right to satire." This is a right elaborated in a jurisprudential way and not constitutionally guaranteed, one of criticism and the news. The satirical genre is defined as merciless criticism of political personalities that "symbolically" emphasizes or deforms the representation of the facts in order to obtain an ironic effect in the public opinion. It is incompatible, therefore, with the truthful parameter of the news, albeit within the rather imprecise limits of moderation—that is, of the verified truth of facts that might be adopted and in defense of the person's honor and dignity.

[14] "When one finds himself debating with a more able adversary, one becomes offensive, abusive, coarse—that is, one passes from the object of the dispute (where one is on the losing side) to the opposing side; one attacks his person in some way" (A. Schopenhauer). An "etotic" meditation the philosopher might say to those who abused the Goncourt brothers with P. Verlaine: "Curses...to this drunkard, to this pederast, to this assassin, to this coward crossed from time to time by fears of hell that make him shit in his underpants." It is a rhetorically profitable tactic, as proved by the popularity of those who have made the insult a genre in the media. The art critic V. Sgarbi, for example, has left the worn apostrophe *maiale* [pig], for the lighter one of *capra* [goat], but he reiterates it with sufficient superabundance that he silences the unfortunate interlocutor.

[15] Borges ends with a malign parenthesis: "(An Italian, to dismiss Goethe, issued a brief article in which he never tired of giving him the nickname 'il signore Wolfgang.' It was almost an adulation, but it meant a refusal to acknowledge that authentic arguments against Goethe were not lacking)."

[16] It is a widespread and old "anti-behavior" of Russian culture to tell someone to go fuck their mother (*mat*), a saying that would be ill-advised in Latin countries. Uspensky suggests wisely that the obscene lexicon converges with the sacred one: it would be a case of ritual incantation to avoid the wrath of Mother Earth, who, to the diabolical threat of incest, would open herself wide and let out the dead. This is a "sepulchral semantics" that would explain the current fashion for zombies!

A *pathosformel* culturally transmitted even to the hardly orthodox songs of Pussy Riot in the church of San Salvatore in Moscow:
"Shit, shit, shit of the Lord
Shit, shit, shit of the Lord
Gundyaev the patriarch believes in Putin,
Would it be better, slut, if you believed in God?"
Etc.

We find a ceremonial anti-behavior addressed to the Mother (the aquatic one this time) in the poetic apostrophes of A. Zanzotto for *Fellini's Casanova*. He had asked him to "wrap the entire rite [of Carnival] in a fabric, in a type of resonant spider-web, sacred and popular" made up of "propitiatory speech, iterative imploring, seductive telephony, evocative litanies, but also irreverence, challenges, insults, sneering provocations, all of it in an uneasy, exorcising skepticism, the feared failure of the event." To the address of the ceremony, the "mother goddess" emerges from the lagoon, and the bystanders proffer rhymed insults: the "*Strussia*"; "*la xe imbriagona, la xe magona*"; "*mona ciavona, cula cagona,*"; "*Baba catàba, vecia supssona.*" As so-called Neapolitan "relatives" do when they ask for the release of the blood of San Gennaro with epithets like "*Faccia gialluta, guappone,*" mixed with exhortations "*omm'e niente squaglia 'stu sfaccimm' 'e sange!*" and threats: "*Nun fa o' fess' San Genna', ti vott' a copp' a bascie.*" Attests R. Saviano: "I was a child and never would have believed you could utter so many insults in a church."

[17] F. Fortini: Title: "*To Carlo Bo.*" Text: "*No!*"

[18] From the electoral duel between Prodi and Berlusconi in the elections of 2006.

[19] Gadda had already had practice in the series of the most loutish insults against scatterbrained and incompetent subordinates in his *Journal of war and prison*, and in the *Pasticciaccio*, the ex-leader has already been disgraced with *Buce, Dictatore impestatissimo* [Most corrupt dictator], *Emir col fez e col pennacchio* [Emir with a fez and plume], *Erediluetico* [Hereditary syphilitic], *Facciaferoce* [Fierceface], *Gallinaccio con la faccia fanatica* [Turkey cock with a fanatical face], *Luetico* [Syphilitic], *Maledito Merdonio* [Cursed shit-devil], *Mascelluto* [Jawboned], *Natoscemo* [Bornstupid], *Negro coi guanti* [Black with gloves], *Rachitoide acromegalico* [Rickety acromegalic], *Rospo* [Toad], *Sterratore analfabeta* [Illiterate digger], *Testa di Morto in stiffelius* [Head of a dead man in a frock coat], *in tight* [...in morning dress], *in bombetta* [...in a bowler], *in pennacchi* [...in plumes], *Truce* [Grim]." For Gadda the Lombard, the *parlare* [speaking] that "would drip from [Mussolini's] balcony" was *pirlare* ["being a prick"].

Here, however, in his resonant satire against Mussolini (though his name is never written!) are the most rancorous epithets; *Alessandrone rincoglionito* [Big dumb-assed Alexander], *Batracemago* [Toadwizard], *Batrace tricacco* [Triturd toad], *Bombarda di tripla greca* [three-striped bombard], *Bombetta* [Derby], *Borioso* [Puffed up], *Cacchio* [Dick], *Cavallini* [Little horses], *Cetriolo* [Cucumber], *Ciuco maramaldo* [Bullying ass], *Ex-bomba* [Ex-bomb], *Estrovertito* [Extroverted], *Faba magna* [Great bean], *Fabulatore* [Confabulator], *Faccia feroce* [Fierce Face], *Fava* [Prick], *Furioso* [Raving Mad], *Gran Kan* [Great Khan], *Gran Pernacchia* [Great raspberry], *Gran somaro nocchiero*

[Great ass-driver], *Gran Tamburone del Nulla* [Great drummer of nothing], *Grande imago* [Great image], *Genio e favante tutore della Italia* [Genius and dicking protector of Italy], *KU-Cé, Ingrognato* [Grumpy], *Maldito* [Badfinger], *Mascellone mago* [Big-jawed wizard], *Mascellone unico* [Single bigjaw], *Mastro Pungolo* [Punchmaster], *Modellone* [Big Model], *Mugliante* [Bellower], *Nullapensante* [Nothingthinker], *Pirgopolinice* (Miles gloriosus) [Pyrgopolynices], *Poffarbacco* [By Jove!], *Priapo Giove Ottimo Massimo* [Most Excellent Priapus Jupiter], *Priapoimmagine* [Imageofpriapus], *Protuberato bucchesco priapo* [Protuberant hole-ridden Priapus], *Pupazzo* [Puppet], *Racimolatore* [Gleaner], *Scipioneria* [Scipio-nity], *Somaro* [Ass], *Stivaluto* [Booted one], *Super balano* [Super acorn shell], *Tauro* [Bull], *Torsolone* [Big torso], *Trombone e Naticone Ottimo massimo* [Most excellent trombone and Bigass], *Tuberone* [Big tuber], *Trebbiatore* [Thresher], *Velopendo* [Soft-palate]. Not to mention lists like: "he, a big horse saddle, the great man, the big man, the big fez, the big hole, the big boot, the provolone, the big man's big brain, the big three-stripe general" Choice names largely expurgated, however (when not censored), from the versions of *Eros and Priapus* amended for publication. Like *Merda di cervellone Caino* [*Shit of Cain's big brain*], which becomes *cervellone* [big head]; sanguinolento porcello [bloody piglet] becomes *brav'uomo* [good man] while *cavallerizzo tuttoculo* [little knight complete ass] falls completely, along with *provolone imbischerito* [provolone made stupid], *maramaldo omicida* [homicidal bully] and finally *Appiccata carogna* [Hung bastard]. In particular, in the first drafts we find broad and un-dulled assertion of the dictator's venereal adventures: *sifilide simbolica* [symbolic syphilitic], *morbo nelle medulle del Sozzo* [diseased in the essence of filth], or of the *kuce-verga* [kuce-dick], *quella scarlatta peste che gli escava il balano* [that scarlet fever that dug out his barnacles], *ex-puttaniere impestato* [contaminated ex-pimp], *Priapo marcio* [Rotten Priapus]. *L'autoerotomane eredicalcolico ed ederoluetico e luetico e in proprio* [the self-sex maniac hereditary alcoholic and hereditary syphilitic and syphilitic on his own] becomes *autoerotomane affetto da violenza ereditaria* [self sex-maniac affected by hereditary violence]; *Pirgopolinice spirochetaro* [spirochetic Pyrgopolynices] is replaced by *Pirgopolinice* [Pyrgopolynices]; *Faccia feroce* [Fierce-faced] by *sterco fetente gloria* [glorious stinking dung]; *l'eroe grasso, sifoloso* [the big, fat syphilitic hero] is replaced by *tiranno* [tyrant]; *l'impestato* [the contaminated] becomes *il bombetta* [the derby]; *il luetico* [syphilitic] becomes just *il frenetico* [the frenetic one].

[20] In *Rage and pride* (2003), after the tragic attack on the Twin Towers, Oriana Fallaci explained to her Italian readers, in the classical ways of satire, an articulated battery of violent insults directed against "Muslims and political figures," adding some of which it appears she had been the object. In the supposed "sermon," Muslims were branded as *scemi e barbari* [fools and barbarians], *stronzi e grulli* [assholes and idiots], *dannati figli di Allah* [damned children of Allah], *fottuti* [fucked], *figli di puttana* [children of whores], *da trattare a pedate nei coglioni* [to be dealt with by kicks to the balls], *ladroni clonati come pecora* [big thieves cloned like sheep], *cani mordaci* [snapping dogs], *conigli* [rabbits]. Their women were *sottomesse scimunite e minchione* [submissive fools and dupes], like the sisters of Osama bin Laden, *brutte con cicciuti seni e immense natiche* [ugly women with fat breasts and immense asses].

As for Italian politicians, they are generally *stronzi* [assholes], *gelosi* [jealous], *biliosi* [peevish], *vanitosi* [vain], *piccini e cretini* [tiny and stupid], *scemi* [fools], *illusi* [dreamers] but also *farabutti* [scoundrels], *imbroglioni* [tricksters], *analfabeti* [illiterates], *beoti* [morons], *squallidi* [squalid], *mediocri* [mediocre], *falliti* [failed], *animali* [animals], *somari* [asses], *coglioni* [assholes]. Among the opposing *cialtroni* [scoundrels] of the left, the Sessantottini are *fessi* [jerks], *inetti e rivoluzio-*

nari del cazzo [inept and revolutionary dicks]. The worst are the Cicale, who treat the author as a *mascalzona* [good-for-nothing], *forcaiola* [reactionary], and *razzista* [racist]. But they, on the other hand, are the *puttane a la page* [whores of the page], *da prendere a calci nel culo* [to be kicked in the ass], *sanguisughe livorose* [spiteful bloodsuckers], *galline* [hens], parasite [parasites], *umiliate da maiali maschilisti* [humiliated by macho pigs], when they are not *avvoltoi* [vultures]. Italy, at least in part, is the land of *piccole iene e dei voltagabbana* [little hyenas and turncoats], *godereccia* [pleasure-seeking], *furbetta* [sneaky], *volgare* [vulgar], *meschina* [petty], *stupida* [stupid], *vigliacca* [cowardly], *opportunista* [opportunistic], *doppiogiochista* [two-timers], *imbecille* [imbecilic], *imbelle* [cowardly], *infingarda* [slothful], *smidollata* [spineless], *edonistica* [hedonistic]. The young Italians of today are *sciagurati* [wretched], *molluschi* [spineless], *inetti* [inept] and *parassiti* [parasites] who like the *schifezza chiamata rap* [filth called rap] and are devoted to the *dannate squadre di calcio e ai dannatissimi stadi* [damned soccer teams and the goddamned stadiums]. *Non vogliono battersi* [they don't want to fight], and therefore they are *cretini e bugiardi* [idiots and liars], *codardi* [cowards], *sciocchi e masochisti* [fools and masochists], *cani bagnati* [wet dogs].

An exhaustive list that rigorously respects the rules of satire: the individualist who states the truth, in the complicit silence of the many, in the name of offended values and starting from the insult of the past, but without hope in the unsustainable present. We notice further, in the case of Fallaci, the abundance of animal metaphors, which is a distinctive trait of the discourse of the extreme right.

[21] "I have the greatest veneration in the world for the gentleman who…sits at his table and with complete calm composes forms of the insult suitable to any sort of provocation and…always keeps them within reach on the shelf of his fireplace, ready for use,' L. Sterne.

[Translated by Gianpiero W. Doebler]

Bibliography

Accattino, A. *Gli insulti che hanno fatto la storia*. Milan: Piemme, 2005.
Alberoni, F. *L'élite senza potere. Ricerca sociologica sul divismo*. Milan: Bompiani, 1973.
Bachtin, M. *L'opera di Rabelais e la cultura popolare*. Turin: Einaudi,1979, 1st ed. 1963.
Benveniste, E. "La blasfemia e l'eufemia," in *Essere di Parola*. Milan: B. Mondadori, 2009.
Borges, J. L. "L'arte di ingiuriare," in *Storia dell'Eternità*. Milan: Adelphi,1997.
Bouchet, T. *Noms d'oiseaux. L'insulte en politique de la Restauration à nos jours*. Paris: Stock, 2010.
Buonanno, G. *Insulto quindi sono. Come e perché conviene ingiuriare l'altro*. Bologna: Editrice Missionaria Italiana, 2013.
Butler, J. "Atti incendiari, parole ingiuriose," in *Parole che provocano*. Milan: R. Cortina, 2010.
Calvino, I. "Le parolacce," in *Una pietra sopra*. Turin: Einaudi, 1980.
Capuano, R. *Turpia*. Milan: Costa e Nolan, 2007.
Casaleggio, G. *Insultatemi*. L'Adagio, e-book, 2013.
Casalegno, G. et al. *Brutti, fessi e cattivi. Lessico della maldicenza italiana*, ed. G. Casalegno and G. Goffi. Turin: Utet, 2005.
Capuano, R.G. et al. *Elogio del Turpiloquio, Letteratura, politica,e parolacce*, ed. R. G. Capuano. Viterbo: Nuovi Equilibri, 2010.
Culpeper, J. *Impolitness, using language to cause offence*. Cambridge: Cambridge U. P., 2011.

D'Alessandro, G. *Bestiario giuridico 2. Le offese nel diritto e le offese del diritto*, Vicenza: Angelo Colla, 2011.
Dematteo, L. *L'idiota in politica. Antropologia della Lega Nord*. Milan: Feltrinelli 2011, 1st ed. 2007.
Derrida, J. and E. Roudinesco, *Quale Domani?* Milan: Bollati Boringhieri, 2004.
Eco, U. "Come dire parolacce in società," in *La bustina di Minerva*. Milan: Bompiani, 2000.
Edouard, R. *Dictionnaire des injures de la langue française. Traité d'injuriologie* 10/18. Paris: Tchou, 1979.
P. Fabbri, P. *Segni del tempo. Un lessico politicamente scorretto*, Rome: Meltemi, 2004.
Fabbri, P. and A. Marcarino, "Il discorso politico," *Carte Semiotiche*, n. 1 (settembre, 1985).
Fisher, S. "L'insulte: la parole et le geste," *Langue française*, n. 144, 4 (2004).
Frankfurt, H. *Stronzate, un saggio filosofico*. Milan: Rizzoli, 2005, 1st ed.1986.
Fuligni, B. et al. *Petit dictionnaire des injures politiques*, ed. B. Fuligni. Paris: Librairie Générale Française, "Le livre de poche," 2012.
James, A. *Stronzi, un saggio filosofico*. Milan: Rizzoli, 2013, 1st ed. 2012.
Maledicta, The International Journal of Verbal Aggression, Wisconsin, USA (1977-2005).
Honneth, A. *Riconoscimento e disprezzo*. Soveria Mannelli (CZ): Rubattino, 1993.
'Insultiamoli tutti', un breviario, ed. Collettivo Carla Ferguson Barberini. Rome: Aliberti, 2011.
Lagorgette, D. et al. *Les insultes: approches sémantiques et pragmatiques. Langue française*, n. 144 (2004).
Lagorgette, D. et al. *Les Insultes en français: de la recherche fondamentale à ses applications (linguistique, littérature, histoire, droit)*, ed. D. Lagorgette. Chambéry: Université de Savoie, 2009.
Lotman, J. *La cultura e l'esplosione*. Milan: Feltrinelli, 1992.
Milner, J.-C. *De la syntaxe à l'interprétation. Quantités, insultes, exclamations*. Paris: Le Seuil, 1978.
Morel, J.-P. *Le meilleur des insultes*. Paris: Fayard, 2013.
Pinker, S. "Le sette parole che non si possono dire in televisione," in *Fatti di parole, la natura umana svelata dal linguaggio*. Milan: Mondadori, 2009, 1st ed. 2007.
Rastier, F. *La misura e la grana*. Pisa: ETS, 2013 (chap. 7: "Semiotica dei siti razzisti e prevenzione della xenofobia").
Rosset, C. "Les insultes de Schopenhauer," in *Faits divers*. Paris: Puf, 2013.
Ruwet, N. *Grammaires d'insultes et autres études*. Paris: Seuil, 1982.
Schopenhauer, A. *L'arte di insultare*. Milan: Adelphi,1999.
Shiqiu, L. *La nobile arte dell'insulto, le arti marziali della parola*. Turin: Einaudi, 2011.
Tartamella, V. *Parolacce. Perché le diciamo, che cosa significano, quali effetti hanno*. Milan: Rizzoli, 2006.
Uspenskij, B. A. *Storia e semiotica*. Milan: Bompiani, 1988.

David Marsh

The Invectives of Petrarch and his Quattrocento Successors

Classical invective was developed by orators employing an established rhetorical framework, which contrasted the topics of praise and blame in public speaking.[1] In forensic and deliberative oratory, such topics were useful but not exclusive. In the courtroom, laudatory themes could aid the defendant, and derogatory ones his accusers; and in public deliberations, antithetical topoi helped urge opposite courses of actions. In epideictic or demonstrative rhetoric, praise and blame offered the central repertory for the public speaker. The antithetical basis of argumentation was further encouraged by rhetorical training in arguing both sides of a question. At first, the Romans were horrified by the apparent moral indifference of a Greek thinker like Carneades, and famously banished him from their city. But a few generations later, the successful mediator of Greek literary culture, Cicero, made arguments *in utramque partem* a basic tool of oratorical training and philosophical discourse.

When Renaissance humanists revived the categories of ancient rhetoric, their social status and political organizations offered little occasion for using forensic or deliberative oratory.[2] By contrast, epideictic rhetoric supplied them with a vast arsenal of weapons that could be deployed in their cultural warfare. Hence the centrality of the epideictic antithesis of praise and blame. While humanists illustrate moral philosophy by lauding notable exemplars of virtue, they also denounce their opponents in the most exaggerated terms of abuse.

The Latin noun *invectiva* is not classical, but it derives from the verb *inuehor* 'to ride against, to attack,' attested as early as Plautus and used by Cicero in the context of courtroom debate.[3]

The prefix *in-* connotes attack and denunciation, as is clear from two passages in Asconius' commentaries on Ciceronian orations. On the (now) fragmentary *In toga candida*, he writes: "Tum Cicero graviter... surrexit atque in coitionem Catilinae et Antoni invectus est.."; and on *In Pisonem* he describes Piso as follows: "reversus in civitatem Piso de insectatione Ciceronis conquestus est et in eum invectus est....Pisoni Cicero respondit hac oratione." As these instances suggest, classical invective is directed literally *ad hominem*, which explains the personal targets implicit in titles such as the *Catilinarians* or the *Philippics*, which famously imitate Demosthenes' attacks on Philip of Macedon.

While Cicero generally pled for the defense–in speeches such as *pro Archia* or *pro Milone*–his denunciatory orations feature the significant preposition *in* (*in Verrem, in Catilinam, in Pisonem,* and *in Vatinium*), and each of the *Philippics* is titled *In M. Antonium oratio Philippica*. Of these speeches, only the five directed against Verres were part of a legal prosecution. The rest were delivered in the senate, but partake more of epideictic defamation than deliberative suasion.[4] Cicero's famous Catilinarian orations are often called invectives in later manuscripts, and they apparently inspired a contemporary Roman to compose two spurious little invectives, purportedly exchanged between Cicero and Sallust.[5] These pseudo-classical texts gained wide acceptance, and we find them cited approvingly in two passages of Quintilian's *Institutio oratoria*. In a discussion of apostrophe (4.1.68), Quintilian lauds Sallust for directly addressing Cicero, which recalls Cicero's opening words to Catiline:

> Quid? non Sallustius derecto ad Ciceronem, in quem ipsum dicebat, usus est principio, et quidem protinus: "Graviter et iniquo animo maledicta tua paterer, M. Tulli": sicut Cicero fecerat in Catilinam: "quo usque tandem abutere"?

(Again, did not Sallust in accusing Cicero address him directly? Indeed, he says forthwith: "I should feel deeply injured by your insults, Marcus Tullius," just as Cicero had done in his speech against Catiline: "How long will you abuse...?")

Then, in discussing various figures of speech (9.3.88-89), Quintilian observes that some, like personification, resemble "figures of thought":

> Quaedam verborum figurae paulum a figuris sententiarum declinantur.... Etiam in personae fictione accidere quidam idem putaverunt, ut in verbis esset haec figura: "crudelitatis mater est avaritia," et apud Sallustium in Ciceronem "o Romule Arpinas": quale est apud Menandrum "Oedipus Thriasius."

(Certain figures of speech differ little from figures of thought... Some have even thought that this applies to personification as well, so that such figures are found in expressions such as "Avarice is the mother of cruelty," and "O Romulus of Arpinum" in Sallust's speech against Cicero, and Menander's "Thriasian Oedipus.")

Evidently Quintilian envisaged Sallust and Cicero present together, addressing and insulting each other directly. With the decline of the senate, deplored by Tacitus in his *Dialogus de oratoribus*, such confrontations survived in the muted form of epistolary exchanges like Jerome's invectives.

What are the mechanisms of vituperation? At the lexical level of vocabulary, we find established vocabularies of insult, or name-calling, while at the conceptual level we find recurrent themes of defamation. The lexicon of Latin invective has been studied by Ilona Opelt and Severin Koster.[6] Let us examine Cicero's use of insults in his accusatory orations. In the first *Catilinarian*, Cicero calls his enemy "scelus, furia, audacia, flagitium"–terms that appropriately suggest subversive violence. The insults of *In Pisonem* are stronger and cruder: "belua, furia, furcifer, Clodiane canis, immanissimum ac foedissimum monstrum,O scelus, o pestis, o labes, asine."[7] (The term "furcifer" recurs in Ciceros' *In Vatinium* 14.) Another "classic" insult–comparison to a pig–is found in pseudo-Cicero's *In Sallustium* 1.3: "Itaque nihil aliud studet nisi ut lutulentus sus cum quovis volutari," and was used by Jerome and Petrarch.[8]

The topics of ancient encomium and invective often rely on the categories of biography.[9] An early example of this is found in pseudo-Sallust's invective (2), where he impugns Cicero's amoral family:

> Verum, ut opinor, splendor domesticus tibi animos tollit, uxor sacrilega ac periuriis delibuta, filia matris paelex, tibi iucundior atque obsequentior quam parenti par est.

> (But, I suppose, your spirits are raised by the brilliance of your home, by a wife guilty of sacrilege and dishonoured by perjury, by a daughter who is her mother's rival and is more compliant and submissive to you than a daughter should be to a parent.)

The Renaissance revival of invective begins with Petrarch's four invectives, in which he assails prestigious authorities: the science of medicine (*Invective contra medicum*), ecclesiastical dignity (*Contra quendam magni status*), Scholastic philosophy (*De sui ipsius et multorum ignorantia*), and French nationalism (*Contra eum qui maledixit Italie*). (Strictly speaking, the *De ignorantia* is not an invective, but it sprang from an actual encounter between the humanist and four of his supposed friends.)

When Petrarch resorted to the genre of invective, he modified the classical model. Most strikingly, his writings lack the elements essential to Quintilian's conception–the open confrontation and direct address to his adversary.

Petrarch's invective is an instrument of *ignominia* – the act of depriving someone of his or her "name." He never names his adversaries, preferring to consign them to oblivion. And while his *Against a Physician* and *Against a Man of High Rank* directly address the enemy, the *On His Own Ignorance* and *Against a Detractor of Italy* are couched as letters to friends. All the same, Petrarch's invectives share with their classical models what we may call their public spirit. Cicero's *Catilinarians* explicitly invoke the safety of the Roman republic. This is the image of Cicero that Petrarch limns in *Against a Physician* 158, when he ironically proposes that the physician may turn rhetorician:

> Nonne ita homo es tu, ut Cicero? Accusat ille Clodium ac Verrem et in *Invectivis* Catilinam, et in *Philippicis* insectatur Antonium – magnos viros ac feroces, ad ultionemque promptissimos – et molem multorum criminum, ac reipublice ruinam illis opponit. Tu defunctum unum nec loqui valentem nec ulcisci, cur non fidenter accuses, quod se ipse necaverit?

> (Aren't you just as human as Cicero? He accuses Clodius and Verres; and he assails Catiline in his *Invectives* and Antony in his *Philippics*. They are powerful, violent men, and quick to take revenge; but he charges them with a huge number of crimes and the ruin of the republic. So why can't you confidently accuse a dead patient, who is incapable of speech or revenge, alleging that he has killed himself?)

For the most part, Petrarch employs insult more than defamation: since he chooses not to name his opponents, he says little about their private lives. His abusive language describes his adversaries with reference to three denigrating topics: human stupidity and madness, bestial traits and behavior, and repellant substances like urine, vomit, and sewage. At the same time, Petrarch attempts to offset his negative censures with a positive vision of his own values, thus complementing his Juvenalian and urban critique with Horatian and rural idealism.[10]

Quattrocento humanists generally followed Petrarch's lead in employing invective.[11] Their revival of ancient rhetoric gave epideictic a central place, since they had little opportunity to plead in law courts and legislative assemblies. By turns, we find praise and blame inspiring numerous humanist tracts and dialogues. For example, Buonaccurso da Montemagno (ca. 1391-1429) composed an oration of Catiline against Cicero ("Catilinae in Ciceronem Oratio") which in a Perugia codex is called an invective.[12] Hence, the invectives of Renaissance humanists appear as counterparts to their compositions in a laudatory vein. To cite one example, when in 1406 Leonardo Bruni was struggling to compose an encomium of Coluccio Salutati, he took refuge in writing his risqué *Oration of*

Heliogabalus to the Prostitutes of Rome. By the same token, the invectives of Poggio Bracciolini (1380-1459) are balanced by his laudatory funeral orations, which in fact follow them in the 1538 Basel edition.

The heir apparent to Petrarch was of course Leonardo Bruni (1370-1444), whose residence in Florence gave new life to local devotion to the Trecento master. Bruni read Petrarch's invectives, and found them wanting. In the first book of his *Dialogi ad Petrum Histrum*, he has the captious Niccolò Niccoli lament Petrarch's rhetorical skills:

> Scripsit preterea *Bucolicon carmen* Franciscus; scripsit etiam *Invectivas*, ut non solum poeta, sed etiam orator haberetur. Verum sic scripsit, ut neque in bucolicis quicquam esset quod aliquid pastorale aut silvestre redoleret; neque quicquam in orationibus quo non artem rhetoricam magnopere desideraret.

> (Francesco wrote a *Bucolic Poem* as well, and also wrote *Invectives*, so that he would be regarded not only as a poet, but as an orator too. Yet he wrote in such a way that there is nothing pastoral or sylvan in his bucolics, and there is nothing in his orations that do not greatly stand in need of rhetorical skill.)[13]

Like Petrarch, Bruni composed a series of works which modern editors call "Scritti polemici."[14] Like Petrarch, Bruni does not name his adversaries, as in his *Oratio in hypocritas* (1417) directed against three unnamed foes, presumably Ambrogio Traversari, Niccolò Niccoli, and a third person. Although the context is personal, Bruni's exordium, with its allusions to conspiracy and destruction, evokes the public spirit of Cicero's *Catilinarians*:

> Ex omni genere hominum, quos variis damnabilibusque vitiis ingeniosa et ad malum prona coninquinavit improbitas, nullum neque perniciosius, neque odibilius esse reor, ne severiori censura animadversioneque plectendum, quam eos, qui cum perverse mentis animique malignantis sint, tamen fingendo id callide conantur et agunt ut sancti et integerrimi homines omnique carentes vitio habeantur. His namque, cum sint totius humani generis infestissimi hostes, et in capita ceterorum hominum ad perniciem fraudemque coniurati, dignum est a cunctis, tamquam adversus aliquam publicam luem, inexpiabile bellum indici.

> (Of all the kinds of men whom clever and corrupting dishonesty has polluted with various vices worthy of condemnation, I think that none are more destructive or more hateful than those who, possessing a depraved mind and malignant spirit, astutely pretend to act in such a way that they are regarded as holy, righteous, and free of any vice. For since they are the deadly enemy of the entire human race and conspire to destroy and defraud the lives of other men, it is just that all declare implacable war against them, as against a public pestilence.)[15]

In his *Oratio in nebulonem maledicum* (1424) Bruni replies to the (spoken) calumnies of Niccolò Niccoli, who again is not named. Much of the tone is Petrarchan, as when Bruni denounces Niccoli for "vomiting" slander: "calumniis in me congestis... vomuisti apud satellites et asseclas stultitie tue" ("Piling up slanders against me, you vomited them up before the companions and followers of your folly").[16] Bruni's invective was inspired by Niccoli's attacks on him and on other men of learning–figures such as Dante, Petrarch, Boccaccio, Thomas Aquinas, Chrysoloras, and Guarino of Verona. Implicit here is something more than a matter of cultural taste. Niccoli's attacks represent an assault on the republic of letters. In a sense, Bruni is transferring Cicero's political context to a cultural one. In defending himself, Bruni observes that he is in good company, for it is an honor to be denigrated by such a worthless buffoon:

> Quis refugiat in eodem a te numero collocari, in quo Dantem et Petrarcham et Chrysoloram collocasti? Vituperatio quidem impuri nefariique hominis et perditissimi scurre insulsissimique nebulonis, qualis tu es, summa laus videri non immerito debet...

> (Who would shrink from being assigned a place in the group in which you placed Dante, Petrarch, and Chrysoloras? The abuse of a vile and wicked fellow, of a depraved buffoon, and of an utterly mindless scoundrel like you must rightly be considered the highest praise.)[17]

This observation, which recurs in Poggio's invectives against Filelfo, echoes similar paradoxes enunciated by Petrarch, who mocks the ineptness of men who can neither praise nor blame others without achieving the opposite effect. In his invective *Against a Physician* 164, he compares the doctor's rhetorical clumsiness with his medical blunders:

> Quos vituperare vis laudas! Non miror, quia et quos curare vis interficis, et – puto – quos interficere velles efficeres immortales.

> (You praise the very people you wish to disparage! I'm not surprised, since you kill the people you wish to cure. I even think you could render immortal those whom you wish to kill.)

Likewise, in *Against a Detractor of Italy* 73, he scoffs at his adversary, whose praise is worthless:

> Multo quidem illaudatus esse maluerim, quam a tali laudatore laudari.

> (By far, I would prefer to be unpraised, rather than praised by such a praiser).

And in *Against a Man of High Rank* 4-5, Petrarch sarcastically gives thanks for being spared a prelate's praises:

> Ubi primum crebro te meum nomen usurpare audivi, suspensus animo timui ne laudares; quod si faceres, actum erat: nullum glorie, nullum tu fidutie relinquebas locum, siquidem infamie non ultimum genus laudator turpis atque infamis. ...Nunc enim quod vituperando me laudas, vereor ne vino potius quam iudicio tribuatur. Si plene igitur me laudatum cupis, siccus impransusque vitupera...

> (When I first heard that you often went about citing my name, I was perplexed, fearing that you might be praising me. If you had done this, I would have been finished. You would be depriving me of any glory or credibility, since having a base and infamous man praise you is one of the worst kinds of infamy.... As it is, when your censures win me praise, I fear they spring from wine rather than your judgment. So if you wish to praise me fully, censure me when sober and fasting…)

Two other features of Bruni's invective are worthy of note. First, although Bruni's exordium begins by addressing this "perditissime scurra" directly–as Quintilian recommended-- he soon appeals to a fictive audience to judge the matter (340): "vos autem qui auditis iudices eritis." Second, in keeping with classical invective, Bruni turns to biographical facts to demonstrate the baseness of his adversary and his family. His grandfather's tavern in Pistoia attracted whores and wastrels (352): "avi caupona... meretrices et ganeos invitabat." Niccoli himself defrauded his brothers of their inheritance, and lives with a Beneventan whore, whom he stole from his brother and who like Circe has transformed him into a beast.

Poggio Bracciolini (1380-1459) is perhaps the best-known polemicist of the first half of the Quattrocento, but in the rhetorical tradition his numerous invectives are balanced by a number of laudatory funeral orations. Like Bruni, Poggio wrote against hypocrites (*Contra hypocritas*), but his target was not Florentine acquaintances but the orders of mendicant friars. His most famous invectves are those directed against Francesco Filelfo (1398-1481) and Lorenzo Valla (1407-1457), both of whom repaid him in various attacks in both verse and prose.

Poggio's writings are all directed *ad hominem*, with no pretense of anonymity. His four invectives against Filelfo (1435) were initially provoked by the latter's attacks on Niccoli, and they offer the sort of biographical defamation that Bruni had employed. Filelfo had already provoked the enmity of the Medici clan, and on their seizure of power in 1434 he was forced to flee to Siena. Here he began to take revenge in the only manner possible, literary attacks in the form of Latin satires filled with venom and obscenity. Poggio's response was immediate and virulent. In his first invective, he calls Filelfo a pig wallowing in mud (an image common in classical invective) and rebukes his use of sexual language:

> Tu nisi esses spurcissimus omnium quo nostra aetas tulit, nunquam profecto te in scoeno uilissimorum uerborum tanquam immunda sus libens uolutasses, uuluam, tentiginem, priapum, et his similia uersibus tuis admiscens...[18]

(If you weren't the foulest of all the people born in our age, you would never had wallowed in the mud of base language like a filthy sow, flavoring your verses with terms like vulva, erection, and phallus...)

Poggio then takes the sexual offensive against his opponent. You accuse Niccoli of loving a woman, he says, but you seduced a Greek one, although you prefer boys, and should not be called Philelphus but Pedarpus ("lad-grabber"). Filelfo may have thought he would be crowned with laurels for his poetry, but his head will be soiled by a a crown of excrement:

> Sperasti, monstrum infandum, hos tuos insulsissimos uersus, in quibus etiam male latine loqueris, allaturos tibi laureolam, qua fanaticum caput redimeres. At stercorea corona ornabuntur, foetentes crines priapei uatis et sacris suis initiati, ut cum homines te uiderint, insusurrent omnes: Hic ne ille est priapieus Apollo, qui non Heliconum, sed merdiconum laticem degustauit, cuius ex ore tam foeda oratio prodierit, tam spurcidicus sermo emanarit?[19]

(You hoped, unspeakable monster, that these vapid verses, written in poor Latin, would bring you a laurel to encircle your frenzied head. But they will be adorned with a crown of excrement, along with the stinking hair of the bard of Priapus and his initiates, so that when people see you, everyone will murmur: "Isn't this the phallic Apollo who tasted not the Helicon but the stream of Merdicon, from whose mouth such filthy speech and such obscene discourse flows?")

In his second invective, Poggio expands his horizon to depict Filelfo in conflict first with the Florentines, and then the Venetians; and Filelfo's affectation of growing a Greek-style beard summons forth comparisons with stinking goats and horned beasts (as in his pun *corniger velut cornutus*).[20] Poggio's third and last invective takes the biographical approach to such an extent that historians have been grateful for its details of the humanist's checkered career.

In the end, Filelfo appears as an exile banished from every decent place in society. Small wonder, Poggio observes, since his mother was a disgraceful slattern, and his early training made him a catamite! While a guest of Chrysoloras, he violated his virgin daughter, and escaped like a new Paris with Helen as his concubine, leaving nothing behind for his creditors but his "behind.": "nates pro pecunia ostentans creditoribus tuis."[21] On his return to Italy, he swindles various men in Venice, Bologna, and Florence, even stealing jewelry from Leonardo Bruni's wife! After a shameful visit by his mother, he escaped to Lombardy; and while walking the streets of Pavia he was in fact doused with a basin of human urine and excrement–thus fulfilling the coronation prophesied in the first invective.[22]

The biographical approach is normal in Poggio, whose use of epideictic rhetoric extended from the vituperation of invective to the laudations of funeral encomia. Petrarch, by contrast, has little use for demonstrative rhetoric. When he was crowned with the poetic laurel in 1341, he used the dated form of the thematic sermon to praise poetry. To be sure, he was interested in biography, but principally in those of classical history. And as Leonardo Bruni would point out a century later "history is one thing, and encomium another *(aliud est enim historia, allud laudatio)*."[23]

Like Bruni, Poggio in his third invective says being attacked by a scoundrel is a badge of honor:

> ...mihique summae laudi ducam a Francisco Philelpho scurruli homine rabulaque turpissimo omnium qui uiuant, illa obiici alteri ac describi, quorum homines norunt ipsum optimum artificem extitisse... Non me illa laedunt, non famam, non laudem minuunt, non honorem, non dignitatem polluunt, sed augent et illustrant... Hoc enim est antiquum artificium, quo mali et tui similes delectantur, ut carpant bonos, quorum in summam uergunt laudem nefariorum hominum detrectationes.
>
> (I consider it the highest praise when Francesco Filelfo, a scoundrel and the basest ranter of anyone alive, blames someone else and ascribes to him all the acts of which he himself is known by all to be the principal architect... His words don't harm me, they don't lessen my fame, they don't besmirch my honor or dignity, but rather increase and enchance them... This is an old ploy favored by evil men and those like you: they carp at good men, but the detractions of scoundrels in fact contributes to their praise.)[24]

The combative Lorenzo Valla (1407-1457) naturally aroused the enmity of rival scholars, and engaged in a series of invectives, most notably against Poggio (*Antidota in Poggium, Apologus*) and Bartolomeo Fazio (*Antidotum in Facium* 1447).[25] The richness and complexity of Valla's invectives defy brief characterization, and much of his argument is conducted along philological rather than rhetorical lines. All the same, he too owes some debt to Petrarch: witness the association of contemporary invective with ancient court cases. In *Against a Physician* (209), Petrarch observes that some talented young orators hoped to make their name by prosecuting prominent citizens:

> Solebant equidem ingeniosi adolescentes ab insigni accusatione aliqua primum nomen auspicari, quasi victori accederet victi nomen, et fama multis quesita laboribus eventum unius iudicii sequeretur. Non infame negotium, ut mos erat, sed unde quosdam valde nobilitatos legimus.

> (In fact, young men of genius used to first make a name for themselves by accusing a prominent individual. They believed that the victor would inherit the renown of the vanquished, and that the outcome of a single verdict would bestow on them fame that had been won by many labors. As this was the custom, it was no disgraceful affair. Indeed, we read that it rendered some men very famous.)[26]

He is referring to the early career of Julius Caesar as narrated in the life by Suetonius.[27] By the same token, Valla begins his *Antidotum in Facium* with an observation that echoes Suetonius and Petrarch:

> ... more veterum adolescentium in causis forensibus auspicandis, qui, ut se disertos, ut probos, ut rei publice studiosos ostenderent, claros viros in iudicium vocabant, criminibus responsuros.

> (It was the ancient custom of youths beginning their legal pleading to call famous men to trial as defendants in order to demonstrate their eloquence, probity, and patriotism.)[28]

With the invectives exhanged by Poggio and Valla, we move from personal and anecdotal abuse into a different sphere toward which Petrarch pointed the way–the debate on texts and their authority. As I observe in my introduction to *Against a Detractor of Italy*, "as a detailed refutation of Hesdin's tract, Petrarch's last invective points the way toward the polemical exchanges of the Quattrocento, in which humanists censured the texts of their opponents."[29] (Today's clashes of internet view has produced the coinage Fisking, or to Fisk, blogosphere slang referring to the point-by-point criticism that highlights perceived errors, or disputes the analysis, in a statement, article, or essay.)

Let us conclude with some notes on a significant "textual" invective, the 1432 *Philippic against Antonio Panormita (Philippica in Antonium Panormitam)* by Antonio da Rho (1395-1447).[30] Titled after Cicero's neo-Demosthenic orations against Mark Antony, this invective pits the author against another Antonius.[31] Recently, Panormita had written to Antonio da Rho to complain of anonymous verses that obscenely censured his *Hermaphroditus*; and suspecting that the culprit was Raudensis, he censured him in turn for making an translation of Suetonius, whose lives of the emperors contain many sordid details. In reply, Antonio da Rho composed 70 pages of prose invective, couched as a point-by-point refutation of four objectionable passages in Panormita's letter! The influence of Petrarch is unmistakable: like the *De ignorantia*, the work is couched as a letter addressed to a friend (in this case, the humanist Pier Candido Decembrio); and it uses allusions to base bodily functions like urine (72) and vomit (186) to pillory its adversary.[32]

In his preface to Decembrio, Antonio da Rho establishes the contrast between his own Christian tolerance and the bestial fury of Panormita, who is later called a Siculus-Suculus ("Sicilian Piglet") and Panormita-Gomorrita (Palermitan from Gomorrah).[33] This is the reason why he answers not to single insults, but to the chief arguments of his opponent:

> Nolo tamen putes, mi Candide, me faecibus sordibusque suis diutius immoraturum.... Futurus sum igitur qui non turpibus petulantibusque uerbis eius singulis... sed capitibus et partibus haud nullis, ne absolute quidem illis omnibus, responsum dedam. Animum quoque sic belle institui meque omnem ita perscripsi, ut Christiani spectato more et sancto potius opem mihi ferrem defensitaremque– scutum tenerem, gladium reiicerem– quam illius exquisita elaborataque flagitia insimularem, honeste quidem. Non enim considero quid ipse mereatur, sed quid me deceat.
>
> (But I do not want you to think, dear Candido, that I am going to tarry long in his scum and slime.... Consequently, I am not going to respond to each one of his foul and abusive words... I shall respond only to the principal points and to some parts, and not fully even to them. In addition, I have trained my mind and defined my whole character so well that in the respected and sacred practice of a Christian I would rather aid and defend myself than denounce, honorably to be sure, his exquisitely elaborate crimes. I retain the shield and cast away the sword. For I do not consider what he deserves, but what is appropriate for me.)[34]

Antonio da Rho represents a new development in Renaissance invective. While he was professor of rhetoric at Milan, in 1433 he compiled a handbook called *Imitationes rhetoricae* that includes a repertory of vituperative language. Under the heading "Obloqui" ("To vilify"), Antonio offers snippets largely drawn from Cicero's *Verrines* and *Catilinarians*, as well as from the pseudo-Ciceronian "Declamation against Catiline." But he also quotes from Jerome–along with Cicero, his principal model–and even from some of his own polemical writings.[35] And in "Words we Ought to Use Only to execrate Vice," he offers an alphabetical list of offensive terms–many of them sexual–running from "anus" to "vitiosus."[36] Opprobrium has left the law court and entered the classroom.

Notes

[1] See Lindsay Cameron Watson, "Invective," in *Oxford Classical Dictionary*, 3d ed. by Simon Hornblower and Antony Spawforth (Oxford-New York: Oxford UP, 1996), p. 762; Ilona Opelt, *Die lateinischen Schimpfwörter und verwandte sprachliche Erscheinungen: Eine Typologie* (Heidelberg: Carl Winter Universitätsverlag, 1965); Severin Koster, *Die Invektive in der griechischen und römischen Literatur* (Meisenheim am Glan: Verlag Anton Hain, 1980); Ennio I. Rao, *Curmudgeons in High Dudgeon: 101 Years of Invectives (1352-1453)* (Messina, Edizioni Dr. Antonino Sfameni, 2007), pp. 99-107, with a census of humanist invectives at pp. 147-59.

[2] Perhaps the most notable manifestation of the epideictic is found in works that debate the merits of antiquity vs. the modern age. Cf. Robert Black, "Ancients and Moderns in the Renaissance: Rhetoric and History in Accolti's Dialogues on the Preeminence of Men of His Own Times," *JHI* 43 (1982), 3-32; and Charles Trinkaus, "*Antiquitas* versus *Modernitas*: An Italian Humanist Polemic and Its Resonance," *JHI* 48 (1987), 11-21.

[3] Plautus, *Mercator* 998: "heia! superbe inuehere" ("Go ahead! Rail haughtily"); Cicero, *De oratore* 2.301: "urgent aduocati, ut inuehamur, ut male dicamus" ("Advocates urge us to inveigh and insult"). On the latter passage, see J. H. G. Powell, "Invective and the orator: Ciceronian theory and practice," in Joan Booth, ed., *Cicero on the Attack: Invective and Subversion in the Orations and Beyond* (Swansea: The Classical Press of Wales, 2007), p. 12.

[4] For a classic treatment of oratorical invective, see M. Tulli Ciceronis *In Calpurnium Pisonem oratio*, edited with text, introduction, and commentary by R. G. M. Nisbet (Oxford: Clarendon Press, 1961), "The *In Pisonem* as an Invective," pp. 192-97. See now also Anthony Corbeill, *Controlling Laughter: Political Humor in the Late Roman Republic* (Princeton: Princeton UP, 1996), and the eight fine essays in J. Booth, *Cicero on the Attack*, cited in n. 3 above.

[5] See Koster, *Invektive*, pp. 177-200.

[6] Opelt, *Schimpfwörter*; Koster, *Invektive*, pp. 358-364 ("Invektivische Apostrophierungen" = invective forms of address).

[7] All these terms as used by Cicero and other are cited in Opelt, *Schimpfwörter*, in her exhaustive discussion of political and juridical insults.

[8] Koster, *Invektive*, pp. 191, 359. Cf. also Jerome, *Commentary on Hosea* in *PL* 25.855: "[haeretici] instar porcorum volutantur in coeno." For animal imagery in Jerome, see David Wiesen, *Jerome as a Satirist: A Study in Christian Latin Thought and Letters* (Ithaca NY: Cornell UP, 1964), pp. 186-7 (the preceding passage is cited on 187). For a list of Jerome's abusive terms, see Opelt, *Schimpfwörter*, p. 229.

[9] See Koster, *Die Invektive, sub indice*, "Lebenslaauf": for example, p. 16 (Aphthonius), 86-89 (Demosthenes, *in Aeschinem*), 127 (Cicero, *in Vatinium*), 225 (Cicero, *in Pisonem*). Cf. also David

Rutherford, *Early Renaissance Invective and the Controversies of Antonio da Rho* (Tempe: MRTS, 2005), pp. 4-6. For the topics of ancient biography, see David Marsh, "The Self Expressed: Leon Battista Alberti's Autobiography," *Albertiana* 10 (2007): 125-140 at 126-7.

[10] Cf. *Against a Man of High Rank* 35: Political deliberations and measures, as well as the administration of public funds, are entrusted to others, who were born for this purpose. To me, nothing is entrusted but leisure, silence, security, and freedom. These are my concern and my business. While others at dawn seek great palaces, I seek my familiar woods and solitude."

[11] See Rao, *Curmudgeons*, esp. pp. 13-39.

[12] See *Prose e rime de' due Buonaccoris da Montemagno* con Annotazioni e Alcune Rime di Niccolò Tinucci ... (In Firenze, Nella stamperia di Giuseppe Manni, 1718): Inc. (f. lxviiiii) "Omnes homines, qui in maximis principatibus vitam agunt"; expl. (f. lxxii) "supplicem insontemque pristinae claritudini omnium civium gratiae et benivolentiae vestrae restituite." It also appears as the "Oratio pro L. Catilina contra M. T. Ciceronem" which is called an 'invectiva' in a Perugia codex (*Iter Italicum* 6:107, IV B 5).

[13] Leonardo Bruni, *Opere letterarie e politiche*, ed. Paolo Viti (Turin: UTET, 1996), p. 114; my translation.

[14] Ibid., pp. 283-393, "Scritti polemici."

[15] Ibid., p. 310; my translation.

[16] Ibid., p. 338. On polemical references to vomit, see Francesco Petrarca, *Invectives,* ed. and tr. David Marsh (Harvard UP, 2003), p. xvi, and *Against a Detractor of Italy* 12 (p. 375): "Unable to control his bile, he has vomited many charges against me...."

[17] Bruni, *Opere*, 344-346; my translation. Note that Bruni omits Boccaccio, who in his *Dialogi ad Petrum Histrum* had appeared as the least of the Three Crowns.

[18] Poggii Florentini, *Opera omnia*, 4 vols, ed. Riccardo Fubini (Turin: Bottega d'Erasmo, 1964), vol. 1 (=1538 Basel ed.), 165. Cf. ps.-Cicero, *In Sallustium* 1.3, cited above.

[19] Ibid., 169, correcting the final clause from "iam foeda...tam spurcidus sermo."

[20] Ibid., 171-4; 173: "o hirce foetulente, o foetide corniger"; 174: "in eos euome... barbatum hircum."

[21] Ibid., 174-9.

[22] 185: "Scies enim, et alii quoque sciunt...quendam...tibi in publico deambulanti humanis stercoris urinaeque plenum uas in Heliconium ac Musis sacrum caput effudisse." In the conclusion of his fourth invective Against Valla (1452-1453), Poggio imagines his enemy seated backwards on an ass, and crowned with the intestines of a slaughtered sheep: cf. my "Further Notes on Leon Battista Alberti's *Dinner Pieces,*" *Allegorica* 14 (1993): 23-37, at 36-7.

[23] Bruni, Epistle VIII, 4 of 1440 to Francesco Picolpassi: cited by Gary Ianziti, "Bruni on Writing History," *Renaissance Quarterly* 51,1998, 367-91 at 370, n. 8.

[24] Poggio, *Opera*, I: 174; my translation.

[25] For the latter, see Lorenzo Valla, *Antidotum in Facium*, ed. Mariangela Regoliosi (Padua: Antenore, 1981); Valla was responding to Facio's four invectives: see Bartolomeo Facio, *Invective in Laurentium Vallam*, critical edition with introduction by Ennio I. Rao (Naples: Società Editrice Napoletana, 1978).

[26] Petrarca, *Invectives*, 176-9.

[27] Suetonius, *Divus Julius* 55, as I note in my edition (p. 502, n. 198).

[28] Lorenzo Valla, *Antidotum in Facium*, ed. Mariangela Regoliosi (Padua: Antenore, 1981), p. 3 (no source cited); my translation.

[29] Petrarca, *Invectives*, p. x.

[30] See Rutherford, *Invective*; and cf. my review in *Neulateinisches Jahrbuch* 10 (2008), 337-338.

[31] Introducing the First Objection of his invective, Antonio da Rho characterizes Panormita in words used by Cicero against Antony in *Philippics* 2.4.7: "humanitatis expers et uitae communis ignarus" ("devoid of humanity and ignorant of the common usages of life").

[32] For a brief summary of such themes, see Francesco Petrarca, *Invectives*, edited and translated by David Marsh (Cambridge, MA and London: Harvard UP, 2003), pp. xiii-xvi. In his peroration (p. 186), Antonio da Rho describes Panormita as a "dog returning to its vomit," a Biblical tag used by Jerome and Petrarch (p. xiv).

[33] Rutherford, *Invective*, pp. 68 ("Suculus"), 186 ("Gomorrita").

[34] Ibid., pp. 54-7.

[35] Rutherford, *Invective*, Appendix VIII, pp. 300-313. On Antonio's use of Jerome, see pp. 20-2.

[36] Ibid., Appendix IX, pp. 314-20.

Kathryn Morgan

Domesticating Invective in Plato's Laws

Plato may seem an odd choice as a focus for an essay on invective, inveterate foe as he was of the entire mode and its various generic instantiations. Nevertheless, the mirror of his disapproval allows us to isolate issues of interest for any consideration of the social function of the invective mode. Much discussion at the CMRS conference that gave rise to this volume centered on the question of whether invective could be described as a literary genre, and in general this move was resisted in favor of considering it as a "mode." Recent work on the function of invective mode in the ancient world and elsewhere has provoked scholarly excitement to reconsider problems of persona and broad cultural function.[1] The issue is, then, to understand how this mode informs the literary discourses in which it appears and how the pose of anarchic and splenetic venting interacts with its contexts (literary and otherwise). Plato's *Laws* is of interest precisely as an attempt to theorize the practice of invective and reflect on its social effects and context. Further, the dialogue models an attempt (associated with its theorizing) to regulate the practice of comic invective. This attempt at regulation sits in the context of a literary work that portrays an intellectual expert generating a legal framework for an entire society, a society in which performance of all types is central, where civic excellence is expressed through public and communal song. The question of how to police the bad as well as celebrate the good is crucial, and it will be instructive to see the reasons why invective is deliberately excluded from the protocols of the ideal city of Magnesia.

Let us begin with some background. We search in vain in Archaic and Early-Classical Greek literature for any systematic analysis of invective, although the practice itself (unsurprisingly) already had a long history stretching back to Homer before Plato's theoretical strictures in the mid-fourth century B.C. with which I shall be concerned here.[2] The poetry of Archilochus (7th century B.C.) and Hipponax (6th century B.C.) was associated with the term *iambos*. Although *iambos* is a word that can describe the iambic metre, it is also used more loosely in antiquity to designate invective poetry. A recent analysis has suggested that it was the fourth century B.C. and in particular the work of Aristotle, Plato's pupil, that saw the theoretical restriction of the scope of *iambos* to abuse.[3] Aristotle talks of the "iambic form" (*iambikē idea*) when he analyzes how the poets of Attic old comedy started to move away from the invective lampoon and towards more structured plots, and it is evident that, for him, *iambos* was a conceptual forerunner of comedy.[4] Connections between Attic old comedy and the archaic *iambos* are indeed strong, and the plays of Aristophanes, (that Plato would have attended as he grew up) supply magnificent examples of invective against contemporary politicians and other easy targets.[5] These were the genres that offered opportunities for poetic invective, but of course, the assembly and the lawcourts were packed with politicians and litigants defaming their opponents; indeed, it seems clear that these orators used the excessive invective of comedy and *iambos* to castigate and humiliate their opponents and rivals.[6]

Plato's world of the first half of the fourth century BCE was thus one in which invective had several established functions. Yet it is also the case that in Athens the city regulated the scope of invective.[7] Laws against slander were certainly operative in the early fourth century, and there may even have been laws against the defamation of magistrates in the 6th century BCE. As Halliwell puts it, shameful speech, or *aischrology* "is a locus of social, educational, psychological, ethical, political and religious concern throughout the whole of Greek antiquity."[8] It seems, however, that comic performances in the theater, were, as a matter of practice if not of law, exempt from such concerns since comedy existed in a particular cultural framework outside a context in which verbal abuse was perceived as actionable."[9] It comes as no surprise, therefore, that Plato would turn to the problem of invective and its contexts. We shall see that, unlike most of his contemporaries, he would not allow that a festival context could insulate comic invective from criticism. In the body of this paper I shall sketch the way Plato has his characters formulate the problem of abuse, comic and otherwise. This will generate a familiar result: comedy and abuse call forth a kind of emotional indulgence and representation that pander to the lowest parts of the human soul. They must be regulated because they are psychically damaging. More specifically, however, I shall concentrate on the society portrayed in the *Laws*, using one lengthy and important passage as a tool to ponder why invective and the persona adopted by the speaker of invective poses a particular problem for the quasi-utopian city whose design is the central task of the dialogue. The problem of invective will be framed not in the general terms of *mimesis*/representation, but in terms of the peculiarities of the invective persona and the social construction of blame in this designer city. In a city where all social and cultural action is understood as a performance, the essential disproportion of traditional invective self-presentation makes it a particular concern.

The Laws *on invective*

My core focus will be *Laws* 934d-936b, the text of a series of laws on abuse. This passage is part of a sequence of laws the nature of whose connection needs specifying. A few pages previously the Athenian Stranger, the driving force behind the conversation and composer of the dialogue's lawcode, had dealt with the respect due to one's parents and the necessity of protecting them from abuse (931a-932d). Next came the problem of how to deal with poisoners, both those who use drugs and those who attempt to cast magic spells (932e-933e). A brief interlude then instructs that penalties should be proportionate to the crime (933e-c). What follows marks a start on a fresh subject: the regulation of lunatics (who are not allowed to appear in public, 934c-d). The Athenian Stranger feels a need to acknowledge the complexity of madness: men are mad in different ways, and one of the results of madness is slander, *blasphēmia*. This leads to the law on slander and abuse that we will shortly consider in more detail (934d-936b). The lawcode then moves on to a law forbidding begging (936b-c) and then to the damage of property (936c-e). All these laws are united by a concern with harm and abuse, both mental and physical, although as noted, there is a break between the law on poisoning and that on lunatics. In the mind of the lawgiver, verbal and physical damage are closely connected.

It is perhaps significant that slandering someone by accusing them of physical abuse of their parents was one of the forbidden categories of slander in fourth century BC Athens, although the text of the *Laws* itself does not make this connection. Indeed, the law on parental abuse makes it a matter of universal concern that any mistreatment shall be reported and punished. Anyone who has knowledge of it shall report it or suffer legal penalties himself. The result is that the very possibility of slander in this area is forestalled; if the accusation were true it would be a matter of legal action and no forum exists for making such an accusation in jest. Plato's city thus has standards for treatment of parents similar to (though more extreme than) contemporary Athens, but no separate category is necessary for slanderous accusations of abuse. The law on poisoning similarly has possible invective resonance. It deals both with physical poisons and those inflicted by words and incantations, and it is the latter that concern us here. We are told that the victims and even the perpetrators of such spells are convinced that they can work real harm (whatever the truth of the matter); thus the terror evoked by seeing a wax figure at a crossroads. The lawgiver will explain that nobody should terrify people as if they were children, and legislates accordingly. Now, curse tablet and wax dolls may seem to be a far cry from the powers of the invective practitioner, but we should remember that both Hipponax and Archilochus, the archaic iambic poets, were credited with considerable powers of influence through their poetry. Archilochus was said to have caused the suicides of his enemy Lycambes and his daughters by his invectives, and Bupalus, the foe of Hipponax was also supposed to have hanged himself. Later epigrams speak of Archilochus' "viper's bile," or conceive Hipponax as a stinging wasp.[10] As the Athenian Stranger will shortly emphasize, words and their associated representations can cause real harm; poison is no less real for being figurative. Even though the invective practitioner does not make an appearance in the law on poisoning, he participates in the same cultural discourse as one who poisons through incantation.

Finally, we should note the importance of the figure of the beggar in iambic discourse and, once again, the possibility that such a figure exists as a shadowy presence behind the law on beggary. The principle behind the law is clear: in a well-regulated state such as the one envisaged, no virtuous citizen would ever be so neglected as to be reduced to poverty. Thus the state will not allow anyone to scrape together a livelihood by endless requests. The law is an attempt to rid the city of a public nuisance: he will be expelled beyond the borders of the land so that the land may be "pure" (936c6). Yet the greedy beggar also plays an historical role in iambic discourse. As Worman puts it, "A dog's life, snappish talk, the ravenous mouth: these rude images cluster in the language of insult from early on in Greek poetry."[11] As early as Homer, there is a connection between the beggar who searches for a good meal and the witty (and sometimes aggressive) speech by which he attempts to win people over, and the connection endures in the poetry of Archilochus and Hipponax.[12] The abject beggar may also be threatened with expulsion from the community. Plato's beggar is threatened with such expulsion, and we may catch here a faint scent of the scapegoat figure (*pharmakos*) that appears in the poetry of Hipponax (5-10W), who wishes that his gluttonous enemy may be chased down to the sea and stoned (128W). Plato's law is, in a sense, a law against abjection, a law against a system of exchange that allows trading witty abuse for food or permits a poet to play with such abjection for invective purposes. There is, simply, no place for hunger, poverty, and the rhetorical systems that profit from them. Thus several of the laws that surround the law on abuse (on parental abuse, poisoning, begging), while they do not deal explicitly with invective, do address concerns that had a literary and social-historical association with the practice. All of this makes clear that the regulation of invective is part of a much wider network of issues centered on social ethics and performance, where public display is important because of its paradigmatic effect.

A concern with lowness and abjection also characterizes the law on madness that leads into the law on abuse. The madman must be confined, we infer, both because he may be a danger to others and because his lack of rational control makes him a bad example, an ethical danger. The connection with abuse will be precise—perhaps more precise than one would have expected. It is not just that both the madman and the verbal abuser are bad examples for society at large, it is that verbal abuse is actually a version of madness. To see how this is so, we need to look at the law in some detail, and it deserves full quotation:

> Many people are mad in many ways. Some because of illness—we have just spoken about them—but there are others who are mad because their temper is bad by nature and also because of a bad upbringing. These people, whenever a petty hostility comes about, speak ill of and slander (*blasphēmountes*) each other raising their voice, although it is not fitting that any such thing occur in a city of law-abiding people—no way, no how. Let this be the law concerning evil speech (*kakēgorias*) in all cases: nobody is to abuse (*kakēgoreitō*) anybody. When people are involved in verbal disputes, let each instruct and be instructed by his opponent and the audience, always keeping away from evil speech (*kakēgorein*). For when they curse each other and employ womanish utterances with shameful words, actual hatreds and enmities, most grievous ones, come into being through speech, although it is a trivial thing. For the speaker, gratifying that unpleasant affair, his temper, feeds his anger with evil banquets and makes this part of his soul savage again, although it had once been tamed by education. He becomes bestialized and lives in discontent, getting a bitter return for his temper. In such situations, moreover, all people are usually accustomed in some way to move on to saying something funny about their opponent. Nobody who has ever acquired this habit has failed to miss entirely seriousness of character or to destroy much of his greatness of mind. Therefore let no one ever make any such utterance in a sanctuary, nor at any public sacrifice, nor yet at contests, nor in the marketplace, nor in court nor in any public gathering. Let each magistrate who is in charge of these areas punish the offender with impunity, or let him never compete for prizes of excellence, on the grounds that he cares nothing for the laws and disobeys the commands of the lawgiver. If anyone does not avoid such language in other locations, either embarking on abuse

(*loidorias*) or defending himself, any elder who comes across them should defend the law, and prevent with blows those who are well-disposed towards their temper, that evil companion.[13] If he does not, let him be subject to the assigned penalty. We're saying this because it is not possible for someone who is involved in abusing (*loidoriais*) someone to do so without trying to make jokes, and this we abuse (*loidoroumen*), whenever it occurs because of anger.

Well then, are we to accept the eagerness of comic poets to make jokes like this at people's expense if they try in their comedies to speak of our fellow citizens in this way without anger? Or shall we make a distinction on the basis of whether they are playing or not and it shall be allowable for someone to make a joke about someone in play without anger, but, just as we said, it should not be possible for anyone to do so in earnest and in anger.[14] Well, about that we must in no way change our opinion, but we must lay down the law about those who will be allowed to compose and those who will not. It shall not be possible for a composer of comedy or *iamboi* or lyric poetry to mock (*k m dein*) any citizen either in word or in image, with or without anger.[15] If someone disobeys let the commissioners of the contests exile him absolutely from the land the very same day or let him be fined three minas payable to the festival of the god whose contest it is. Those we previously proclaimed should have a license to compose something shall be allowed to mock each other without anger and in play, but they shall not be allowed to do so in earnest and when they are angry. Decision in these matters shall be turned over to the supervisor over the entire education of the young. Whenever he approves something its composer shall be allowed to make it public. Whenever he disapproves, its composer shall neither present it himself, nor shall he be shown to have taught it to anyone, slave or free, or let him have the reputation of being bad and disobedient to the laws." (934d-936b)

This tremendously rich passage reflects several aspects of ancient discourse on invective, as well as themes familiar from elsewhere in Plato. In the former category we may place connections with female (and thus inferior) deportment, banquets and eating, and animals, in the latter the connection of comedy and invective with an inferior disposition of the soul. Indeed, one might say that an inferior psychic disposition is partly constituted by indulging female and other appetites. Those who curse each other with shameful words are making use of female utterances. A modern reader is likely to pause here in amazement at the misogyny, but in fact women had long been associated with insatiability and the indulgence of the appetite, as well as with chattering and (over) clever speech.[16] What is interesting here is that the Athenian Stranger seems to move beyond the stereotype of women as clever chatterboxes, and focuses instead on mutual cursing as a female characteristic, as one might speak of "screaming fishwives." Indulgence in shameful speech results in a loss of control that causes alienation from the self. The disputants are men no longer. Just as abusive disputation causes the small to become great, it causes men to become women. The speaker here has isolated an important facet of our present inquiry: the inevitable tendency of an invective situation to cause exaggeration. Intemperate screaming is projected onto women, and there may also be an implication that what a woman would say is overblown and unsubstantiated.[17]

The passage also plays subtly on two other aspects of ancient invective as it pictures the speaker of invective feeding his anger with evil banquets and becoming like a wild beast. It has been observed that the Greek literary tradition portrays those who engage in abuse as devouring their food like an animal. It also associates such speakers strongly with gluttony. Plato, then, is deploying a well-developed critical discourse to characterize his invective speakers,[18] but is doing so in terms of his own psychology, where the appetitive part of the soul figures as a beast. Yet, as has also been remarked, the invective speaker's accusation of greed and animal characteristics in his victim or object is itself a regular move.[19] Abuse and abuser converge, and this is one important reason why the practice of invective can be seen as ethically damaging. The insults and mockery one flings reflect on oneself. Invective is thus a transformative mode. It changes the speaker and, crucially, has a propensity to translate between the spheres of the rhetorical and the real world: real hatreds arise from trivial and empty words. Like a glutton, like an animal, the invective speaker is insatiable and recognizes no natural limit to his appetite for abuse.

The picture of the appetitive part of the soul as bestial, irrational, and uncontrolled is of course familiar to readers of Plato from the psychology of the *Republic* and need not be rehearsed at length here.[20] It is, however, worth noting that at *Republic* 395d-396a, in a discussion of the kind of imitation that should be allowed in the education of the future rulers of the state, we find (in a long list of rejected objects of *mimesis*) the same collocation of verbal abuse connected with women (a young guardian will not imitate one who is abusing [*loidoroumenēn*] her husband), together with a concomitant rejection of the imitation of madmen, and those who speak ill (*kakēgorountas*) and lampoon (*kōmōdountas*) each another, speaking foul words (*aischrologountas*). It matters not that these would only be performances—representation encourages slippage towards reality. We may also recall here the observation of Nehamas that Aristotle, more liberal than Plato in many areas connected with literature will, at *Politics* 7.1336b, join him in his concern that the young not be exposed to invective and comedy.[21] In the passage of the *Laws* under consideration here, Plato's concern is extended from the young to all citizens, and extends beyond the mimetic realm to the general operation of society. A law-abiding city depends on all its citizens having their emotions, especially anger, under control, and nothing can be allowed that would encourage them to develop bad emotional habits. The role of education in the ideal city is to tame the base part of the soul. Abuse, then, is a kind of madness because, like madness, it allows the passions to run riot. When people are afflicted by this species of social madness, rhetorical inflation occurs: the smallest grievances cause great vocal effusions. This has the effect of sidelining rational interaction. Verbal disputation should, we are told, be a process of give and take related to education. When, however, abuse is involved this does not happen; the parties involved scream at each other (like women). The power of invective to create its own reality out of nothing undoes the job done by civic education.

The section of the *Republic* considered in the previous paragraph helps us understand the nature of the transition from invective to comedy in our *Laws* passage. It places its discussion of lifestyle (as opposed to poetic) imitation in the context of a discussion of poetic representations, where the former is merely a less stylized version of the latter. It thus reinforces the perception of a continuum between role-playing in everyday life and in poetic productions governed by generic rules. The discussion in the *Laws* moves from a treatment of angry abuse in various civic venues to a scrutiny of the claims of comic poets. What we might call informal invective is a reflex of passion in the first instance, but as already remarked, has a structural tendency to turn itself into a public performance. So it is that the impulse to mock one's opponent enters the picture: the bestialized abuser almost always moves on to saying something funny about the object of his ire, and the role of an audience (already implicit in the occurrence of abuse in public locations) thus becomes even more important, since it is the audience that registers and reacts to the humor. When the Athenian Stranger introduces the issue of comic poets, he is drawing out the implications of formalizing the performance of abuse. Now we are dealing with a fairly well-defined genre (comedy) with its own protocols. Because the subject of comedy is brought up in connection with the question of laughter and abuse it seems likely that what are envisaged here are the invective extremities of Attic Old Comedy, whose heights of artistic vituperation may well have been reached during Plato's youth.[22] As we shall shortly see, stylized and generic protocols only serve to mire the problem of invective in confusion and complexity.

Let us examine first the association of invective with raising a laugh. The Athenian Stranger tells his interlocutors that this practice is destructive of one's seriousness of character and greatness of mind. The language here draws on the resonance of the adjective *spoudaios,* "serious," here translated as "seriousness of character." What is *spoudaios,* serious, is the opposite of what is *geloios,* laughable.[23] It might seem almost tautologous to say that habitually raising a laugh destroys one's seriousness, but *spoudaios* also means "good" or "excellent" in a moral sense. Thus someone who engages in invective will inescapably be drawn to saying what is laughable. This ruins not just his seriousness, but his goodness. This sequence of analysis, taken with what comes before it, forms an extended mediation of the psychology of abuse, justifying the ban on it. The law is then restated in an expanded form to take into account a possibility that was not at first countenanced: that the invective situation might not simply involve two people screaming at each other, but might be a more crafted performance (thus moving us, as we have seen, towards the territory of comedy). What if our abuser is not just calling his opponent a greedy coward, but is insulting him in such as way as to make the bystanders laugh? The presence of an audience for invective was already presumed when those who were present at verbal disputes were mentioned. We remember that the disputants had to educate not only their opponents, but their audience. The introduction of laughter raises the stakes since it makes the audience active rather than passive. The invective speaker tries to raise a laugh from them, thus implicating them in his own lack of moral seriousness and worth. As audience they respond, and they will in part be judging the success of the abuser's comic expertise (rather than pondering the facts of the situation). Any effort to claim that an admixture of satiric comedy might render moot the blanket condemnation of abuse expressed in the first formulation of the law fails. Humor also corrupts, and even when invective is humorous it is still forbidden.

Enforcement of the law is specified in a way that underlines the social implications of abuse: no one shall make a derisory statement in any public location (temple, court, marketplace and so on), and the Athenian Stranger stresses that enforcement is the job of the magistrates. Failure to enforce on the part of the magistrate is in turn an offence (an aspect to which we shall return); we are dealing with a through-going regulation of derision in every formal public forum. Nor does public regulation mark an end to the constraint. Invective shall not occur even in places outside the view of government officials. When it does it is a civic responsibility for any senior memory of the community to stop it, even to the point of using physical chastisement. It makes no difference whether the offender started the derision or is merely responding; he is "kindly disposed towards his anger." The problem with laughter is that it muddies the ethical waters. Since what is laughable is opposed to what is serious, the presence of laughter might incline one to say that comic invective (that is, invective that is funny) is not serious and thus that we cannot take it seriously. Yet we are clearly told that the invective speaker has given in to his temper, something that needs to be taken very seriously indeed. The psychically lethal combination is that of humor and anger. From the lawgiver's point of view, the combination is a lie: damaging abuse masquerading as something other than the serious problem it is.[24]

Might one come at this problem from a slightly different angle, that of persona? Might one say to the Athenian Stranger, "Invective is not the problem you seem to think it is. Of course when people get angry at each other they abuse each other, and we may grant you that a well-regulated city will not want to see too much of this sort of loss of control. But you don't seem to realize that invective may be performed in a way that does not implicate the soul in damaging behavior. What if someone abuses just for effect, just to attain a rhetorical goal; what if he's putting it on?" This would, however, have no purchase for Plato, because for him, it is almost impossible just to "put something on." The problem is complicated by the nature of the representation involved in performing invective. As we have seen, invective creates its own reality, and it is part of that process that the abuser exaggerates and makes the small great. What begins as words becomes deeds. Although he would not put it this way, the Athenian Stranger who formulates the law has isolated a characteristic of an invective persona, the way the invective speaker must, in order to be successful, inhabit the reality he creates. This is what damages the soul. One might say this of any form of performance, of course, but in invective there is the additional problem that there is a fundamental disproportion between the reality to which invective reacts and the words with which it expresses itself. By its very nature this form of speech act undermines the harmony of the self and of society. No wonder, then that it is considered a type of madness. If the issue of persona is implicit, as I think it is, even in an examination of the psychology of non-literary invective where anger simply expresses itself in speech, how much more pressing this difficulty will become in the case of stylized literary invective informed by a set of generic protocols. Plato's Athenian Stranger has put his finger on a problem that will continue to loom.

The complex juxtaposition of the *spoudaion* and the *geloion*, the serious and the laughable, in the Athenian Stranger's formulation of his law leads to a paradoxical yet revealing play on words.[25] He tells his interlocutors that "it is not possible for someone who is involved in abusing (*loidoriais*) someone to do so without trying to make jokes, and this we abuse (*loidoroumen*), whenever it occurs because of anger." My translation here strives to bring out a pun: the Athenian says that he abuses someone who abuses someone in anger. Most translations of this passage do not linger over the wordplay. We may take the version of Saunders as an example: "when a man is embroiled in a slanging match he is incapable of carrying on the dispute without trying to make funny remarks, and when such conduct is motivated by anger we censure it."[26] To be sure, this rendering is more elegant, but it misses the play. We must ask, then, why such punning would be significant. We note first that the Athenian is not deriding the offender in anger himself, so he need not be the object of our disapproval (we need not abuse him in turn). He is, we may charitably assume, speaking with all good intention. Yet the choice of the word *loidoroumen* (in "this we abuse") creates a little joke that fulfills the theoretical profession of the previous sentence that it is unusual to abuse someone without trying to be funny. We have to admit that the rhetoric here is both (somewhat) comic and serious, and the same two poles will be held in tension through out the rest of the passage, as the Stranger considers the possibility that one can be funny as long as one is not ... angry. Only at the end of the passage is the "angry" option connected with seriousness, when we are told that mockery will not be allowed when people are serious and angry, by which he means "seriously angry." So: anger often leads to abuse and abuse to comedy, although there is also a possibility that humorous abuse may exist in the absence of anger. We will need to consider how coherent a possibility this last option is.

The Athenian's formulation thus has its own austere philosophical humor as it employs the language of abuse to discuss abuse. Indeed, this analysis may be pressed even further. We have already seen that when the Athenian specifies the effects of abuse on the soul of the abuser, he uses commonplaces of iambic discourse to characterize the objects of his disapproval. The abuser becomes like a beast and feasts his greedy anger on an evil banquet. It is now clear that this critique is itself a form of censure or blame, and the distinction between censure and abuse is a delicate one (cf. the use of "censure" for "abuse" in Saunder's translation quoted above). The philosophical speaker declares that the abuser is a glutton and a beast. How, then, can he escape the cycle of assimilation whereby the speaker of invective is tainted by the same qualities of bestiality and greed? One answer might be his restraint (we have seen that although he censures, he does so in accordance with dictates of reason rather than anger). Another possibility is that we may credit the philosopher with a developed notion of the operations of the human soul. When Achilles calls Agamemnon greedy and a dog—among other things—in the *Iliad* (1.225, 331), he is engaging in pure abuse and at the mercy of his rage. The philosopher, however, may have (and in the *Republic* does have, explicitly so) a model of the soul in which a particular part of the soul has a natural tendency to greed and bestiality. Although speaking of animal appetites is certainly morally evaluative, when placed in the context of a structured explanation of the workings of the soul as a whole (both in itself and within society) his language could be argued to negotiate successfully the fine line between description, censure, and abuse.

This is not to ignore the degree to which Plato and his oeuvre are themselves implicated in strategies of criticism and abuse that might broadly be termed iambic. Dialogues that are conventionally assigned to the early and middle periods of Plato's production have drawn particular scrutiny in this respect, as Plato strives to define and distance Socrates' (and his own) philosophical project from those of the sophists active in the so-called sophistic enlightenment of the second half of the fifth century. It has long been realized that Plato uses all his very considerable literary resources to cast sophistic intellectuals in an unflattering and disreputable light.[27] Most recently, Worman has argued that Plato "participates directly in an iambic discourse about public speaking shaped largely by old comedy in the fifth century and adopted by orators and rhetorical theorists in the fourth." Intellectual conversation in the dialogues is not infrequently depicted as a "feast," while Socrates depicts his opponents' techniques as a pandering chef's indulgence and constructs himself as a crude outsider.[28] Against this background it is easy to see that references in the *Laws* to indulgent and uncontrolled invective partake self-reflexively in the same ambience but it is also evident that the atmosphere of the conversation between the interlocutors is very different from that in some of the more combative and earlier dialogues. The Cretan, Spartan, and Athenian interlocutors are experienced men of even temperament, and are, importantly, disinclined to take offence. We see this clearly in the early stretches of the dialogue, where criticism of various forms of constitution is accompanied by the assurance that it is directed at all (630d 633a) and by the determination to receive it gently (634c), not with malice but with goodwill (635b). The proper tone, then, for intellectual discussion and especially for criticism is neither defensive nor aggressive. What is at stake is, as we would say, nothing personal (except to the extent that all interlocutors are affected by virtue or vice in society).[29] When the Athenian "abuses" the abusers, he is speaking at a theoretical level (note the generalizing plural of "we abuse"), and objects of his criticism are not in his immediate audience. Even if they were, they would be encouraged to accept the justice of the critique. The Athenian's pun reflects his attempt to reformulate the conception of abuse, emptying out of it its emotionalism and outrageousness, calming and domesticating it until it means censure and can serve the purposes of a rationally ordered city. In the last part of this paper, we shall see that something of the sort is happening on a larger scale in the *Laws* as a whole, where the agonistic and traditional Greek discourse of praise and blame is reformulated to reinforce the civic performance of virtue.

Comedy

We must now return to the problem of theatrical comedy and formalized invective performance. The final part of the law on invective is generally considered as a contribution to Plato's conception of and objections to the genre of comedy, and this is indeed true, but less frequently do scholars make the problem of invective central. Yet the passage treats comedy as a kind of knock-on effect of invective, and it is useful to examine it in this light. The question is whether an exception can be made to the overarching law banning abuse. The exception might be justified in the case of humor that is given a generic frame, that is, performed as part of comedy (or as we shall see, iambic or even lyric poetry). If the poets say something funny about a citizen without anger it might be acceptable; it would not be in earnest: "are we to accept the eagerness of comic poets to make jokes like this at people's expense if they try in their comedies to speak of our fellow citizens in this way without anger?". As Halliwell has pointed out, Plato seems here compelled to recognize the prevailing Athenian sense that comic freedom of abuse had to be conceded. Even this much of a concession, he thinks, is remarkable, that Plato acknowledges, even as he curtails, the idea of festival license.[30] We may also remark that the text seems to grant that poetic invective might be a matter of "play" and could be said not to involve anger.

At this point in our passage (365d3-6) only comic poets are under consideration, but interestingly the scope immediately broadens in the words that follow: "Or shall we make a distinction on the basis of whether one is playing or not and it shall be allowable for someone to make a joke about someone in play without anger, but, just as we said, it should not be possible for anyone to do so in earnest and in anger." The example of the comic poets seems to have undermined the substructure of the entire law: if one accepts that a poet can mock and do so without anger and only in play, then why not extend this privilege to all? Anger (usually) implies mockery, but mockery might not entail anger. They will, therefore, remain firm in their opposition to angry abuse and try to specify who will be permitted the non-serious variety. The result is not at all what one might expect. One might have thought that the Athenian Stranger, once he had acknowledged the notion of festival license, might have allowed non-serious mockery of citizens. What happens instead is that the scope of the prohibition is extended beyond comedy. Neither comic, iambic, or lyric poets shall be allowed to compose anything along these lines. Now, earlier in the *Laws* comic performance had been banned for citizens (816d-e) for the same educational reasons mentioned earlier, that one cannot be funny and serious at the same time, and imitating the ridiculous is damaging. Any such performances in the city must be executed by slaves or foreigners. We now realize that these comic performances will not contain any mockery of citizens (much less of the city) whatsoever. The range of content and plot will thus be extremely restricted.

In sum, then, no citizen should make a habit of humorous speech or engage in invective when he is angry. No professional poet may compose invective against or make fun of citizens, whether he is angry or not. It is hard to overstate the paradoxical significance of this regulation. It is precisely professional poets whom we might have expected to have been insulated from the ban by virtue of the formulaic nature of their genre, where an invective persona might be said to be a pose. It is, however, precisely professional poets who are to be subject to the ban in its most basic form. I shall return to the reasons for this paradox, but in order to do so we must glance briefly at that select few to whom mockery will be permitted. These are constituted by "those we previously proclaimed should have a license to compose something." They will "be allowed to mock each other without anger and in play, but they shall not allowed to do so in earnest and when they are angry." Who are those who were previously licensed? Earlier in Book 8 (829c-e), in a discussion of praise and blame to be awarded on days of civic contest, it had been specified that the only people who would be allowed to compose such discourses in the city would be citizens over the age of fifty: not professionals with musical expertise and no civic achievements, but rather those who distinguished by personal merit. This is to be the rule even at the expense of musical polish. Only the virtuous may compose performances of praise and blame. It is, therefore, these paragons who will be allowed to mock citizens, but without anger.[31]

It is hard to cash out the implications of this counsel of perfection.[32] On what basis will people mock the citizens without anger? Are these compositions to be associated with the previously mentioned blame compositions? Perhaps this is why only virtuous elders may do so, because only they have the moral standing to make this kind of judgment, as musical professionals do not. The effect of this would then be to reinforce the connection between censure and mockery. The passage is in fact quite vague about what the content of such performances would be, and one may conclude that the details do not particularly interest the Athenian and his interlocutors. What does tax them is the nature of invective performance and its psychological effects upon composer and audience. Why should poets be singled out as forbidden to engage in mockery when we might have expected the reverse? Here is where the problem of generic framing becomes important. In a recent book, Rosen has drawn a distinction between invective in e.g. lawcourts, where real harm is intended, and poetic invective which, he argues, is fictionalized and should not therefore be taken seriously. "It is," he says, "the "persistent tension between fiction and reality that distinguishes poetic from non-poetic forms of mockery, and allows us to consider such forms as a fundamentally separate human activity from such non-poetic forms as we find either in the ancient law courts or on the street."[33] Poetic satire, on this reading, makes quasi-biographical claims for the speaker of the invective, but the audience knows to hold these in tension with the literary frame.

We have already seen that our passage of the *Laws* gives some purchase to the notion that poetic invective is a genre apart, but what is fascinating is the way that Plato has anticipated and blocked this move, almost as if it is the poetic framing, the generally accepted social and literary presuppositions of the genre, that render it problematic. No professional poet may compose invective against citizens, whether he is angry or not. We might say that, for us, the notion of invective as a possible form of play, coupled with the significance of *mimesis*, representation, anticipates a more developed notion of an invective persona. We are aware that we are operating in a situation where we know not to take any representation seriously. This, however, makes no difference to the lawgiver, and there are (at least) two reasons why this might be so. The first is the way invective works in the soul of the speaker, creating, as we have said, its own reality on the basis of overstatement; because of its practiced disproportion between speech and reality. Invective may not only be the result of anger on the part of the abuser, but works to create anger in its butt. The second emerges from Rosen's perceptive analysis of the dynamic tension between fiction and reality in poetic invective. His analysis focuses precisely on the elements that make such invective especially troublesome. Anger is anger and we know that it is bad. Play is play, and although we may find it inappropriate we know not to take it seriously. Poetic invective, however, plays at making us uncertain about its intentions; this uncertainty is inherent in the mode and is, for Plato's Athenian Stranger, unacceptable. For him, a sophisticated response would be beside the point; some portion of the audience is likely to take the invective seriously, and even one such response would be too many.[34] Indeed, even for modern audiences it has proved difficult to pin down the invective intentions of the fifth-century comic playwright Aristophanes. Do his plays of the 420s B.C. with their violent outbursts and extremely energetic satire of the politician Cleon aim to undermine his standing in the city? Was Aristophanes prosecuted by Cleon for defamation on the grounds that "he mocks our city and insults the people" (*Acharnians* 630)?[35] I am not concerned here with the answers to these questions, but observe merely that the invective mode characterizes itself by assuming seriousness, and does so with such success that, it seems, both then and now nobody is absolutely sure how to take it.[36] For the Stranger, genre is not the solution but the problem.

Conclusion: The Performative City

We have seen that the only way to insulate abuse and mockery from harmful effects is to divorce it from angry emotions and block the muddying of the waters that occurs by bringing poetic genres into the picture. The object of abuse can only accept it when he is sure it is not a result of serious anger, and the only way to be sure about this is to assign its composition and performance to human monuments of civic virtue. Once one bans anger as part of the mocker's self-representation, as one must in Plato's city, what is left of *loidoria*, abuse? It becomes domesticated into mere censure, part of a wider civic discourse of blame reinforcing general civic ideology. I shall draw to a close, then, with some consideration of how praise and blame work in the designer city. I want to suggest that one of the reasons Rosen's distinction between literary mockery and invective and its "real" counterpart cannot operate in the city of the *Laws* is that this city leaves no space for an area of life that is *not* scrutinized as a performance. It is another question whether such a distinction could ever have operated unproblematically in the world of Classical Athens, where, for much of the fourth century the theater was the location of the civic assembly and where the conceptual structures of the theater penetrated almost every aspect of civic life.

The planned city of Magnesia institutionalizes structures of praise and blame with great seriousness.[37] Life itself is seen as a kind of performance, one that is musical in a large sense, including both formal choruses that develop the right state of physical and moral grace in the citizen, and informal performances, ranging from commendation of fellow citizens to reporting malefactors to the proper authorities. The supervision of the laws consists largely of a right distribution of honor and dishonor (631e). Praise and blame provide the framework within which life operates, generating and evaluating citizen performances. In this city everyone is a performer and everyone should be a critic. As David Cohen has remarked, in the *Laws* "Plato entirely collapses the private sphere into the public"; there is no area of activity immune from intrusion by the state.[38] Perfect civic performance, therefore, involves not just individual accomplishment but continual supervision and judgment of others. Since life as a whole is the object of praise or blame, the standards that generate praise or blame must be internalized.

The city is characterized by a broadly agonistic structure. It is engaged in a "contest" for virtue in which all citizens must compete. The object of this contest is the fair reputation of the city. Those who successfully compete will be praised, while those tainted by envy will be blamed. A danger to this project is the envious citizen who engages in slanders. Because he thinks (731) that he must prevail through his slander (*diabolē*) of others, an envious man strives less himself towards true virtue, and discourages his fellow competitors through unjust censure. This condemnation of slander has obvious connections with the issue of abuse. A slanderer will play the game of invective, damaging both himself and the objects of his ill-will. He or she will compromise the process of successful participation in the contest that is civic life. When the system is functioning correctly, there are prizewinners: those who join the magistrates in their task of chastising and censuring the unjust. The network of praise and blame thus exists in a second order as official arrangements for scrutiny and judgment are continually reinforced by and mapped onto formal and informal institutions of praise and blame. Citizens who spend their lives obeying the laws will praise and blame certain activities in the way suggested by the lawgiver, and will in turn praise or blame other citizens who are praising and blaming correctly or incorrectly. Praise and blame, then, are issued both formally and informally. Occasions of formal praise are specified in the lawcode, yet the lawcode also provides more general guidance: certain sorts of actions are to be praised (or blamed) by all citizens on an ongoing basis. Yet this task of praise is itself the object of assessment on the part of the "law," which will praise those who give honor correctly and blame those who do not. This structure is at work, as we have seen, in the penalties laid down for those (both magistrates and laypersons) who fail to enforce the laws on invective. A magistrate who fails to do so will be disqualified from competing for prizes of excellence, while in the absence of a magistrate, any elder passer-by must stop the abuser or be penalized himself. If the commissioners of contests fail to prevent unauthorized comic or iambic performances, they too will be fined.

This broader picture of civic performance does much to contextualize the issues involved with invective. Since censure is a major tool of socialization in the city of Magnesia, the problem of abuse is especially acute, and invective in its strong sense must be regulated and eradicated. Censure must always be taken seriously. If it is uttered by those who have lost control and formulated it in terms of invective it feeds negative emotions, creating hatred with a consequent loss of reception on the part of the object of censure. Its association with humor creates the risk of the wrong kind of civic performance, a strange hybrid of the laughable (and thus not serious) with the angry (serious in the wrong way). Invective is a competitor with the city's own structures of blame. When the Athenian Stranger says he abuses those who abuse, he bleeds out the potential vituperative content of the word, enacting in his speech the reformulation of invective for philosophical purposes. A more wide-ranging context of evaluation is also helpful in contextualizing the problematic issue of persona. In the world of the *Laws* the entire structure of civic performance is focused on closing any possible gap between what people *are* and what they *say* or *do*. No corner of the civic space, no recess in the bedroom, no place on the stage can be allowed where a citizen might behave in an unapproved way. No citizen is given room not to mean what he says. The regulation of invective is perhaps not surprising in a society where there is no freedom of speech and little opportunity for role-playing. What is more interesting than this bare regulation is the intellectual route by which Plato has his characters arrive at this destination. Their analysis, both implicitly and explicitly, reflects and appropriates an entire network of comic and iambic associations. It plays on connections with the womanish, the animal, the mad; it foregrounds the complex interactions of play, seriousness, anger, and humor together with their social repercussions. These issues will, doubtless, find their echoes elsewhere in this volume, but it is fitting to give room right from the start to Plato's subtle and provocative analysis, an analysis whose complexities are at once surprisingly modern and disturbingly retrograde.[39]

Notes

[1] Worman 2008; Conley 2010.

[2] See Worman 2008: 26-40, for proto-iambic discourse in Homer.

[3] Rotstein 2010: 102.

[4] *Poetics* 1449b with Rotstein 2010: 108-11. Note that Aristotle says that comedy was not at first taken *seriously* and was performed by volunteers.

[5] Rosen 1988; Worman 2008: 62-120.

[6] Rowe 1966; Harding 1994 (who asserts, however, that abuse in the comedy and the orators was not meant to be taken seriously, but was manifestly humorous); Worman 2008: 213-74 (Worman's focus here is primarily on the second half of the fourth century, particularly the exchanges of Aeschines and Demosthenes).

[7] Halliwell 1991.

[8] Halliwell 2008: 217.

[9] Halliwell 1991: 54.

[10] Rosen 2007b: 462-6.

[11] Worman 2008: 25.

[12] Worman 2008: 36-7, 40-8.

[13] Reading *hetairō* (England's emendation) for *heterō* in the manuscripts. England 1921, vol. 2: 561.

[14] On the correct text here see the note of Saunders (1972: 116), who translates "Are we then to distinguish . . ." I have retained the "or" of the manuscript: "Or shall we make a distinction . . ." Saunders, following England (1921, vol. 2: 562), is keen to emphasize that there is no real alternative expressed here. On my interpretation the "or" marks a widening of scope of argumentative scope.

[15] On the vexed interpretation of this sentence, see Rotstein 2010: 208-10, 241-7.

[16] Worman 2008:12-3, 51-7, 75-83.

[17] As at Aeschylus, *Ag.* 483-7.

[18] Cf. Worman 2008: 178-84.

[19] Steiner 2002: 300-02.

[20] At *Rep.* 588c2-10 the appetitive part of the soul is compared to a complex and many headed beast. The discussion of the man ruled by his appetites and desires culminates with the descriptions of the democratic (558c-563d) and tyrannical man (571a-576b).

[21] Nehamas 1999: 283; cf. Halliwell 1991: 95. The passage runs, "But younger ones must not be allowed to be spectators of *iamboi* or comedy, until they reach the age at which they will be allowed to share the privilege of reclining and drinking, and at which their education will make them entirely immune to the harm that arises from such things."

[22] Cf. Mader 1977: 50-2; Nightingale 1995: 173-5.

[23] Mader 1977: 46.

²⁴ Compare Socrates' interesting analysis of laughter at *Philebus* 49e-50a: when we laugh at a weakness, we feel pleasure rather than pain. Yet such laughter may also express malice. This is, then, a strange mixture of contradictory qualities, as is the mixture of serious and laughable in the text under consideration here. For an extended analysis of the significance of the *Philebus*' treatment of laughter, see Mader 1977: 13-28.

²⁵ As Jouët-Pastré 2006 (*passim*) has shown, the interaction of play and seriousness is a leitmotif of the dialogue.

²⁶ Saunders 1970: xx.

²⁷ So, for example Rossetti 2000, with a particular emphasis on how ridicule is deployed to attain this goal. Nightingale 1995: 186-90 demonstrates persuasively the intertextual relationship between *Gorgias* and *Protagoras* and specific old comedies of Aristophanes and Eupolis.

²⁸ Worman 2008: 155 (quote), 160, 172-84, 211.

²⁹ A major, and as it turns out, infuriating aspect of Socrates famed irony in the early and middle dialogues is his refusal to take offence.

³⁰ Halliwell 1991: 95.

³¹ The interpretation here is based upon taking the phrase "those we previously proclaimed should have a license to compose" to refer to the virtuous citizens described at 829c (England 1921: 563). Saunders (1972: 117) thinks rather that the referent is the slaves and foreigners assigned the performance of comedy at 816d-e. Yet the mention of "reputation" at the end of the passage makes it unlikely, in my view, that the slaves or foreigners of 816 are meant. How then are we to meet Saunders objection that it is implausible to assume that the composers are the virtuous elders of 829c because if only certain citizens are licensed to engage in comedy, the phrase "each other" (in "shall be allowed to mock each other without anger and in play") "entails the curious and unlikely situation that they may satirize only others who have the same license to satirize *them*"? David Blank proposes to me that the reciprocity involved may be precisely the point, but I suggest a different explanation is possible. At 829c we are told that citizens at festivals shall "compose speeches of praise and blame for each other." A few lines later the Athenian specifies that, as discussed earlier" such compositions may only be created by a certain class of virtuous elders. Now, it makes no sense in this context to suggest that these elders will be both praising and blaming each other; it is surely the entire citizen body that is included in the scope of their critique (one might imagine that they would praise each other, but certainly not blame or censure). In spite of the reciprocal pronoun, then, praise and blame of all citizens is envisaged, and I suggest that the same is the case at 936a, which explicitly (on my reading) refers us back to this passage. Jouët-Pastré 2006: 94 concludes "seule les moqueries entre poètes resteront permises," but I do not see what basis this has in the text unless she too assumes that "those we previously proclaimed" refers to the slaves and foreigners of 816d-e.

³² As Mader 1977: 46 points put, we may wonder, after reading this passage, what place is left for comedy. Jouët-Pastré 2006: 89-90 suggests, surely correctly, that comedy will model behavior to be avoided. Mocking laughter would then mark estrangement from the subject matter.

³³ Rosen 2007a: 27. Cf. Rosen 2007b: 476, "Such poets seem to delight in this blurring of fiction and reality, and the result is a particularly vivid form of poetry that encourages its audience to see poet and target as *real* players in a *real* drama capable of taking on a life of its own." Jouët-Pastré 2006: 94 also highlights the confusion of fiction and reality in the invective mode and the implications for interpretation of the *Laws*.

³⁴ One is reminded of Socrates' argument in the *Republic* (378d) that allegorical interpretations of objectionable myths are beside the point and do not support the admission of these stories into

the ideal city: "for a young person is not able to judge what is not and what is not an undersense [allegory]."

[35] For a recent survey of the problem arguing some historical basis, see Sommerstein 2004.
[36] Cf. Nehamas 1999: 283-288; Nightingale 1995: 180-4.
[37] The argument here is a summary of K.A. Morgan, forthcoming (see below).
[38] Cohen 1995: 55.
[39] I wish to record my thanks to David Blank, Alex Purves, and Mario Telò for their helpful comments and suggestions.

Bibliography

Cohen, D. *Law, Violence, and Community in Classical Athens*. Cambridge: Cambridge UP, 1995.
Conley, T. *Toward a Rhetoric of Insult*. Chicago: Chicago UP, 2010.
England, E. B. *The Laws of Plato*. 2 vols. Manchester: Manchester UP, 1921.
Halliwell, S. "Comic Satire and Freedom of Speech in Classical Athens." *JHS* 111(1991): 48-70.
-----. *Greek Laughter*. Cambridge, Cambridge UP, 2008.
Jouët-Pastré, E. *Le jeu et le serieux dans les Lois de Platon*. International Plato Studies, v. 23. Sankt Augustin: Academia Verlag, 2006.
Mader, M. *Das Problem des Lachens und der Komödie bei Platon*. Stuttgart: Tübinger Beiträge Zur Altertumswissenschaft v. 47, 1977.
Morgan, K. A. (forthcoming) "Praise and performance in Plato's *Laws*."
Nehamas, A. "Plato and the Mass Media." In *Virtues of Authenticity: Essays on Plato and Socrates*. Princeton: Princeton UP, 1998: 279-99.
Nightingale, A. *Genres in Dialogue. Plato and the Construct of Philosophy*. Cambridge: Cambridge UP, 1995.
Rosen, R. *Old Comedy and the Iambographic Tradition*. Atlanta, Ga.: Scholars Press, 1988.
-----. *Making Mockery*. Oxford: Oxford UP, 2007(a).
-----. "The Hellenistic Epigrams on Archilochus and Hipponax." In *Brill's Companion to Hellenistic Epigram*, edited by P. Bing and J. S. Bruss. Leiden: 2007 (b) : 459-76.
Rossetti, L. (2000) "Le ridicule comme arme entre les mains de Socrtes et de ses élèves." In *Le rire des grecs. Anthropolgie du rire en Grèce ancienne*, edited by M.-L. Desclos. Grenoble: Jerôme Millot, 2000: 253-68.
Rotstein, A. *The Idea of Iambos*. Oxford: Oxford UP, 2010.
Rowe, Galen. (1966) "The Portrait of Aeschines in the Oration on the Crown." *TAPhA* 97: 397-406.
Saunders, T. J. *Laws*. Harmondsworth: Penguin Books, 1970.
-----. (1972) *Notes on the Laws of Plato*. *BICS* Supplement, 1972, No. 28.
Sommerstein, A. "Harassing the Satirist." In *Free Speech in Classical Antiquity*, edited by R. Rosen and I. Sluiter. Leiden: Brill, 2004.
Steiner, D. (2002) "Indecorous Dining, Indecorous Speech. Pindar's First *Olympian* and the Poetics of Consumption." *Arethusa* 35: 297-314.
Worman, N. *Abusive Mouths in Classical Athens*. Cambridge: Cambridge UP, 2008.

Paul Perron

Swearing, Invectives and Blasphemy: A Cross-Cultural Bilingual Example in Contemporary Quebec Society

After hearing so many different and interesting presentations in terms both of the texts studied and the methodology underpinning them I would like to paraphrase what Roland Barthes (1966) wrote about narratives in the *Structural Analysis of Narrative*: Invectives of the world are numberless. They appear in many guises and can be articulated through spoken and written language, moving or fixed images, or gestures – as well as a combination of any or all of these. Invective is present in myth, legend, fable, tale, novella, epic, history, tragedy, comedy, mime, painting, stained-glass windows, cinema, comics, news items and conversation. Invective is present in every age, in every place, in every society, all classes; all human groups use invective. Invective is international, transhistorical, transcultural: it is simply there, like life itself (1982: 251-2).

Yet, as Barthes notes, in spite of the intimidating task of dealing with the plethora of narratives across extremely diverse cultures and different ages, one way of approaching the problem of their "universality," as well as their infinite manifestations and forms is to attempt to work out an heuristic model, which in itself is a daunting enterprise, basing it, as he did, on the structural linguistics of the mid-twentieth-century. In counter-distinction to Barthes' approach, though, in order to deal with the specificity of the literary issue at hand, I would like to sketch briefly a hypothetico-deductive descriptive method of studying invective from a socio-semiotic perspective by focusing on an actual court case that occurred in Montreal in November 2008, and was reported in Canada's national newspaper, the *Globe and Mail* on two different occasions. The case in question will constitute a norm or "judgment" for defining the necessary and sufficient conditions for the occurrence of invective in general and will serve to better identify, describe and define literary invectives as a particular and specific class of verbal apostrophe. The court case plays out, in a discursive mode, a number of issues raised in Kathryn Morgan's illuminating paper on "Domesticating Invective in Plato's Laws," as well as some of the other issues that were raised over the last three days.

The first news item appeared as a report on Friday, Nov. 7 and, the second, as an editorial piece, or "Comment" on Monday, Nov. 10, 2008. While recognizing the fundamental discursive differences between an alleged report and an editorial comment that would each merit fairly detailed separate analyses,[1] time dictates that I remain focused and concentrate on their discursive articulation. Moreover, this particular case on invective also gave rise to a political video by Michel Rivard, a well-known Quebec composer and singer. My reasons for choosing these non-literary examples in a colloquium on "Savage Words: Invective as a Literary Genre" is that from my perspective verbal texts and videos such as Michel Rivard's "Culture in Danger,"[2] make use of the same strategies of employment, setting into discourse and enunciation (as literary texts do and as Paul Ricoeur states in *Time and Narrative*) how the main difference between fictional, historical discourses and newspaper accounts does not lie in their structural or descriptive features but in their finality. Historical discourses, and I would add here newspaper discourses, usually have a truth claim or wanting-to-make-believe finality, whereas literary discourse does not necessarily make such a claim. However, though Michel Rivard's two videos do not make the same truth claim as historical discourse, they do nonetheless function at an allegorical level where the interplay of the iconic and the discursive, as well as the ending, leads a viewer to interpret the whole at a political level.

The phenomenon of invective has given rise to a large number of studies of all types, one of the best known in the Anglo-Saxon world arguably being Nicolas Stonimsky's *Lexicon of Musical Invective. Critical Assaults on Composers since Beethoven's Time* first published in 1953. In this work the author concentrates on biased, unfair, ill-tempered and singularly unprophetic judgments made by critics on famous musicians. A practicing composer, conductor and musician, he provides us with a common sense thematic analysis based on a very general but sound intuition that "objections levelled at every musical innovator are all derived from the same psychological inhibition which may be described as the Non-acceptance of the Unfamiliar." (p. 3) This intuition, though interesting, is not theorized enough to enable us to work out a coherent methodology to analyse texts in detail. Again, how should one proceed?

I would like to paraphrase and apply to the proteiform invective what Jean-Paul Sartre states, in *Being and Nothingness*, about Marcel Proust's genius, claiming that this author's works, even if reduced to the sum of their manifestations, correspond nevertheless to the infinity of possible points of view that one can take on them, and that he calls their "inexhaustibility" (1966: lvi). First, one caveat followed by a methodological assertion: I am not comparing Proust's talent or genius to that of the person who wrote the following report, the editorial piece, or the short video. In addition to what Sartre states about Proust, for him a work can be analyzed from an "infinity of possible points of view;" secondly, a theory, a methodology is a construct that permits one to articulate a work from a particular perspective and tease out its signification along those lines. Thus, without further justification, the following analysis will be based on the theories and methodologies of the Paris School of Semiotics under the leadership of Algirdas Julien Greimas from the 1960s on and that continues in various guises today, some 17 years after his demise.[3]

Hence, I will be dealing with a "live" case of invective and not a literary "genre," as the title of the conference suggests, but I trust this will enable us to begin to come to grips with literary invective in terms of discourse analysis, not as genre but as invective. David Marsh began his informative presentation with the example of two "real life" male drivers that he heard insult each other at a crossroads just outside the UCLA campus, as he was strolling back to his hotel. They began arguing about who had the right-of-way; fortunately, instead of assaulting one another, they bantered back and forth each making stronger and stronger claims about the legitimacy of his rights; then brought closure to the debate by questioning the actual legitimacy of their respective interlocutors, calling each other a "mother-fer," before driving off in different directions. "Swearing," which I will deal with, can be considered a micro-narrative or micro-invective, condensing and concentrating all the forces of literary invective in a brief utterance that presupposes the development of literary invective, which Giuseppe Mazzotta defined as "a formalized structure with an argumentative thrust." Others, during this colloquium, without actually using the following descriptive categories, have developed the notion of literary invective as an imaginative rhetorical exercise that depicts the subject inveighed against in negative terms. This could, in turn, be articulated in more formal terms, classified by Pierre Fontanier (1830) in his work on the figures of discourse, dealing with the literary portrait, which he defines as a combination of prosopographia (physical portrait) and ethopeia (moral portrait).[4] In literary invective, these two levels of the portrait are expanded into a narrative (family, social, moral) that iterates, using all possible real or imagined rhetorical tropes, the nucleus "I don't like! I detest! I despise! I hate!" what you do, what you are, what you represent. Swearing as invective does not generally make use of prosopographia or ethopeia, but presupposes them and concentrates all its thrust (rhetorical or other) in a concise, pithy, ironic verbal attack on the other. In this paper, I will delineate similarities and differences of invective, which is situated on a tensive, most often moralized, scale or hierarchy that stretches from swearing, insult, blasphemy to stylized literary diatribe.

A further fundamental difference can be observed between micro-invectives —swearwords— and literary invectives in regard to how aspectualities or temporal tensive categories function. Literary invectives make use of, develop and iterate the inchoative, durative and terminative verbal aspects, narrating beginnings, transformations and states, whereas swearing collapses these three temporal aspects (past-present-future) – which mark the beginning, the duration and the termination, or the tri-dimensional temporality of an action – into the gnomic or the eternal present and absolute truth of non-spatial, non-temporal state of affairs or state of feelings "it is" or "you are" as you were and as you will be, giving it its force or thrust. Hence, the eternal present of the swear-word gives it the thrust and force of a state that was true in the past, is true in the present and will always be true in the future, thus collapsing and concentrating temporality into an immutable state of perpetual, timeless being.

The following is a word for word transcription of the two texts that appeared in the *Global & Mail*. First, Ingrid Peritz' report from Montreal on November 7, 2008:

> *The two solitudes of swearing: in Quebec, the* f-word*'s not so bad*
>
> It is the most crude of curses in the English language, a *four-letter expletive* usually avoided in polite company.
> Yet in Montreal, the *f-word* is apparently not a swear word at all.
> A municipal court judge has ruled that a man who repeatedly tosses the expletive at two police officers during a confrontation was not swearing, because he wasn't taking God's name in vain.
> "While generally recognized as wrong, impolite and coarse, the words '*fuck you*' do not at all constitute a blasphemy, since by definition a blasphemy invokes God or sacred things," Judge Pierre Bouchard said.
> The recent decision led to the acquittal of the man, 37-year-old Charles Yves Dupuy, who had been charged with obstructing justice.
> Mr. Dupuy was approached by two police officers on patrol in Montreal in May 2006. He began to curse at the officers who responded by threatening to give Mr. Dupuy a ticket and then asking him to identify himself. Mr Dupuy refused. His lawyer argued that Mr. Dupuy was not obliged to identify himself because dropping the *f-bomb* did not contravene any municipal bylaw against swearing in public.
> "It is not a curse word, it's an insult," the lawyer, Hélène Rouillard, said in an interview yesterday.

"Cursing is saying things like *tabernacle, calice, ciboire* – everything that comes from the church. If I said *calice de tabernacle* to a police officer, he could give me a ticket." Indeed, curses in Quebec are generally directed toward the institution that historically dominated the province.
So while English speakers would typically swear by invoking sex and bodily functions, French-speaking Quebeckers tend to summon up the Catholic Church and its rituals.
The two solitudes of swearing emerge on the airwaves in the province; it is not uncommon to hear French-language hosts and guests casually throw around the *f-word*, even on Canada's public broadcaster, Radio-Canada.
"To French Canadians, it means nothing, its not our language, our code," said Jean-Pierre Pichette, an ethnography professor who has compiled a dictionary of French-Canadian swear words. "Among French Canadians, the big boss, the supreme authority, was God. So cursing was sort of a verbal revenge against authority."
To him the *f-word*[5] "is the name of an animal that Brigitte Bardot likes to defend," he said, referring to "*phoque*," the French word for seal.
As for Mr. Dupuy, he admitted in court to having a prior criminal record that included assault on a police officer. But he held his tongue in front of the judge.
Before acquitting him, Judge Bouchard noted that Mr. Dupuy acted in an exemplary way, and testified "with respect and courtesy toward everyone."

One could obviously take this account at face value and begin to analyse the report, however, the editorial piece that appeared in the *Globe* a few days later on Monday, Nov. 10, 2008 provides a good deal of supplementary information that might help us better understand the nature of invective, swearing and blasphemy in modern day Quebec culture, and serve as part of our corpus to help us better understand the nature of literary invective.

Profanity and police. Offensive, but no offence

A recent decision from the Municipal Court in Montreal has drawn notice for how the judge distinguished between blaspheming (which would contravene a municipal bylaw) and the "wrong, impolite and coarse" but prevalent *f-word*. While providing a helpful distinction for others within Montreal's city limits seeking to stay on the right side of the law when it comes to expletives, the decision really stands for a citizen's rights to be free from police intimidation.
According to the police officer's testimony, Alain Abrigu saw Charles-Yves Dupuy, a black man in his mid-thirties, seated in front of some shops while on patrol in Montréal-Nord, and perceived Mr. Dupuy as having a "frustrated air" upon spotting Officer Abrigu and his colleague. After hearing Mr. Dupuy speaking but making out only two words – *fuck you* – the officer approached him to ask what he had said. Again, all he understood of Mr. Dupuy's alleged response were the last two words. The officer told Mr. Dupuy that, if he "continued," he would get a ticket, and he told the court that Mr. Dupuy did continue in a mix of Creole and French, again ending with those two En-

glish words, which were still the only ones he remembers hearing and understanding. Soon enough, other officers were called to the scene and Mr. Dupuy was arrested and charged with blaspheming and obstructing a peace officer under the Criminal Code. Mr. Dupuy's version of events was the one the judge found more convincing. Mr. Dupuy testified that he had ordered some Haitian takeout, bought a pack of cigarettes and was smoking one of them while waiting for his food to be ready when he was approached by the officer. Mr. Dupuy testified that he never swore at the officer but simply refused to speak to him. Judge Pierre Bouchard said the tribunal had no reason not to believe Mr. Dupuy, saying his testimony was plausible and credible and delivered with respect and courtesy.

Mr. Dupuy was entitled to ignore Officer Abrigu. He was not obliged to speak to him – either for the sake of politeness or because the officer (by his own account) marched up to him and demanded that he repeat what he had said. In fact, even if Mr. Dupuy had really sworn at the officer – he should not have been charged with obstruction of justice or any other offence.

The *f-word*[6] is not a curse word, it's an insult said Hélène Poussard Mr. Dupuy's lawyer. And that perceived insult prompted the police officer's response. But police must not abuse their authority by inflicting it on those who insult them. As Officer Abrigu said in his own testimony, "We are used to being insulted." An apparent attempt to throw his weight around: intimidation and false charges was a most improper response.

* * *

Both of these accounts share a number of features that characterize literary invective as defined in the contributions of a number of colleagues in this volume, notably irony and euphemism,[7] that was developed in detail by Gianluca Rizzo in his chapter on "Issues of Language and Genre in Macaronic Invectives." Yet, even a cursory examination of the two newspaper accounts of the events that allegedly occurred between Mr. Dupuy and the police officers, whether they happen to be attributed quotes, or reported, indirect dialogue, clearly show that we are dealing with inter-subjective communication between various subjects, which could be the starting point of a formal reflection on invective that we could define in the most general terms as the result of a real or imagined co-presence and interaction between two or more speaking or gesturing actors, when narrated by a voice either *in absentia* or *in praesentia*. Hence the situation of enunciation in both reports on Mr. Dupuy's day in court, whether it is the trial, heard and narrated by the reporter (narrator) for eventual readers (narratee or audience), or the opinion piece written to comment on the former, can be considered a spatio-temporal shifting out and shifting in of the appropriation of all the resources of language by an "I," founding his/her subjectivity on this interpersonal relationship addressing a "You" who, in turn, can appropriate all of the resources of language, thereby founding his/her subjectivity on this communicative act.[8]

Invective can be considered a form of verbal interaction defined as an infraction of regular conversational interaction based on accepted conventions or rules between interlocutors or participants. These conventions or rules are defined historically, socially, geographically, regionally and vary according to age and groups, but they do regulate verbal interaction, the aim of which can vary according to Jakobson's referential, poetic, phatic, metalinguistic, emotional and conative functions. From this perspective, one could study "invective" as a form of enunciation that recognizes conversational conventions but subverts and puts into question their underlying factual, ideological and logical presuppositions. Conversational or dialogical interventions, as Grice[9] and others have shown, are grounded in social rites based on the principles of alternance, internal coherence, internal and external stringing of contents, along with the principles of injunctions and sincerity, specific socio-affective relations and links between inter-actants. Contrary to contractual inter-subjective dialogue, invective functions, at first blush, not at the cooperative or fiduciary level, but at a polemic one, that while recognizing the conventions noted above, nonetheless thwarts and radically contests them.

From a socio-semiotic narratological theoretical perspective, "invective" is a pathemic, polemical form of inter-subjective communication between two or more enunciating actants that posits the existence of shared axiological and ideological micro-semantic universes, in which a subject "I" appropriates all of the resources of language to found him/herself as subject, through the act of enunciation. As such, the inveighing subject can only found him/herself in a relation of real, or simulated co-temporous, inter-actional, polemical co-presence with an inveighed subject "You." Yet, the roles are logically exchangeable, for "You" can become an "I" in responding or not to the inveighing subject by means of invective in the mode of conflict; or he/she can diffuse, neutralize the other by engaging in a contractual relation and projecting shared conversational conventions; or, as Don Beecher has demonstrated in his paper "The Art of Declining Invective in Ben Jonson's *Poetaster*," or one can simply desist.

Again, at first glance, real or perceived conflictual relations seem to be a necessary condition for invective. However, there does exist a playful or ludic aspect to invective, based on simulated conflict; for example, individuals who play sports can, and do, inveigh against each other, but instead of disparaging and deconstructing conventions or the values of the group, this constitutes a recognition or reinforcement of the contractual relations and values that regulate their interaction. Youth culture, as well as other social groups, also function in this way and in standard French there are a whole series of sexual expressions that can either be construed as derogatory invectives or as positive, admiring, superlative ones: "Oh! le couillon, Oh! l'enfoiré, Oh! le con, Oh! l'empapaouté, Oh! l'andouille," etc. This other neglected role of invective in group formation and consolidation would certainly merit further study.

In the two newspaper reports, the initially passive subject had ordered Haitian food, and waiting for it, stepped outside to smoke a cigarette in a stable space, minding his own affairs, which could be considered as being in a monologue-ical, stable state. This space is suddenly transformed with the emergence of a seemingly hostile, dialogical, active subject who proceeds to interrogate the former. A new socio-spatial structure, or a break, occurs in the stable system as a result of the invasion of an intrusive, aggressive subject (police officer), and a new form, or dialogical conflictual structure emerges that can be considered resulting in morphogenesis. The aggressive subject's interrogation provokes a verbal reaction from the previously passive non-dialogical subject that is considered inappropriate by the former who is in a position of authority. The situation of this particular act of enunciation, and not its spatio-temporal dimension, but rather its socio-economical, psychological, and I dare say, racial dimension is clarified, as a "black man in his mid-thirties Mr. Charles-Yves Dupuy" is allegedly interrogated by white officers, "Mr. Agribu and his colleague." They are both representatives of law and order, duly sanctioned by a society whose core values they are mandated to uphold. Perceiving a threat, the supposedly passive subject inveighs against the aggressive one, using "the most crude of curses in the English language, a four-letter expletive usually avoided in polite company." The inveighed subject listens to Mr Dupuy, "but making out only two words – fuck you – the officer approached him and asked him what he had said." Again, the last two words were all he understood of Mr Dupuy's alleged response. According to the officer, Mr Dupuy continued to address him in Creole and French; ending with the last two English words and the policeman said he would be arrested if he continued. He purportedly did; Mr Dupuy was arrested and charged with blaspheming and obstructing a peace officer under the Criminal Code.

A closer examinations of these events allegedly leading to Mr. Dupuy's arrest reveals that in order for an invective to be perceived as such, both inveigher and inveighed must posit a shared axiology or a shared system of values that varies, as we have seen, geographically, historically, culturally, economically, ideologically, in small or large groups, etc. because without axiology there can be no invective. Also, the system of values is scalar and moralized – high-low – as this crudest of all curses is "usually avoided in polite company." For a subject to inveigh he/she has to recognize the inveighed's presupposed system of values and for the inveighed subject to perceive the invective he/she has to be aware of his/her own system of values and perceive the inveighing subject as intentionally verbally contesting it by using "crude language usually avoided in proper company." In the case in point, the police officer perceives the alleged invective as a radical questioning of his status and role of mandated subject who is upholding the values that found civil society. He thus applies what he believes to be the letter of the law by arresting and charging the inveigher with obstructing justice.

And the wheels of justice grind inexorably and slowly. 28 months later Mr. Dupuy, ably represented by his lawyer, Hélène Rouillard – Hélène Poussard in the editorial – and Officer Abrigu, seemingly without legal council, have their day in court presided over by Judge Pierre Bouchard as sanctioning instance. He will hear evidence and pass judgment before an audience, public voice, on the status of swearing, inveighing and blasphemy under Montreal municipal bylaws, which constitute the cultural, geographic, historical, specific legal, or value system used to weigh and evaluate the allegations and accusations of behaviour considered as transgressions, infringements upon or contraventions of the norm. Judge Bouchard, in effect, will rule on the case and sanction one or other protagonist.

Mr Dupuy's lawyer Hélène Rouillard/Poussard argued that swearing, and in this case using the f-word, is a form of invective that is an insult but that insults are not a reason for charging someone with obstructing justice, or any other offence. She also argued that perceived insult prompted the officer's response. In addition, in his own testimony Officer Abrigu said: "We are used to being insulted." This led the accused's lawyer to argue that the officer apparently threw his weight around to intimidate and levy false charges, which was a most improper response. Insults in the form of swearing or invective, though they at one and the same time recognize and radically contest the other's system of values, and though frowned upon by the polite company that establishes social conventions and rules, is not a criminal offence.

Yet, it is the judge's weighing of the evidence before the court audience as reported to the readers of the *Globe & Mail* that is most useful in defining invective or swearing, insofar as one can formulate his reasoning and judgment in terms of modal theory, or modalities that motivate the actions of the two main interacting subjects. Hence, if we assume that for a inveighing subject to "perform" a successful or unsuccessful inter-subjective invective he/she must possess the modal competencies of *knowing* (knowledge), *wanting* (desire), *having-to* (duty) and *being-able-to* (ability) to do so. And the same holds true for the inveighed subject. Thus the inveighing subject must presuppose that the inveighed has an analogous common knowledge of the value system of the one that he or she inveighs, otherwise the invective is misunderstood or misfires and cannot be perceived as such. Hence, knowledge of values constituting a norm as well as deviance from the norm —a common encyclopedia, for example— has to be shared both by the inveigher or the inveighed for invective to occur. If there is a largely asymmetrical relationship in their respective awareness, or, if either or both subjects are not culturally sensitized to their interlocutor's value system, then invective misfires. This is what an expert witness, an ethnographer, Jean-Pierre Pichette, states regarding the use of the f-word: "'To French Canadians, it means nothing, it's not our language, our code…f-word is the name of an animal that Brigitte Bardot likes to defend," he said, referring to "*phoque,*" the French word for seal, an argument that Judge Bouchard was sensitive to. Either Officer Abrigu was more sensitized to the fact that "English speakers typically swear by invoking sex and bodily functions," which is also generally the case in France, or as the title of the Nov. 7 article as well as its contents implies he could be an English speaker since he does not understand any of the words spoken by Mr Dupuy in Creole or French, but only the last 2 English words fuck you, whereas "Quebeckers tend to summon up the Catholic Church and its rituals… [for them] cursing is a sort of verbal revenge against authority. "

In addition, the inveighing subject has to want, or desire to inveigh against the inveighed subject; there clearly has to be intent or motive. Although, Mr. Dupuy admitted in court to having a prior criminal record that included assault on a police officer, which proves a previous intent, he was deferent, polite, well behaved and courteous during his hearing. His good behavior was considered by the judge as a proof of his civility, his regard for social proprieties or values and as counterproof to the accusations brought against him by Officer Abrigu. Judge Bouchard stated: "the tribunal had no reason not to believe Mr. Dupuy, saying this testimony was plausible and credible and delivered with respect and courtesy." Again, it is evident that the allegedly inveighing subject possesses the modality of being-able-to inveigh or swear against a police officer that would constitute verbal polemic as he admitted during the hearing that he had already been arrested for assaulting a policeman, physical polemic. Here, polemic, whether verbal or physical, constitutes not only aggressive behavior but is also both a recognition of the officer's role as representative of social values who has been mandated and sanctioned by society as defender of law and order; and a radical questioning of that very role and those values.

Yet, Mr. Dupuy's general behavior in court is considered by Judge Bouchard to be exemplary as well as his testimony that is respectful and courteous toward everyone leads the judge to a conclusion that what the evidence he gave was plausible and credible, which made it highly unlikely he would insult Officer Abrigu. The officer's version of events was judged not to be as plausible and believable as the accused's; and his understanding of what Mr. Dupuy actually said was considered somewhat inadequate and one sided. Moreover, the officer was seen as having used intimidating and excessively forceful tactics in his dealings with Mr. Dupuy even though they did not come to blows. It was apparent to the judge that the officer did abuse his power or authority by throwing his weight around, intimidating and laying false charges against Mr. Dupuy, which was a most improper response.

The final modality to be evoked by the judge is /having to/ or duty. Once more, Mr. Dupuy is seen as exercising a very controlled and credible response to the officer's aggressive behavior, who perceived his duly constituted and sanctioned authority as upholder of society's laws to be challenged and radically questioned by the f-word invective. Mr. Dupuy thus holds "his tongue before the judge" thereby exercising "exemplary behavior" and showing "respect and courtesy toward everyone," clearly demonstrating that he recognized, esteemed, honored and could uphold the dialogical conventions and rules that govern interpersonal communication as well as the specific, defining, accepted values of the group, thereby consolidating the societal relations of the *demos*, or the "people," contrary to the Officer's polemico-conflctual response that, as we have seen, is considered excessive, since he perceives the alleged invective as challenging the very core values of the group and applies an unwarranted sanction.

A few cursory remarks before playing the video that illustrates a number of the points that were raised in this paper. First of all, I have attempted to sketch or even *bricolate*, as Claude Lévi-Strauss would say, what could be considered a logico-semantic narratological model of the analysis of invective based, on the one hand, on principles of conversational interaction, along with enunciation theory, that posit the existence of rules or conventions that govern and consolidate societal values. On the other hand, I have linked the values in question to the notion of a discursive micro-semantic universe and constructed a model of meaningful verbal interactions in an inter-subjective frame where subjects found their subjectivity by appropriating all the resources of language when saying I in an inter-subject relation with a You and an excluded third Him/Her and, in the case in point, by appropriating all the resources of invective. Finally, I have then made use of modalities that over-determine actants and posited the verbal interaction between two modally competent subjects. However, one aspect that has not been covered, for want of time, is the pathemic, or passional dimension of invective, for example, anger, jealousy, hate, fear, contempt, etc., which would be necessary to complete the model proposed.

Notes

[1] My verbal presentation concluded with a brief video that appeared on YouTube made by the Quebec, composer, songwriter, musician, Michel Rivard entitled "Culture in Danger" before the last Canadian Federal election in the Fall of 2008. There is neither time nor space to transcribe, describe and analyse in written form the complexity of a multifaceted video that combines both verbal and iconic dimensions. The decision by the Harper Conservative government to cut cultural programs to the tune of $49 million and redirect funding to targeted cultural areas produced a very negative and bitter reaction from artists and many ardent proponents of culture, contributed to the election of a minority government. What is interesting, is that the most vehement reaction came from Quebec where the Harper Government that had been wooing the electorate of the province did not win a single new seat of the 10 it previously held in the Federal Parliament in spite of a vigorous and focused campaign supporting the notion of the Quebec nation, which reinforced the hands of "Independentists", "Sovereignists" or "Separatists," as you like.

[2] Two versions of different lengths of Michel Rivard's video can be viewed on http: //.www.youtube.com/watch?v=Uhgv85m852Q.

[3] See for example Greimas 1987, 1990, Greimas & Courtés 1982, Greimas & Fontanille 1993, as well as Perron & Collins 1989.

[4] A long tradition exists in rhetorical theory regarding the literary portrait. In 1830 Pierre Fontanier defined the two aspects of the portrait: *Prosopogaphia* is "a description of the face, the body, the features, the physical qualities or simply the exterior, the bearing, the movement of an animated being either real or fictional, that is to say a being created from pure imagination" (Fontanier, 1968, 425). *Ethopeia* is "a description of the morals, the virtues, the talents, the flaws, even the good or bad qualities of a real or fictional being" (1968, 427). He also notes that often the term "portrait" refers to either ethopeia or prosopographia alone, but for him, as for me, the term portrait combines the two and it is "the description, both physical and moral, of an animated, real or fictional being" (1968, 428) (translation mine).

[5] Emphasis mine.

[6] Emphasis mine.

[7] In Ingrid Peritz's brief account she refers to "a four-letter-expletive" once, the "f-word" three times and the "f-bomb" once, but never does she personally use the word "fuck." The word "Fuck You" and "*phoque*" or seal, pronounced "fock" in French are quoted directly from native French speakers with typically Francophone or dyed-in-the-wool Quebec names Judge Pierre Bouchard and Jean-Pierre Pichet, an ethnography professor, whereas it is attributed to Mr. Charles-Yves Dupuy, another Francophone, or rather allophone Quebecois, since he happens to be of Haitian and not "pure-laine" or native pre-conquest 1759 Quebec settler origin, when France lost New-France to the English. In the unsigned editorial piece the euphemism "f-word" is used twice and again word "fuck you," quoted once, is indirect discourse allegedly that Mr. Dupuy "continued" to use, which is reported by Officer Abrigu who, after calling other officers to the scene, arrested and charged him "with blaspheming and obstructing a peace officer under the Criminal Code.

[8] See Émile Benveniste (1966) "De la subjectivité dans le langage" p. 258-66.

[9] See Paul H. Grice (1989).

Bibliography

Barthes, Roland. 1982 [1966]. "Introduction to the Structural Analysis of Narrative" in Susan Sontag, editor, 1982, *A Barthes Reader*, McGraw-Hill Ryerson Limited, Toronto, p. 251-295.

Benvenist, Émile, 1966. *Problèmes de linguistique générale*. Paris : Gallimard.

Fontanier, Pierre. 1968 [1830]. *Les Figures du discours*. Paris : Flammarion.

Greimas, Algirdas Julien. 1987. *On Meaning. Selected Writings in Semiotic Theory*. Translated by Paul Perron & Frank Collins. Minneapolis: University of Minnesota Press.

----1990. *The Social Sciences. A Semiotic View.* Translated by Paul Perron & Frank Collins. Minneapolis: University of Minnesota Press.

Greimas, Algirdas, Julien & José Courtés. 1982. *Semiotics and Language. An Analytical Dictionary.* Translated by Larry Crist, Daniel Patte and others. Bloomington: Indiana University Press.

Greimas, Algirdas, Julien & Jacques Fontanille. 1993. *The Semiotics of Passions. From States of Affairs to States of Feelings*. Translated by Paul Perron & Frank Collins. Minneapolis: University of Minnesota Press.

Grice, H. Paul. 1989. *Studies in the Way of Words*. Cambridge, Mass.: Harvard University Press.

Perron, Paul & Frank Collins. 1989. *Greimassian Semiotics*. New Literary History. Vol. 20. No. 3.

Ricoeur, Paul. 1984, 1985, 1988. *Time and Narrative*, Vol. I, II, III, Translated by Kathleen McLaughlin and David Pellauer. Chicago and London: The University of Chicago Press.

Sartre, Jean-Paul. 1966. *Being and Nothingness*. Translated by Hazel Barnes. New York: Washington Square Press.

Slonimsky, Nicolas. 2000. *Lexicon of Musical Invective. Critical Assaults on Composers since Beethoven's Time*. London and New York: W. W. Norton & Company.

Ennio Rao

The Humanistic Invective: Genre, Mode, or Meta-Genre?

Until about 30 years ago, there was good reason to lament the almost absolute neglect into which the Humanists' invectives had fallen. Were it not for the pioneer studies of Lorenzo Mehus in the eighteenth century and Giuseppe Zippel's and Remigio Sabbadini's "spigolature" (gleanings) in the late nineteenth and early twentieth centuries, the humanistic invectives could have been declared dead and forgotten. But the situation brightened when Pier Giorgio Ricci edited several of Petrarch's invectives in the late 1940s and 1950s. The last three decades of the twentieth century finally witnessed an intensification of scholarly interest that is continuing into the new century, resulting in a steady stream of editions, translations and studies by Rao, Mariangela Regoliosi, Ari Wesseling, M. C. Davies, Giuliana Crevatin, David Marsh, David Rutherford, Silvia Fiaschi, Francesco Bausi, and Virginia Bonmatí Sánchez.[1]

Besides a critical edition of Facio's invectives against Valla, I have devoted a nuts-and-bolts study to the humanistic invectives,[2] in which I tackle the problem of classifying them as a genre. So I was delighted to receive the invitation from Professor Ciavolella to participate in a conference that specifically examines this thorny problem.

Classifying the invective is no easy task, since historically we find elements of it imbedded in epic poetry, tragedy, comedy, iambic poetry, satire, epigram, and oratory, to name a few types of literary endeavor that we easily recognize and classify from their particular form, content and technique. The invective is indeed as old as the history of Western literature, as we find elements of it in Homer's *Iliad*, notably in the first three books: in the bitter exchange between wrathful Achilles and haughty Agamemnon, in the objurgations of Odysseus against evil-tongued Thersites, and in the accusations of cowardice launched by Hector and Helen against Paris.

Genre has been the subject of controversy ever since Plato distinguished between two modes of representing an object or person: 1) by description, or 2) by impersonation. Plato himself became aware that this simple division left out too much, so he later inserted a third division: the mixed mode, in which narrative alternates with dialogue (*Respub.* 3.392-94). Western theory on the subject has alternated between cautious acceptance and recognition of genre's usefulness for imposing order, and utter rejection. Theorists have approached it prescriptively until the end of the eighteenth century, and descriptively thereafter. Put another way, they have debated whether genre is a normative or empirical category, and have raised the question of the possibility of "impure" genres and if genres can be transgressed. Application of a strict canon has resulted in the stifling of creative impulses in Italian Renaissance tragedy and personal woes for such authors as Torquato Tasso.

The question of genre has involved the greatest literary critics and thinkers of every age, from Aristotle, Horace and Quintilian to Donatus, Dante and Scaliger. In more recent times it has entertained the attention of Giordano Bruno, Boileau, Samuel Johnson, Hegel, and Schlegel, down to Croce, Northrop Frye, Mario Fubini, Walter Binni, Claudio Guillén, and Fredric Jameson.[3] Some critics have attempted to skirt the issue of "genre" by using terms such as "mode" and "canon." I am familiar with the alternating fortunes of the various factions, but will wisely stay away from the fray, limiting myself to a description of the humanistic invective and to the definition of *invectiva* in Western critical literature from the *Rhetorica ad Herennium* to the Humanists' own contemporaries. I will then conclude with my definition of the humanistic invective and will attempt to classify it.

In the year 1352, Petrarch became the first humanist to pen an invective. During an illness of Pope Clement VI, Petrarch addressed him a letter in which he warned him to guard himself against the crowd of doctors attending him, who are no more than ignorant quacks, but rather to place his reliance in the one considered to be the best. News of the letter came to the ears of a physician, who proceeded to write a public defense of his profession, cautioning Petrarch to confine himself to his own province of poetry, whose stock in trade is lies.

Petrarch did not suffer this retort in silence, but invoking the example of St. Jerome wrote what became the first of four invectives.[4] He denied having insulted the science of medicine. On the contrary, he protested his respect for the *real* science of medicine, adding that he had no admiration for the modern practitioners of what had been reduced to a mechanical art, with such sordid practices as sniffing urine. Petrarch opined that modern doctors would be severely censured by the ancient founders of medicine. The doctor answered, but

Petrarch quickly crushed his protestations with three lengthy vitriolic invectives in which he ridiculed current medical practices and beliefs and defended poetry, calling to witness the high regard in which the ancients held their poets, at the same time making show of his vast knowledge of both pagan and Christian authors.

A century later, in 1451, Poggio Bracciolini and Lorenzo Valla engaged in a marathon duel through a series of invectives that overshadow all previous efforts in the medium. The two humanists had long been enemies. Poggio, being very envious of his younger and more brilliant rival, had twice sabotaged Valla's efforts to find prestigious positions in the Roman curia and in Ferrara. Now that they were both apostolic secretaries and ate, as it were, from the same table, it was inevitable that their mutual resentment should erupt into open warfare.

The occasion soon presented itself. A Catalan youth, a pupil of Valla, had annotated some of Poggio's letters, pointing out several errors of grammar and syntax. Poggio, holding the master responsible for his pupil's work, unleashed a scathing invective against Valla.[5] He declared himself honored to be criticized on grammatical points by Lorenzo, thus placing him in the hallowed company of Cicero, Sallust, Livy, Donatus, Jerome, Lactantius, Guarino Guarini, Leonardo Bruni and many other great writers previously attacked by Valla. Defending the correctness of some of his expressions criticized by Valla, Poggio cast ridicule on the latter's work on style, *De elegantia, vel ignorantia potius linguae latinae*. Poggio concluded with the description of a mock-triumph of Valla, somewhat reminiscent of Seneca's *Apocolocyntosis*. He imagines Valla borne on a cart made of giants' bones along a street covered with rams' fleeces, holding a sphinx in his right hand and a phoenix in his left, his brow wreathed with laurel branches from which hang sausages. The cart is pulled by elephants and surrounded by the Muses dressed as slave girls, bearing lyres nibbled by mice. Pallas waves away flies with a sword, while crows, owls and seagulls circle the sky above, accompanying with their cries Valla's song. The cart is preceded by the chief authors and philosophers in chains: there is Aristotle, Cicero, Lactantius, all grammarians, historians, poets and theologians. Satyrs, fauns and donkeys sing their songs. When the cart reaches the Capitol, Valla shuts his prisoners in a dark jail and dedicates a huge bull's head to Jupiter. He finally demands a bronze statue and his enrollment in the ranks of the gods.

Valla replied with a monumental invective, which he entitled *Antidotum*.[6] Declaring at first his reluctance to take the field against a miserable buffoon, old enough to be his grandfather, Valla undertakes a defense of himself and an exposé of Poggio as a perfidious liar, master of lust, adulterer, drunkard and corruptor of youth. He then purports to show Poggio's utter ignorance of the liberal arts, particularly of grammar and rhetoric, by listing and correcting several errors found in Poggio's works. The device used is the dialogue. Excerpts of Poggio's invectives are put in his own mouth and Valla confounds his adversary in the presence of assenting judges.

Valla showed some moderation in this initial reply, focusing chiefly on a discussion of literary matters. Poggio, however, set no such limits to his poisonous pen in his next reply, no less than three *Orationes* (II, III, and IV).[7] Well aware of Valla's superiority in matters of grammar, he totally avoided such questions, resorting instead to his particular specialty, satire. After routine criticism of Valla's slanderous language, he paints a ridiculous picture of Valla lamenting his plight to his concubine after reading Poggio's invective and finally being heartened by her to reply, using whatever arguments, true or false. Then Poggio criticizes Valla for creating in his *Antidotum* a false courtroom atmosphere, while in truth he denied Poggio the right to defend himself. He reprimands his adversary for his self-praise, reminding him that he is held in low esteem by the chief humanists. Alluding to Valla' confrontation with an ecclesiastical court in Naples stemming from his refusal to believe that the Apostles' Creed had been composed by the Apostles, each contributing one verse, a confrontation that resulted in Valla's full acquittal, Poggio maliciously suggests that he was beaten with broomsticks before the Inquisition and asks him to show the scars on his back. In the *De vero bono*, Poggio charges, Valla condemned monastic life and placed prostitutes above nuns. In other works Valla had cast scorn on Jerome, Boethius, and Augustine. At a mock trial presided by Cacus, Rhadamanthys and Pluto, Poggio dooms Valla to hell, where Arius and other heretics await his arrival.

The description of Valla in hell continues in the third *Oratio*. The resident demons, marveling at Valla's evil genius, decide to send him back to earth to carry on their wicked work. They do so after giving him due honor. Having emerged into the upper air, Valla climbs Parnassus to prove his superiority in poetry. It being a very hot day, he stops to drink at the fount of Helicon. Apollo and the Muses try in vain to induce him to spit out the water. Unable to show Apollo his poetic powers, Valla follows a secret pathway pointed out to him by Cerberus which leads him to the Elysian Fields, where his sudden appearance causes great panic among the blessed souls. When he introduces himself as theologian, philosopher, orator, grammarian, historian and poet combined, the souls decide to listen to him. When they assemble and give the place of honor to Homer, Valla protests, claiming the distinction for himself, since he excels in many fields, while Homer's exclusive province is poetry. Then the examination begins, Aristotle leads Valla to agree that he is an animal; other writers lead him to humiliating conclusions about himself. Tired of the carryings-on, Valla decides to entertain the souls with song and accompanies himself on a lyre fashioned from a donkey's jaw and his own hair as strings. To draw inspiration, he drinks the contents of a chamber pot. When the latter breaks accidentally, he is unable to continue his song. The souls place him on a donkey, crown him with the intestines of a sheep and send him triumphantly to the upper world. There Valla hangs the crown on his house, which he dedicates to the god Sterquilinium.

As soon as Valla heard of Poggio's new attack, he countered with two compositions that he entitled *Apologus*, consisting of two "scenici actus."[8] Parodying the philosophical dialogue, Valla introduces Poggio engaged in solemn conversation with Guarino, one of Guarino's pupils, a cook, and a stable servant. As Guarino reads excerpts from Poggio's letters, the schoolboy, the cook and the stable servant find fault with their language and style. The distraught Poggio falls asleep. In the second dialogue, which takes place in a garden, Poggio takes leave of his interlocutors, Valla and Guarino, to go home and fetch his masterpiece, the *Historia tripartita convivalis*, in which, among other subjects was discussed the question of whether the spoken language of ancient Rome differed from the written language. Poggio had argued that the Romans spoke the written language, adding that grammar was not an artificial set of rules, but a codification of usage. Valla opposes this position. According to him, Latin grammar was not descriptive, but prescriptive. He distinguishes between use and art, the former common to all, the latter achieved through pursuit of studied elegance.

One would expect Poggio to take the cue from this work and treat some equally serious subject. Instead, in his fifth invective[9] he resorted once again to base *ad hominem* insults, rehashing the old accusations of heresy and pride and taunting Valla for having dared to criticize Cicero, Virgil, Jerome and Augustine.

When Valla could finally examine the text of Poggio's second invective, which the latter had deftly concealed from his rival despite its wide circulation, putting aside the translation of Herodotus that he had undertaken at Pope Nicholas V's request, Lorenzo penned his *Secundum antidotum*.[10] Valla returns to the attack of Poggio's position regarding the nature of Latin speech, while defending himself against charges of sacrilegiousness, impiety, and ignorance. He concludes defending his moral integrity and attacking Poggio's private life, which is as obscene as his infamous *Facetiae*.

Happily, after scouring the Latin language for two years in their search for obscene words with which to hail down scorn upon one another, Poggio and Valla finally succumbed to the invitations and the protests of fellow humanists to lay down their weapons.

As even these extremely brief synopses have revealed, the Poggio-Valla invectives are far longer and more complex than the pioneer invectives of Petrarch. They represent indeed a sizable portion of the two humanists' *opera omnia*, which include many other essays in the medium.

If the scope, creative fancy and erudition of their invectives make Poggio and Valla masters of the genre, they were not without rivals. For between 1352 and 1451 more than eighty invectives were written, most of them in the latter fifty years. The invective had in fact become in the fifteenth century the favorite weapon of the humanists in their numerous disputes, whether the matrix of their enmity lay in political, religious, literary differences, or simply in personal antipathy. The authors of the invectives represent a veritable *Who's Who* of humanism. Some of them were so skilled that they helped refine the conventions of the invective while conferring to it a prodigiously rich variety of forms, creating a gallimaufry that greatly expanded its traditional contours. The evolution, nay the revolution wrought upon the invective is one of the most remarkable facts about the humanistic period.

To examine this evolution or revolution, we should examine how the humanists found the invective and how they left it. What are the antecedents of the humanistic invective and how was the invective defined by the ancients and in the Middle Ages?

The prototype of the humanistic invective is to be found in two writings believed to have been exchanged between the Roman historian Sallust and Cicero.[11] These writings are now generally considered spurious, but they were held to be genuine by Quintilian and by the humanists. The medieval manuscript tradition gave them the title of *invectivae*, but the term *invectiva* is of late classical coinage, being used both as an adjective (the feminine form of *invectivus, -a, -um*) and as a feminine noun (*invectiva, -ae*). It is used in both forms to describe and define a reproachful *oration*. (It is used once to describe the *Ibis* of the poet Ovid). In the majority of cases, *invectiva* is used as the title of Cicero's orations against Catiline.

The late classical and early Christian periods abound with writings that bore the title of *invectiva*, or that were referred to as such. Even in such an age of common polemics, one man stood above all others, St. Jerome. He had a real talent for the invective. He felt that he had a lofty mission as a moral reformer and as a defender of orthodoxy. Consequently, he felt that he was not bound by the usual rules of charity, but that he had a God-given license to indulge in malice and scurrility in the pursuance of his goals. Besides his own powerful rhetorical arsenal, Jerome, a great admirer of the classical pagan authors, deployed their satirical material; in addition he quarried the vast invective elements from the Bible, for he always enlisted God as his second in his private quarrels. This peculiar combination of pagan and Christian elements is the trademark of Jerome's invectives, which were usually delivered in the form of open letters against his adversaries: Helvidius, Jovinianus, Rufinus and Vigilantius.[12] Other noteworthy examples of invectives are Julian the Apostate's orations against Constantius and two poetic invectives by Claudian, not to mention several writings by Arnobius, Tertullian, and Paulus Orosius.

The later Middle Ages were no less rich in works of an invective nature. Suffice it to mention the invectives of Berengarius in defense of his master Abelard against Bernard of Clairvaux, and those of Gerard de Berry against Hubert Walter, archbishop of Canterbury. We must pass over the countless passages of invective nature found in the works of such authors as Alain de Lille, Dante and Marsilio of Padua, which dot the period preceding the advent of Humanism.

The question arises: Were the humanists aware of this wealth of late classical and Christian material, and if so, to what extent (if any) were they influenced by it? Petrarch, the first humanist, professed to know these invectives and made several references to them. The friar Antonio da Rho knew Jerome's invectives and felt a particular kinship with that author, to whom he refers as "Hieronymus meus." The other humanists, however, whether or not they were familiar with earlier invectives, as they were certainly familiar with most of their authors, made no mention of them. Their higher standards of Latinity gave them an attitude of contempt with regard to those writers whose works in their opinion fell hopelessly short of classical elegance and represented the decadence of the Latin language. The only invectives earlier than their own which they cared to acknowledge are the two exchanged between Sallust and Cicero, Cicero's attacks against Verres, Catiline, and Mark Antony, and Petrarch's.

In spite of this attitude of superiority by the humanists, a comparison between late classical and Christian invectives with their productions will nevertheless show some striking similarities, particularly in content. (After all, how many novel ways are there to insult an enemy?) The major difference lies in the more abundant usage of scriptural and theological material by the Christian authors and in the better Latinity and extraordinary variety of forms employed in the fifteenth century. Thus, the more "classical," the purer the Latin of a pre-humanist author, and the more able he is to break away from the narrow confines of the traditional genres, the closer will his work be to the humanists'.

I must now address the question suggested by the title of this paper: Is the humanistic invective to be considered a literary genre? Or are we to demote the word *invectiva*, the title of so many humanistic works, to the status of an adjective, modifying (improbably) an implied noun, such as *oratio, satura, epistola*, etc.? To find the answer it might be useful to review the opinions of various rhetoricians from Roman times down to the middle of the fifteenth century. The earliest work which should entertain our attention is the *Rhetorica ad Herennium*,[13] until recently attributed to Cicero, the seminal work which provided the terminology used with slight variations throughout the history of Latin rhetoric. (Cf. Cicero's *De inventione*). The *Author ad Herennium* divides all speeches or *orationes* into three categories: "iudicialis," "deliberativa," and "demonstrativa" or epideictic. He describes the last variety as including "laus" (praise) and "vituperatio" (censure) and therefore dealing with external circumstances, physical attributes and qualities of character of a person whom we choose to praise or censure. To external circumstances belong descent, education, wealth, titles to fame, citizenship, friendships and the like, and their contraries. Physical attributes are merits or defects of the body. Qualities of character are wisdom, justice, courage, temperance, and their contraries. The *Author ad Herennium* then proceeds to discuss the various parts of an epideictic speech. Its introduction might include a justification for censure, on the grounds that the author has been compelled by the petulance of his adversary to take such a measure, or because he wants to make known to everyone the latter's evil character. Its "divisio" should set forth that which the author intends to praise or censure. Then the main body of the speech should recount the events, describing at the same time the faults of character of the adversary, thus painting his portrait based on external circumstances and physical attributes. The conclusion should be in the form of a brief summary.

Later rhetoricians, in similar fashion, assigned praise and censure (the latter being synonymous with "invectiva") to the "genus demonstrativum." Thus Priscian, Emporius, and Sulpicius Victor, with slight variations.

A notable development in the thirteenth century is the wholesale application of the term *invectiva*, which had hitherto been confined to the field of oratory and in a few instances to poetry, to epistolography as well. The *dictatores* Buoncompagno da Signa, Thomas of Capua, and Matteo de' Libri, all established this trend, which was consecrated by Brunetto Latini, Dante's teacher, in his *Rhetorica* (1262).[14] Latini insisted that Cicero's teachings not be limited to forensic speeches, but that they be applied not only to epistolography, but also to diplomatic embassies, and even to the "canzoni amorose," which have the character of a "controversia" and whose purpose is to persuade. We should not then be surprised to find the humanists, the true heirs of the *dictatores*, giving the form of letters and other genres to writings to which they attached the title of invective or that were considered such.

The rhetorical treatises of the fifteenth century, in line with the humanists' avowed aspiration to a thorough imitation of classical models, represent a return to the terminology and classification of the *Rhetorica ad Herennium* and of Cicero's rhetorical works. Thus, both Gasparino Barzizza's *De compositione* (1423),[15] and George of Trebisond's monumental *Rhetoricorum libri quinque*[16] (before 1435), return to the threefold division of oratory, according to which the invective fell under the "genus demonstrativum" of speeches. Gian Mario Filelfo, Francesco's son, in a short treatise, *Praecepta artis rhetoricae*,[17] divided the "oratio invectiva" into three classes: "familiaris, familiarissima et gravis," depending on the language and style, and gave examples of each. Bartolomeo Cavalcanti, in his *La retorica*,[18] gave various rules for the composition of the invective, all drawn from the *Rhetorica ad Herennium*'s discussion of "vituperatio." Francesco Negri, to mention yet another rhetorician, in a treatise on epistolography,[19] distinguished between two kinds of invective: "invectiva criminis," sent to a friend or enemy in condemnation of a fault or a crime, and "invectiva contentionis," written to a person "cuius ignorantiam reprehendere volumus super aliquo loco humano."

It is certainly clear from the preceding review of the various definitions and descriptions of "invective" that neither the classical, nor the medieval, nor the humanists' own is adequate for its humanistic variety, although some are more useful than others. Some define satisfactorily a few specimens – especially if couched as an oration or an epistle – but none is elastic enough to account for the remarkable variety of forms achieved in the invectives of the humanists, particularly Poggio and Valla. It is a case of the treatise writers not keeping pace with developments in the material under scrutiny and being more orthodox in their definition of "invective" than its practitioners, being prescriptive rather than descriptive.

An adequate definition of the fifteenth-century humanistic invective might be: a composition in prose or verse, whose chief purpose is to reprehend or accuse an adversary, dead or alive, or to answer charges received against one's person, family, country, or any other object of personal affection. Its usual means of publication was by distribution among mutual friends and acquaintances, seldom to the adversaries. It came in a great variety of forms, most often that of an undelivered oration. In many cases the invective took the form of an open letter sent to a third party.

The greatest development in form was achieved between 1440 and 1453, but even earlier we find the more versatile humanists breaking out of the traditional strictures that the title "invective" implied. Depending on their rhetorical skills and their personal temperament, we find them using the form of the philosophical treatise and the "dissertatio." A favorite form with Valla and Poggio was the dialogue, since it afforded an opportunity to vilify and confound the opponent by putting into his mouth weak and ridiculous arguments from which he could not extricate himself. Because of the mordant nature of the invectives and the choleric state that usually bred them, we seldom find in them well-modulated, subtle Socratic irony. We find, rather, the excoriating sharpness of Juvenal and the causticity of Martial's epigrams. Poggio had a particular admiration for the satirist Lucian, some of whose works he translated from the Greek. Poggio's own humor was very akin to Lucian's, so we find affinities with the satirist's works, particularly in Poggio's invectives against Valla, where we also recognize the slapstick humor of Aristophanes and of Seneca's *Apocolocyntosis*. Yet another form, used effectively by Bartolomeo Facio, Valla and Coluccio Salutati, is that of the commentary, or textual exegesis, consisting of the quotation of excerpts from the opponents' work, followed by comments of a grammatical, stylistic or other nature.

These forms are by no means the only ones used. Nor were they used one at a time, for often we find several within the same invective, as we saw in the invectives exchanged between Valla and Poggio.

If we keep in mind the central fact that these literary essays, despite their prodigious variety, share a common title, *"invectiva,"* we will then resist the temptation to ascribe to the term a merely adjectival, descriptive function and to deny it a definitive, identifying property. And when we further consider that this common title was attached to extremely tradition-bound men of letters whose respect for classical models approached worship, we must conclude that just as the Romans could state that "satura tota nostra est" (satire is totally our own invention), when they examined that hodge-podge which found no exact correlative in Greek literature, so the claim can be made for the humanists that they were the creators and practitioners (to use a fashionable prefix) of a "meta"-genre. Taking a term that an old (albeit late classical) tradition already used with considerable flexibility, they used it to define a composition so elastic as to be able to draw at once from many disparate forms; a composition apt to give expression to their innermost feelings, often during indiscreet moments of excessive passion.

It may be easy to dismiss the humanistic invectives as mere rhetorical exercises. After all, they were not taken too seriously and we have no record of any of its authors being prosecuted for libel. Yet, they are to be reckoned as belonging to the long tradition of ludic literature that springs periodically whenever a new age dawns on mankind and old and new ideas clash with one another. Moreover, the invectives allow us to catch the humanists, to use a popular expression, "with their hair down," laying bare to us their petty hatreds and jealousies, as well as their fierce loyalties and allegiances, constituting at the same time invaluable historical and literary records, as well as indispensable biographical documents.

Notes

[1] For a full bibliography on these works, see Ennio I. Rao, *Curmudgeons in High Dudgeon: 101 Years of Invectives* (Messina: EDAS, 2007).

[2] Bartolomeo Facio, *Invective in Laurentium* Vallam. Preface by P. O. Kristeller (Napoli: Società Editrice Napoletana, 1978; and *Curmudgeons...* (Messina: EDAS, 2007).

[3] See Alastair Fowler, *Kinds of Literature: An Introduction to the Theory of Genres and Modes* (Cambridge, MA: Harvard UP, 1982), and the collection of essays edited by David Duff, *Modern Genre Theory* (New York: Longman, 2000).

[4] *Invectiva contra medicum,* ed. Francesco Bausi (Firenze: Le Lettere, 2005).

[5] "Poggii Florentini Invectiva in L. Vallam prima," Poggio Bracciolini, *Opera omnia* I, ed. Riccardo Fubini (Torino: Bottega d'Erasmo, 1964) 188-205.

[6] "Antidoti in Pogium ad Nicolaum Quintum Pontificem Maximum Liber I," Lorenzo Valla, *Opera omnia* I, ed. Eugenio Garin (Torino: Bottega d'Erasmo, 1962) 253-274. Modern edition by Ari Wesseling (Assen: van Gorcum, 1978).

[7] *Op. cit.* 206-234, 234-242, and *Opera omnia* II (1969), where the fourth oration bears the title of "Poggii invectiva quarta in Vallam," 325-366.

[8] *Opera* I 366-389.

[9] "Oratio V," *Opera* I 242-251, where it bears the title of "Poggii fl. Invectiva V in L. Vallam."

[10] *Opera* I 325-366.

[11] Sallustius, *In Ciceronem et invicem invectivae,* ed. A. Kurfess (Leipzig: Teubner, 1962).

[12] These invectives are all found in Migne's *Patrologia Latina* XXIII.

[13] Ed. Harry Caplan (London: Heinemann, 1954).
[14] *La rettorica,* testo critico di Francesco Maggini (Firenze: Le Monnier, 1968).
[15] *Opera,* ed. G. A. Furietti (Romae, 1723; Rpt. Bologna: Forni, 1969).
[16] *Rhetoricorum libri V* (Venetiis: Aldus Manutius et Andreas Torresanus, 1523).
[17] *Novum epistolarium* (Mediolani: Pachel & Scinzenzeler, 1484) (Hain 12969).
[18] *La retorica* (Vinegia: Gabriel Giolito de' Ferrari, 1559).
[19] *De modo epistolandi* (Venetiis: I. Tridino, 1517).

Bibliography

Barzizza, Gasparino and Guiniforte Barzizza. *Gasparini Barzizii bergomatis et Guiniforti filii opera.* Ed. J. A. Furiettus. Romae: Salviani, 1723. Rpt. Bologna: Forni, 1969.
Bracciolini, Poggio. *Opera omnia.* Edizione di Riccardo Fubini. 4 Volumes. Torino: Bottega d'Erasmo, 1964-1969.
Brunetto Latini. *La rettorica.* Testo critico di Francesco Maggini. Firenze: Le Monnier, 1968.
Cavalcanti, Bartolomeo. *La retorica...Divisa in sette libri: dove si contiene tutto quello, che appartiene all'arte retorica.* Vinegia: Gabriel Giolito de' Ferrari, 1559.
Duff, David (ed.). *Modern Genre Theory.* New York: Longman, 2000.
Facio, Bartolomeo. *Invective in Laurentium Vallam.* Critical Edition by Ennio I. Rao. Preface by Paul Oskar Kristeller. Napoli: Società Editrice Napoletana, 1978.
Filelfo, Gian Mario. *Novum epistolarium.* Mediolani: Pachel & Scinzenzeler, 1484.
Fowler, Alastair. *Kinds of Literature: An Introduction to the Theory of Genres and Modes.* Cambridge, MA: Harvard UP, 1982.
Greek Iambic Poetry. Edited and Translated by Douglas E. Gerber. Cambridge, MS: Harvard UP, 1999.
Jerome, Saint. *Adversus Jovinianum libri duo.* Migne, *Patrologia Latina* XXIII, Cols. 205-338A.
_____. *Contra Rufinum.* Migne, *Patrologia Latina* XXIII, Cols. 395-492A.
_____. *Contra Vigilantium.* Migne, *Patrologia Latina* XXIII, Cols. 337-352C.
_____. *De perpetua virginitate Mariae, Adversus Helvidium liber unus.* Migne, *Patrologia Latina* XXIII, Cols. 181-206.
Koster, Severin. *Die Invektive in der griechischen und römischen Literatur.* Meisenheim am Glan: Hain, 1980.
Maggini, Francesco. *La rettorica italiana di Brunetto Latini.* Firenze: Galletti e Cocci, 1912.
Negri, Francesco (Franciscus Niger). *De modo epistolandi.* Venetiis, Io. De Tridino, 1517.
Petrarca, Francesco. *Invective contra medicum...* A cura di Francesco Bausi. Firenze: Le Lettere, 2005.
_____. *Invectives.* Edited and Translated by David Marsh. Cambridge, MA: Harvard UP, 2003.
Rao, Ennio I. *Curmudgeons in High Dudgeon: 101 Years of Invectives.* Messina: EDAS, 2007.
Rhetorica ad Herennium. With an English Translation by Harry Caplan. London: Heinemann; Cambridge, MA: Harvard UP, 1954.
Trapezuntius, Georgius (George of Trebizond). *Rhetoricorum libri V.* Venetiis: Aldus Manutius et Andreas Torresanus, 1523.

Valla, Lorenzo. *Opera omnia*. Con una premessa di Eugenio Garin. 2 Volumi. Torino: Bottega d'Erasmo, 1962.

———. *Antidotum primum: la prima apologia contro Poggio Bracciolini*. Edizione critica di Ari Wesseling. Assen: van Gorcum, 1978.

West, Martin Litchfield. *Studies in Greek Elegy and Iambus*. Bernin & New York: de Gruyter, 1974.

Gianluca Rizzo

Issues of Language and Genre in Macaronic Invectives

> "With the single exception of Homer, there is no eminent writer, not even Sir Walter Scott, whom I can despise so entirely as I despise Shakespeare when I measure my mind against his. The intensity of my impatience with him occasionally reaches such a pitch, that it would positively be a relief to me to dig him up and throw stones at him, knowing as I do how incapable he and his worshippers are of understanding any less obvious form of indignity."[1]

This – in so many words – is what George Bernard Shaw thinks of the Bard. The passage is taken from the review of a Cymbeline's production, which Shaw published in 1896, centuries after Shakespeare's death. What should we make of it? It would seem that this *stroncatura* comes too late to be considered the product of a militant critic. Is it an invective directed against Shakespeare? Is it a satire aimed at the cult following Victorian England formed around some of his works? Is it, perhaps, an epigrammatic assessment of the Bard's achievements, with a taste for paradox? Irony is involved in this statement; no one could deny it. Sarcasm, no doubt, can be detected too. And a good measure of bitterness for a fellow dramatist of some success, even though he has been dead for centuries, must have contributed to the choice of such a worthy adversary. But what is it *exactly*? Which of these categories does it fall under?

If we were forced to label it, and then asked to justify our decision, we would be hard pressed to find a satisfactory set of arguments. Does this mean there is no difference between invective, satire, epigram and verbal assault? Between irony, sarcasm and the pure and simple indulgence in that ancient and noble art of profanity? On the contrary: there must be a way to differentiate between these different types of texts (and textual strategies). And yet, a sensible distinction will prove to be very difficult to articulate.

If we were to attempt a typology, we would most likely have to rely on extra-textual indicators, such as the audiences these texts were intended for, the cultural climate in which they were produced, and the intentions of their authors. In particular this last criterion would prove to be very misleading, knowing, as we all do, how fond writers are of lying about their own creations (in other words, lying about their own lies).

However, distinguishing between these different types of texts is not, perhaps, the most productive way of talking about "savage words." Perhaps a better way would be to clarify what makes these textual strategies so similar to each other, and what distinguishes them from works of a different nature. Let us pursue this line of investigation, and provide a plausible description of the commonalities these texts share.

First, they all perform the same function. Pragmatically speaking, they all serve one single purpose: expressing the speaker's dislike of someone or something. In this respect George Bernard Shaw's attack on Shakespeare is exemplary in its clarity. Yet, assaulting one's opponent, even if only verbally, is one of those behaviors that are not tolerated in polite society. To put it in more precise terms, verbal assault is, at its core, an anti-social behavior, and therefore it is sanctioned by what psycho-linguists call "interdiction." For a better definition of this phenomenon, and the bearing it will have on our discussion, we will turn to a very interesting essay written in the '60s by Nora Galli de' Paratesi and entitled "*Le brutte parole*" ("*The ugly (or bad) words*"):

> We call *interdiction* the compulsion to avoid speaking of a given subject, or rather the act of referring to it by using words that suggest a given idea without pointing to it directly. Such interdictions can either be imposed externally or internally. It is the psychological motivation for a series of linguistic behaviors.[2]

Verbal assault is one of those areas of language subject to interdiction. When engaging in such a practice, a speaker (or an author) will feel compelled to adopt a set of rhetorical strategies that will allow him to say that which otherwise could not be said in the public arena, while at the same time avoiding the personal consequences of openly engaging in anti-social behavior. In obtaining both these goals *euphemism* will prove to play an instrumental role. In Galli de' Paratesi's words, we will define euphemism as:

> [...] that linguistic phenomenon by which certain words are avoided and substituted with other words. Thus, the word *euphemism* includes all those linguistic manifestations caused by a psychological *interdiction*. More often than not, in everyday speech, we use *euphemism* to mean that word or expression used to substitute the word or expression subject to interdiction: in this sense we prefer the term *euphemistic substitute* or more simply, *substitute*. We call *means* or *modes of substitution* those linguistic means used by the speaker to create different *substitutes*.[3]

The fact that satire, epigram and invectives are all expressions of a similar anti-social behavior, and that they all use the same strategy to linguistically overcome an interdicted discourse, explain on the one hand why these different genres hold certain affinities and, on the other, why it is so difficult to set them apart. Galli de' Paratesi's essay also offers a very detailed description of how these "modes of substitution" actually work. Among the most popular of these "modes", we find one she calls "substitution by ineffability": when confronted with an interdicted term, the speaker will avoid mentioning it, and will substitute it with a pause of silence (the three dots in writing), or with the first letter of the word that designates it. Examples in English would be the F word or the S word, just to mention a few.

This strategy works only on the level of lexicon. What happens when we try to apply this same "mode of substitution" to a whole text? We can find a good example of a "substitution by ineffability" extended to a whole text in the first humanistic invective ever written, a text that revived the whole genre, giving it new vigor: Petrarch's *Contra medicum*. In book one, on the very first page, the Poet writes:

> Quia tamen cogis ad id, ad quod nunquam sponte descenderem, et loqui aliquid necesse est, ne, si – quod interdum in animum venit – propter contemptum rerum tuarum tacuero, tu tibi forsan ex mea taciturnitate complaceas, petita non a te sed a lectore venia si quid contra morem meum dixero, respondebo ad aliqua. Multa enim tam inepte dicis, ut quisquis ea responso digna duxerit, ipse merito videri possi ineptior.

This strategy has proved to be so successful that almost all the *orationes invectivae* written after this point include a similar disclaimer at their very opening. By saying he has been dragged into the controversy in spite of his best efforts, Petrarch is actually building himself an alibi for what he is about to say, for the anti-social behavior he is about to engage in. Once the disclaimer has been put forth, however, the typical humanistic invective will address the core purpose for which it has been written: discrediting the character and the work of the addressee. In pursue of this objective humanists have not been shy by any means. On the contrary, they employed their best rhetorical skills in order to devise the most inventive insults, worthy of their disdain for the adversary. A quick look at Antonio da Rho's *Philippica in Antonium Panormitam* will help us understand the general tone they kept in these matters:

> And so we discern that this measly teacher of ABCs (*hunc grammaticulum*) is, as I would put it, a pure ass, who has not yet quit the benches of primary school or ceased to be a schoolmaster. He understands nothing about what a knowledge of the sundry histories means, what usefulness they impart, or what kind of flavor they possess.

> Long-eared animal that he is, Panormita certainly hears the sounds of these histories and the ancient trumpets; for what purpose they blast he hears nothing.[4]

I chose one of the politer passages, since I didn't want to offend my reader. This is taken from the very beginning of the *oratio*, just a few pages into the first of four "objections": at this point he is just warming up. So much for euphemism, one could say. Well, yes. And still, we must not forget one crucial element: Latin. One of the "modes of substitution" listed by Galli de' Paratesi as a possible source for euphemism is the "use of foreign words" or, better said: code-switching. It is a phenomenon common to most languages: when something cannot be said in your own language with decency, try using your neighbor's language, which is just a *flatus voci* anyways. That will make things less offensive. For instance, think about the use of French words (or French sounding *grammelot*), both in English and Italian, when it comes to matters relating to the bed chamber. The same strategy applies here. Humanists are using Cicero's and Virgil's language to call each other names. Nothing inappropriate can be said in Latin, can it? In addition, who but a few other humanists will be able to understand and appreciate these flowers of rhetoric?

However, scholars weren't the only people using Latin for euphemistic reasons. It was a very well received practice in preaching, as well; especially if we think that even Cherubino da Spoleto (who died in 1484), in his book of advice to fellow preachers entitled *Sermones quadragesimales*, writes:

> In regards to these things you, preacher, try to speak in an appropriate manner (*honeste*) whenever possible; what you can't say in an appropriate manner in vernacular, say it in Latin.[5]

Thus, the interdiction attached to verbal assault (or to indecency and anti-social behavior of any kind) is resolved by humanists through the macro-strategy of code-switching, which pervades the totality of their texts.

However, euphemism is not used only as a means to justify and engage in a fundamentally anti-social practice. It also plays a key role in the other crucial dimension of invective: variation. All these texts, as we said at the very beginning, share the same meaning. Ultimately, they all say: I don't like you! When handled by men of letters, this meaning must be embellished. In fact, each author needs to appropriate it and couch it in his or her own style. Hence, the importance of variations. After all, how many ways of saying "I don't like you" are there? Well, as it turns out, plenty. And how do authors generate all these different variations? By "modes of substitution," the same techniques used to form euphemisms, only that in this case they are turned upside down. Instead of serving the purpose of avoiding offence to one's audience, they are exploited to create better and new ways of attacking one's adversaries, of creating, in other words, *dysphemisms* tailored towards one's enemy.

If we go back to Antonio da Rho's *Philippica*, we'll remember how he calls Antonio Panormita, among other things, a "*grammaticulum*" and a "*purum onagrum*" in the passage we quoted, while in another passage, a few lines down, he calls him a "*simia literata*" a "literate ape." All these insults have been formed by applying euphemistic (or, better, dysphemistic) "modes of substitution." In the case of "*grammaticulum*," through the mode that Galli de' Paratesi calls "grammatical alteration," by adding the suffix "*-ulus*" Antonio da Rho transforms the word "*grammaticus*" which means teacher of Grammar (Latin) – a perfectly respectable profession – into an offensive epithet. "*Purum onagrum*" and "*simia literata*," instead, belong to the *metaphorical* "mode of substitution," where the stereotypical qualities of the two animals are metaphorically attributed to Antonio Panormita.

These are the key rhetorical strategies humanists used in order to (1) deal with the interdictions connected to the verbal assault while (2) exploiting at the same time the productive capabilities of euphemism, to create an infinite (and infinitely offensive) set of insults. They were able to do so, without suffering the social consequences for breaching the rules of linguistic interdiction, by abiding to the advice Cherubino da Spoleto gave to his colleagues: by "saying in Latin what vernacular cannot say in an appropriate manner."

But what if a careless preacher were to invert the terms of Cherubino's advice? What would be the effect of such a speech on a church audience? And what if, instead of a preacher, we imagine a student, a doctor, or a professor who would not only do the opposite of what Cherubino suggested, but out of sheer malice, would also mix Latin and vernacular in such a way that the resulting language wouldn't resemble either of them? What if such a language were used to publicly ridicule a fellow citizen, or a colleague? We call the result of such an experiment a Macaronic invective.

Before describing more in detail this kind of text, let us briefly mention the history of this language. Before being a literary tool, it has undertaken several transformations. At the earliest stage it was a temporary, provisional code of communication devised by the clergy who, while forced to deliver their sermons in Latin, could not be understood by their own flock. Especially in the telling of *exempla* (exemplary tales), priests would insert long passages in the vernacular, to make sure that the message they were trying to convey would reach their audience. At the same time this hybrid, ungrammatical language was widely used by notaries and administrators, in dealing with their clients and with one another. In their case, the need to make the documents they were compiling understood, coupled with their own lack of knowledge of Latin, would produce some hilarious, and involuntary, linguistic monsters. However, the environment that contributed the most to the diffusion of macaronic Latin, and accounted for its evolution into a literary tool, was the university classroom. Here the prevalent language was Latin, but, due to pedagogical issues as well as a sheer goliardic spirit, vernacular and macaronic expressions were also largely used.

For an amusing example of the general linguistic atmosphere in Italian universities at that time we can turn to the *reportationes* of Pietro Pomponazzi's lectures. Here is a brief sample of the kind of similes he was very fond of, while lecturing on philosophy: "*do exemplum quod, etsi turpe sit, satis tamen est accommodatum: quando tangis mulierem, sentiens illud molle, exit ipsum quod prius latitabat*[6]".

Those observations we made regarding the humanistic invective apply also to these macaronic texts. The same code-switching techniques reach here an unprecedented level of complexity. The dichotomy of Latin vs. vernacular is constantly negated by this flexible language, thus making it an ideal tool for breaking any type of linguistic interdiction, from social ones to religious, from scatological to sexual. We will come back to this observation later on in this article.

Since their first appearance, macaronic texts display the same characteristics as the humanistic invectives: they are directed against a specific person, most of the time identifiable; they attack the adversary according to the same outline followed by the humanists, they use the same channels of circulation, etc. The only major differences are that while performing these functions, macaronic texts: 1. show a particular indulgence in all sorts of dysphemistic behavior; 2. they avoid any sort of self-justification at the beginning; and 3. the "mode of substitution by ineffability" is rarely employed. Here everything is profusely nominated: lists of synonyms, accumulations of exaggeratedly scatological images and blasphemy are essential characteristics of macaronic poetry. Still, it is worth repeating, all these sprawling dysphemisms are generated according to those same "modes of substitution" mentioned earlier. Let us take a look at the texts now, as much as decency will allow, and let us try to identify some of these "modes of substitution" at work.

Scholars agree that the oldest macaronic text (and here we understand macaronic as the literary, deliberate kind of hybrid language) is the *Tosontea*, by a certain Coradus, written against Ludovico Carensio.[7] Coradus' character is attacked through a rhetorical strategy common to most humanistic invectives: reconstructing the family history of one's adversary, rather creatively it must be said, in order to have his defects and vices come as a natural consequence of his gene pool. In this particular case, Coradus is accused of being the son of a *facchino* (street porter) and of having been a *facchino* himself, before receiving some education by one of his patrons, the logician Mengus.[8] After stealing some of Mengus' knowledge, along with a copy of his book on logics and some money from his purse, Coradus goes to Padova, and begins to give public lectures on logics, obtaining a considerable following among students. Let us look at the incipit of the poem. After a very brief *captatio benevolentiae* (4 lines), and a summary of the argument (2 lines) Coradus writes:

> Vitam, facta, genus et garbos cantare Toseti
> incipio. (vv. 7, 8)

Besides the obvious reference to the incipit of the *Aeneid* (arma virumque cano…), there is no sign of the customary declaration of reluctance to engage in the exchange of invectives. The *Tosontea* is particularly interesting for its description of the university environment that, no doubt, surrounded the author while the piece was being written. And the author must have been familiar with the output of humanist invectives, since it exploits not only the *topos* of attacking one's parents to ridicule one's character, but also the common places of physical description to stress moral and psychological vices and defects. When Toseto's father addresses his son he says:

> "Tonse puer" dixit "quum sit tibi ciera fachini
> et spallas habeas grossas, restabis et ipse
> mecum. Nam poteris nostram governare brigadam:
> huic te nam arti promptum natura creavit."[9] (vv. 28-31)

Nature endowed Toseto with all the qualities of a street porter: wide shoulders (*spallas habeas grossas*) and "*ciera fachini.*" However, an even better example of this type of dysphemistic description is provided by Tifi Odasi's *Macaronea*. While relating a *beffa* – plotted against Giampiero di Comino degli Odasi, a relative and friend of the author, belonging to his same *macaronica secta* – Odasi sketches a brief and vivid description of the numerous characters involved. A portrayal of the victim's lover reaches an unsurpassed height in the *ars macaronica*, providing one of the least amicable descriptions in the history of Italian literature. Let us take a quick look:

> A caput incipiens, nigros habet illa capillos,
> lendinibus plenos semper sudore covertos,
> et scarpellatos habes omni tempore ocellos
> inque oculorum gemino cantone puinas.
> In viso poteris porros plantare puzanti,
> nam semel in toto visum sibi lavat in anno,
> plenaque formaio retinet dentalia semper." (vv. 501-507)

In this brief passage the euphemistic "modes of substitution" is brilliantly used for the creation of dysphemisms. In order to describe the pitiful state of personal hygiene kept by the "*masara cusini spiziari*," Odasi compiles a long list: he starts with her hair, which wasn't exactly clean, her skin, covered in freckles and sweat, he then moves on to consider her eyes, her face and finally her teeth. Taken individually, these traits would have been enough to qualify the *masara* as a person of poor manners. Yet, by listing them one after the other, Odasi destroys the euphemistic potential of these expressions and amplifies their grotesque quality, transforming the character into a list of dysphemisms.

The constant switching between Latin and vernacular short-circuits the euphemistic modes of substitution, as it was envisioned by preachers such as Cherubino da Perugia. It creates a linguistic environment in which it is not immediately clear which language is being used as a euphemistic substitute, and which one is being substituted. The confusion is further complicated by the accumulation of images, all focusing on the same interdicted topic, thus offering endless variations of substitutes that, rather than avoiding offence to the audience, seem aimed at obtaining the opposite effect. And still, it must be noted that, technically speaking, all these substitutes amount to euphemisms, even if they are in their reversed dysphemistic form.

Other macaronic texts, more or less contemporary to the two just mentioned, are the *Virgiliana*, the *Nobile Vigonce Opus*, the *Macaronea contra Savoynos* and the *Macaronea contra macaroneam Bassani*. Both the *Virgiliana* and the *Nobile Vigonce Opus*, belong to the same university goliardic environment, and closely resemble the *Tosontea*. In both cases, a student of the Padua university is singled out and ridiculed for his debatable morals, his lack of intelligence and his presumptuous behavior.

Unfortunately we don't have enough space to engage in a close textual analysis of these works. And yet, we can't forego the two *Macaronee* by Bassano Mantovano and Giovanni Giorgio Alione (*Macaronea contra savoynos* and *Macaronea contra macaroneam Bassani*, respectively) without noting that, out of the entire production of macaronic poetry, these two closely resemble a proper humanistic invective; they also posses a more political motivation, as they testify to the growing tension between French Piedmontese and Italian Lombards in Northern Italy. Unlike any other macaronic text, they display a short declaration of reluctance to engage in the dispute at their very opening, and they keep an overall more decent demeanor (and therefore of less interest to us).

Until now we have been talking about the macaronic production of verses preceding Teofilo Folengo's *Macaronee*. When compared to Folengo's, these texts lack complexity and appear to be nothing more than the adolescence of macaronic poetry. What makes Folengo's macaronic so superior? First of all, his language is much more refined. And by refined I don't mean less inclined to infringe on the rules of interdiction. Rather, it is a more sophisticated literary tool, able to take the potential inherent to the *Macaronee* by Odasi or Fossa beyond the boundaries of Renaissance Italian cities.

His heroicomic epic entitled *Baldus* narrates the adventures of an Orlando type of characters, from his infancy to the greatest of his feats: destroying hell and all its demons. Along the way Baldus collects several exceptional friends, most remarkably: a giant (similar to Morgante), a creature half man half dog, a buffoon and a rogue by the name of Cingar (gipsy). In narrating these adventures, Folengo uses the meter of classical epic poetry, the hexameter, with an accuracy rivaling that of the most talented humanists. His language, however, couldn't be more different from theirs. In his hybrid concoction, the Latin of Virgil coexists with that of the notaries and the scarcely educated clergy, and everywhere one feels the invigorating injections of vernacular speech, which manages to revive and question the language received from tradition and authority.

I would like to discuss one passage in particular: Baldus and his companions have already embarked on the journey that will take them to confront evil and destroy hell. They find themselves in a limbic space between the world of the living and the realm of the dead. In this *antinferno* they encounter an old man, accompanied by a young woman. Curious about their story, they stop to interrogate the couple. They reveal themselves as Pasquino and his daughter, the very same Pasquino who was the addressee (and the putative author) of so many satiric and invective poems in Rome. After his death, the population of Rome petitioned the pope to obtain a passage to Paradise for their beloved Pasquino. And so the pope allowed him to build an inn, just outside of the Paradise's gates, so that the clergy making its way to heaven would have a place to stop and refresh before being admitted to god's presence.

> Raro pontifices vidi regesque ducasque,
> raro signores, marchesos, raro barones,
> raro capellutos, mitratos, raro capuzzos,
> qui mihi scudiferas possent aperire crumenas[10]...

Clearly, Pasquino wasn't happy with his new job. The only people arriving were penniless hermits and decrepit penitents, unable either to pay for, or appreciate the rich and sophisticated food served at his inn. No wealthy popes, kings, dukes or abbots would ever make it to his tavern.

Once, a particularly poor anchoret ("cui brocoli, sardae, fighi, fava frantaque curae"), refusing to pay Saint Peter a fee in order to be admitted to Paradise, provokes the wrath of the father of the Church. While indulging in a long tirade against poverty (especially when it afflicted the Church), the holy man allows a group of young angels to slip past him.

> At Petrus in colera miserum de limine sburlat,
> mox ait: "Hinc abeas, destructio fava menadae,
> non es, nec maium fueris dignatus Olympo,
> donec apud chiericos madonna Simona manebit,
> quam dum permittit mundo sic vivere Luscar,
> nec tu, nec tua stirps poterunt intrare chidentrum.
> Vade, nec ultra chioches portam, ne forte chiocheris".
> Talia dum fierent, exibant extra seraium,
> deque schola coeli guizzabant mille putini,[11] ...

These angels ("qui male vestiti, qui nudi, malque politi, / malque petenati, magri, tegnaque coperti") climb over the gates of heaven to invade and pillage Pasquino's kitchen, protesting that they have been underfed and mistreated. That was the last straw. Pasquino decides to leave his post. When Baldus and his companions meet him, he was on his way to hell, hoping that, by relocating his *taberna*, he would earn a better living. After retelling his story, Pasquino magically disappears, taking with him the young and beautiful daughter and the hero's fellow travellers. Baldus continues his journey, encounters a character named Pizzacappelletto, who reveals that Pasquino was in reality the demon

Demogorgon who "*solet ut cauda vivaces battere fadas, atque styras ipsas asinarum more cavalcat.*"[12]

This is a crucial passage in the poem, for a number of different reasons. First, because of its language; as we mentioned earlier, the macaronic mixture of vernacular and Latin, when inserted in the classical frame of the Virgilian hexameter, generates an interesting effect of estrangement, which projects a surreal light on the characters and the narration. Also, and more importantly, it intensifies that "short-circuit" effect between substitute and substituted that we already mentioned when talking about pre-Folengo macaronic verses. It must be pointed out that, on the linguistic level, refusing to choose between a language used as a source for euphemistic substitutes and one that will act as the language in which these substitutes are inserted, is not just a stylistic devise. It bears very important consequences regarding the ideological structure of the *oratio invectiva*. More specifically, it equates to a refusal to choose between one side (and one side only) in any given dispute. The planned confusion systematically implemented by Folengo attacks the core assumption of invectives, in which there can only exist one privileged, and therefore dominant, point of view at any given time.

In other words, if the languages employed throughout the text function both as substitutes and substituted, the strategy of code switching for euphemistic purposes is rendered ineffective. The two levels of the discourse – the plain language that expresses the socially acceptable content and the impolite and anti-social language that should be substituted by a euphemism – are systematically confused. As a consequence, it is impossible to take an absolute stand in any given dispute. The language itself will prevent the author from doing so. Even if Folengo were to formulate an absolute statement in his macaronic tongue, the reader could never be sure whether that statement was uttered in all seriousness or ironically.

This intuition about the ideology of *Baldus* is further confirmed if we turn our attention from the language to the events described in this episode. Saint Peter's tirade against the poverty of the clergy; the angels fleeing paradise in search of food; the old anchoret excluded from heaven because of his virtue; Pasquino, first paradisiacal inn keeper and then the demon Demogorgon; all these episodes reflect an upside-down universe, where values have been shuffled, and justice and truth have failed to distinguish themselves from evil. This is especially true if we look at Pasquino's transformation into a demon. If we read his character as the embodiment of the invective spirit, particularly when aimed at the established power, we must then interpret his transformation as Folengo's refusal of this verbal practice. But why would Folengo deplore the *pasquinate*, a type of text that one would easily associate with his own macaronic style? Pasquino is presented to the reader as a ruffian, expert in those arts necessary to please powerful men, owner of an inn catering to an affluent clientele. He feeds his guests, provides them with young women, and acts as a buffoon for their amusement. However, at the same time, Pasquino is the scourge of the powerful, the only one who openly denounces their vices. Finally, to further complicate matters, we find out at the end of the episode that Pasquino is in reality a demon. Ruffian, scourge and demon; Folengo seems to question the relationship between *poesia pasquinesca* (and therefore his own poetry, which he states to be similar to the *pasquinesca* in more than one passage in the Baldus) and truth. Not only is his language inherently incapable of asserting absolute truths, but one of the characters that closely resemble the poet himself is also presented as an unreliable source, someone who is in no position to criticize others or formulate judgment about the world and human kind. Does this mean that Folengo refuses to denounce the vices of his own time, and act as a civil conscience for those who seem to have lost their sense of justice? On the contrary, he constantly criticizes his fellow Christians, while including himself and his own works among those who should be criticized.

If we have been successful (and accurate) in describing the working mechanism of invectives and its relationship with macaronic poetry, then we have shown how this latter has been constantly eroding the practice of invectives from within. First, by blurring the line between the two languages (Latin and vernacular) the macaronic has weakened the euphemistic value held by Latin, while at the same time reducing the dysphemistic capabilities of vernacular. In other words, macaronic poetry has rendered this dichotomy useless. Second, by systematically refusing to privilege one point of view over another, by presenting those who should be good as evil and those who should be evil as pitiful, Folengo refuses to succumb to the most fundamental characteristic of invectives: that of pitting censor against censored, absolute good against absolute evil. And here, in my opinion, lies one of the highest achievements of macaronic poetry, the ultimate proof of its astounding modernity.

Notes

[1] It appeared for the first time on September 26th, 1896 in the *Saturday Review*, and was entitled "Blaming the Bard." It was reprinted in 1907 in the *Dramatic Opinions and Essays*, Vol. II, and more recently in *Shaw on Shakespeare: An Anthology of Bernard Shaw's Writings on the Plays and Production of Shakespeare*, edited by Edwin Wilson (New York: Applause Books, 2002).

[2] Nora Galli de' Paratesi, *Le brutte parole* (Milano: Mondadori, 1969). The translation, here and in the following passages, is ours. The Italian reads: "Noi intenderemo per *interdizione* la coazione a non parlare di una data cosa o ad accennarvi con termini che ne suggeriscano l'idea pur senza indicarla direttamente. Tale interdizione può venirci imposta dall'esterno oppure essere un fatto interiore. Essa è comunque il momento psicologico di una serie di comportamenti linguistici," p. 25.

[3] Ivi, p. 25-6. "[...] quel fenomeno linguistico per cui alcune parole vengono evitate e sostituite con altre. La parola eufemismo quindi, riassume quell'insieme di manifestazioni linguistiche di cui l'interdizione è la causa psicologica. A volte nel linguaggio comune, si intende per *eufemismo* il termine che viene usato al posto di quello colpito da interdizione: in questo senso preferiamo usare *sostituto eufemistico* o semplicemente *sostituto*. *Mezzi* o *moduli di sostituzione* sono invece i mezzi di cui si vale il parlante per creare i sostituti."

[4] David Rutherford, *Early Renaissance Invective and The Controversies of Antonio da Rho* (Tempe: The Renaissance Society of America, 2005), p.69. Here is the original Latin: "Cernimus itaque hunc grammaticulum, purum, ut ita dixerim, onagrum, nondum ludi puerilis subsellia aut pedagogium exuisse. Quid sibi velit historiarum notitia, quid usus afferant, quid habeant condimenti nihil callet; sonos illarum et antiquas tubas – auritus ut est – exaudit quidem; quorsum erumpat nihil exaudit."

[5] Cherubino da Spoleto, *Sermones quadragesimales*, Venezia, Arrivabene, 1502, c. 174r, citato in Lucia Lazzerini, *Il testo trasgressivo* (Milano,: Franco Angeli, 1998), p. 89, n. 30:"In omnibus his tu, predicator, conare honeste dicere quantum potes; et quod non potes honeste dicere vulgariter, dicas latine."

[6] This simile was used in the context of an explanation of the cause and effect relation. The curious reader whose Latin got too rusty will excuse me if I won't dare translate this particular passage.

[7] Son of a ser Lorenzo Fornaciaio of Padua (1463-1539)

[8] Identified as Domenico Bianchinelli, of Faenza.

[9] "Toseto", he said, "you have the appearance / And the wide shoulders of a street porter / Stay with me and together we will take care of ourselves: / Nature made you specifically for this job."

[10] Lib. XXIII, vv. 326-9. "Rarely I have seen popes, kings and dukes, rarely noblemen or marquees, rarely knights, rarely cardinals, bishops, rarely friars, who could open for me their purses full of money...."

[11] Lib. XXIII, vv. 347-355. "But Peter, blind with anger, pushes the poor thing out of the gateway and then says: "Go away, you useless bum! You are not worthy of being accepted in heaven, and never will be, as long as Madame Simony will stand by the clergy, and as long as Charles will allow her to perseverate in her life style. You and your kind will be excluded from this place. Go away! And do not knock on this doors ever again!" While this things were happening, a thousand little angels escaped from the paradise's school...."

[12] Baldus, XXIII, vv. 401-2.

www.ingramcontent.com/pod-product-compliance
Lightning Source LLC
Chambersburg PA
CBHW030524080526
44586CB00011B/307